Exhibition as Social Intervention
'Culture in Action' 1993

Joshua Decter and Helmut Draxler

With additional essays by Hafþór Yngvason and Joe Scanlan; interviews with artists Mark Dion (conducted by Stephanie Smith) and Simon Grennan of Grennan & Sperandio (conducted by Lucy Steeds) and artist Daniel J. Martinez in conversation with Michael Brenson; statement by curator Mary Jane Jacob; and an introduction by David Morris and Paul O'Neill.

Exhibition Histories

Exhibition Histories

Afterall Books presents *Exhibition Histories*, a series dedicated to shows of contemporary art that have – since the first documenta in Kassel, Germany, in 1955 – shaped the way art is experienced, made and discussed. Each book in the series draws on archival material, bringing together numerous illustrations, texts from the time and newly commissioned essays to provide detailed exploration and analysis of selected exhibitions. The shows under consideration have all responded to and influenced artistic practice whilst provoking debates about the meaning and importance of art within culture and society more broadly.

The history of modern art has conventionally focused on artistic production, emphasising the individual artist in the studio and the influences on his or her practice. *Exhibition Histories* complicates this approach by arguing for an examination of art in the moment and context in which it is presented to a public. Exhibitions offer art its first contact with an audience, and in so doing they place art within explicit or implicit narratives and discursive frameworks. Every decision about the selection and installation of work, the choice and use of the venue, the marketing strategy and the accompanying printed matter informs our understanding of the art on display. The various agents and diverse factors that give form to an exhibition and determine its subsequent influence are addressed in these books from multiple standpoints: the voices of artists, curators and writers are all brought to bear. In some instances the shows selected for study already have established reputations and our work involves analysing why this is so and whether it is justified. In other cases the opportunity is taken to illuminate lesser-known exhibitions that have, nonetheless, suggested new paradigms and that can stake an equal claim to historical importance.

This series is the result of a research project initiated by Afterall at Central Saint Martins and developed with the Academy of Fine Arts Vienna and the Van Abbemuseum, Eindhoven. It currently benefits from collaboration with the Center for Curatorial Studies, Bard College. Through archival study, interviews, symposia and seminars, we have amassed the materials to allow us to select exhibitions for examination and to give shape to the resulting books. The findings, analyses and narratives we propose are by no means exhaustive; rather, we see these books as a spur to further research into the exhibition form, and ultimately as a contribution towards a better understanding of contemporary art and its histories.

Front cover image
Iñigo Manglano-Ovalle and Street-Level Video, documentation of *Tele-Vecindario: A Street-Level Video Block Party*, Erie Street, Chicago, 28 August 1993 © the artists; photography: John McWilliams

Back cover image
Simon Grennan, Christopher Sperandio and Local 552 of the Bakery, Confectionery and Tobacco Workers' International Union of America, documentation of *We Got It! The Workforce Makes the Candy of Their Dreams*, 1992–93 © the artists; photography: John McWilliams

First published 2014 by Afterall Books in association with the Center for Curatorial Studies, Bard College

Afterall
Central Saint Martins
Granary Building
1 Granary Square
London N1C 4AA
www.afterall.org

Afterall Editorial Directors
Charles Esche and Mark Lewis

Afterall Publishing Director
Caroline Woodley

Afterall Manager
Joyce Cronin

Exhibition Histories
Series Editors
Tom Eccles, Charles Esche, Pablo Lafuente, Paul O'Neill and Lucy Steeds

Associate Editors
Line Ellegaard and David Morris

Research Interns
Rafa Barber and Piotr Florczyk

Copy Editor
Deirdre O'Dwyer

Design
A Practice for Everyday Life

Print
Grafiche SiZ

British Library Cataloguing-in-Publication Data
A catalogue record for this book is available from the British Library

Distribution
Koenig Books, London
c/o Buchhandlung Walther König, Köln
Ehrenstr. 4, 50672 Köln
Tel. +49 (0) 221 / 20 59 6 53
Fax +49 (0) 221 / 20 59 6 60
verlag@buchhandlung-walther-koenig.de

Switzerland
AVA Verlagsauslieferungen AG
Centralweg 16
CH-8910 Affoltern a.A.
Tel. +41 (44) 762 42 60
Fax +41 (44) 762 42 10
verlagsservice@ava.ch

UK & Eire
Cornerhouse Publications
70 Oxford Street
GB-Manchester M1 5NH
Tel. +44 (0) 161 200 15 03
Fax +44 (0) 161 200 15 04
publications@cornerhouse.org

Outside Europe
D.A.P. / Distributed Art Publishers, Inc.
155 6th Avenue, 2nd Floor
USA-New York, NY 10013
Tel. +1 212 627 1999
Fax +1 212 627 9484
www.artbook.com

ISBN 978-3-86335-448-0 (Koenig Books, London)
ISBN 978-1-84638-138-X (Afterall Books, London)

Exhibition Histories was initially developed with Teresa Gleadowe as Research Consultant and as a Series Editor with Stephan Schmidt-Wulffen and Sabeth Buchmann. It was launched in 2010 with the support of the following institutions: Academy of Fine Arts Vienna, Van Abbemuseum and Musée d'Art Moderne Grand-Duc Jean

Exhibition as Social Intervention
'Culture in Action' 1993

Exhibition Histories

Contents

Introduction: Exhibition as Social Intervention — David Morris and Paul O'Neill

Chicago's scattered-site exhibition-event 'Culture in Action' officially took place over a period of approximately one hundred days, between May and September 1993. But many of its eight projects extended far beyond this standard timescale for a public exhibition: most began a year earlier, and at least one continues to operate today, more than twenty years later, albeit in modified form.[1] Described as a public art programme,[2] 'Culture in Action' involved many hundreds of individuals in its production and realisation, and provided little or nothing in the way of traditional display. As such, it offers a welcome perspective on our current post-participatory condition, in which the borders between the author-producer and participant-receiver of duration-specific public art praxis are no longer clearly delineated and the end work is the result of fields of interaction between multiple actors and agencies.[3]

Processual and cooperative practices, such as those seen in 'Culture in Action', present us with numerous questions, such as: does the artwork's objecthood disappear into operational methods, interventionist procedures and hard-to-find participatory moments? What happens to art when it is intended to engage with people and places under neither the relatively confined conditions of the museum or gallery, nor nomadic conditions such as biennial curatorship – when it instead gathers its audiences over a longer period? What happens when public participation becomes a negotiated space of co-production within multiple networked flows of social encounters?

—

[1] For the latter, see the description of Iñigo Manglano-Ovalle's project in this volume, p.122.

[2] The full title was 'Culture in Action: A Public Art Program of Sculpture Chicago'.

[3] For an assessment of more recent cooperative, duration-specific public art projects, see Paul O'Neill and Claire Doherty (ed.), *Locating the Producers: Durational Approaches to Public Art,* Amsterdam: Valiz, 2011. See also Tom Finkelpearl's recent book, *What We Made: Conversations on Art and Social Cooperation,* Durham, NC: Duke University Press, 2013.

[4] Irit Rogoff articulates the curatorial as critical thought that does not rush to embody itself, instead raising questions that are to be unravelled over time; Maria Lind's notion of the curatorial involves practising forms of political agency that try to go beyond the already known; Beatrice von Bismarck's understanding of the curatorial is as a continuous space of negotiation, contributing to other processes of becoming; and Emily Pethick's proposition of the curatorial presupposes an unbounded framework, allowing for things, ideas and outcomes to emerge in the process of being realised. See I. Rogoff, 'Smuggling – A Curatorial Model' in Vanessa Joan Müller and Nicolaus Schafhausen (ed.), *Under Construction: Perspectives on Institutional Practice*, Cologne: Verlag der Buchhandlung Walther König, 2006, pp.132–33; M. Lind, 'The Curatorial', *Artforum*, vol.48, no.2, October 2009, pp.103–05; B. von Bismarck, 'Curatorial Criticality: On the Role of Freelance Curators in the Field of Contemporary Art', in Marianne Eigenheer (ed.), *Curating Critique*, Frankfurt a.M.: Revolver, 2007, pp.62–69; and E. Pethick, 'The Dog that Barked at the Elephant in the Room', *The Exhibitionist*, no.4, June 2011, pp.81–82.

Such problems mark the contested territory of the expanded field of curatorship today.[4] The debate cannot be reduced to a set of positions that exist in opposition to exhibition-making; rather, they support forms of research-based, dialogical practice in which the processual and the serendipitous overlap with speculative actions and open-ended forms of production. 'Culture in Action' was an experimental exhibition, in the sense that Michael Brenson describes as 'movement into an unknown',[5] and it continues to raise questions within myriad strands of complex public, site-specific, socially engaged and community-based art discourse (contributing artist Mark Dion notes that he receives near-monthly enquiries about 'Culture in Action').[6] Most importantly, perhaps, it was a durational public art event that does not allow for hasty assessment. Its projects tended to develop slowly, with inconstant results – primarily accessible to those who happened to be there at the time, an audience that would also often be an active co-producer of the work, and secondarily to those prepared to attend, equally slowly, to the documentation of the projects, which emerged through artists' word of mouth, a catalogue and published critiques, and now the present volume.[7]

'Culture in Action' can be situated within several simultaneous histories, as Joshua Decter explains in his contribution to this book: the conventions of large-scale public sculpture exhibitions; what might be termed 'public art'; and conceptual and process-based artistic developments between the 1960s and 90s.[8] Its ambition was 'to expand the limits of what could be identified or recognised *as art* in urban social contexts – beyond the studio, gallery, museum or alternative space'.[9] By 1993, the precedent for complex durational engagements with particular sites and 'publics' had been established for some time; 'Culture in Action' did not inaugurate this kind of work, yet it made what was happening visible on a wider scale.

Looking back over the past twenty years, we find many terms that have been inscribed upon such practices, including 'conversational art' (Homi K. Bhabha), 'dialogical aesthetics' (Grant Kester), 'new genre public art' (Suzanne Lacy), 'new situationism' (Claire Doherty), 'connective aesthetics' (Suzi Gablik), 'participatory art' (Claire Bishop) and 'collective creativity' (WHW).[10] Equally, 'the educational turn' in contemporary art and curating

—

[5] See Daniel J. Martinez and Michael Brenson in conversation in this volume, p.205. See also John Cage's definition of an experiment as something 'not ... to be later judged in terms of success and failure, but simply as of an act, the outcome of which is unknown'. J. Cage, 'Experimental Music: Doctrine', *Silence: Lectures and Writings*, Middletown, CT: Wesleyan University Press, 1973, p.13.
[6] See Mark Dion in conversation with Stephanie Smith in this volume, p.182.
[7] See the comprehensive documentation and images of each 'Culture in Action' project in this volume, pp.67–157.
[8] See Joshua Decter, 'Culture in Action: Exhibition as Social Redistribution', in this volume, pp.14–43.
[9] *Ibid.*
[10] See Homi K. Bhabha, 'Conversational Art', in Mary Jane Jacob and Michael Brenson (ed.), *Conversations at the Castle: Changing Audiences and Contemporary*

(Paul O'Neill and Mick Wilson) and the emergence of an art of 'social cooperation' (Tom Finkelpearl) have, in different ways, attempted to encapsulate the social, durational and processual qualities inherent in more immaterial forms of both curatorial and artistic co-production, predominantly experienced beyond the art institutional setting or the traditional gallery frame.[11]

In his contextualising contribution to this volume, Helmut Draxler proposes that 'Culture and Action' occurred at the tail end of a period in which two particular categories of art practice came to the fore: the *exhibitionary* and the *discursive*.[12] The exhibitionary includes 'ways of arranging and presenting objects or displaying information; ways of addressing, assembling and guiding people; and ways of interacting symbolically with those objects or information via conversation, education, marketing or critique', in which the discursive has become a means of intervening into the exhibitionary situation through voiced debates and targeted questioning. As Draxler argues, the emergence of these categories announced a newly decentred and dispersed cultural field, which remains current today.

Such projects might occur at the points at which the main event is critiqued from within, or when the restrictive scenarios, into which art and curatorial labour are forced, are circumvented in some way. On the part of its curator, Mary Jane Jacob, 'Culture in Action' was, in part, a means of sidestepping the established approach of the commissioning public art agency, Sculpture Chicago – an approach that was dominant in the US at the time.[13] It took more than eighteen months for her to convince the project's governing board of the benefits of an arts programme in which there might be no demonstrable outcome at all, or at least none that could be determined in advance.[14] Yet some of its critics at the time perceived these unplanned outcomes as quite the opposite, seen for instance in Joe Scanlan's concerns

—

Art, Cambridge, MA: The MIT Press, 1998, pp.38–47; Grant H. Kester, 'Dialogical Aesthetics', *Conversation Pieces: Community and Communication in Modern Art*, Berkeley, CA: University of California Press, 2004, pp.82–123; Suzanne Lacy, *Mapping the Terrain: New Genre Public Art*, Seattle: Bay Press, 1995; C. Doherty, 'The New Situationists', in C. Doherty (ed.), *Contemporary Art: From Studio to Situation*, London: Black Dog, 2004, pp.7–14; Suzi Gablik, 'Connective Aesthetics', *American Art*, vol.6, no.2, Spring 1992, pp.2–7; Claire Bishop, *Artificial Hells: Participatory Art and the Politics of Spectatorship*, London: Verso, 2012; and What, How and for Whom (WHW) (ed.), *Kollektive Kreativität / Collective Creativity* (exh. cat.), Frankfurt a.M.: Revolver Archiv für aktuelle Kunst, 2005.

[11] See P. O'Neill and Mick Wilson (ed.), *Curating and the Educational Turn*, Amsterdam and London: de Appel and Open Editions, 2010; and T. Finkelpearl, *What We Made, op. cit.*

[12] See Helmut Draxler, 'The Turn from the Turns: An Avant-Garde Moving Out of the Centre (1986–93)', in this volume, pp.44–64.

[13] See M.J. Jacob, 'Chicago is Culture in Action', in this volume, pp.172–81. For more on the public art context at the time, see Hafþór Yngvason, 'The New Public Art: As Opposed to What?', in this volume, pp.158–63.

[14] M.J. Jacob, 'Chicago is Culture in Action', in this volume, p.179.

over the show's proximity to 'recent (government) guidelines that art be useful and have immediately measurable effects'.[15]

Certain aspects of the programme can be understood in terms of a host-and-uninvited-guest tactic of coordination and invention, enabling parasitic curatorial or artistic labour to exist alongside, or in confrontation with, pre-existing cultural forms, originating scenarios or prescribed exhibition contexts. Just as Jacob made up 'plausible outcomes' for her funders where necessary, participating artists operated independently of these prescribed outcomes in order to proceed in the way their projects required.[16] In some cases, the artists would find themselves bypassed by their collaborators in view of larger agendas; Simon Grennan describes here how his and Christopher Sperandio's project with a group of confectionary-factory workers became a tool within a larger power struggle between union president Jethro Head and factory manager Charles E. Brashears.[17] Examples such as this productively complicate the idea of instrumentalisation often associated with preselected or 'sited' community interactions, in which art projects begin to intersect with such a multiplicity of interests – including already-established groups and communities – that the questions raised are necessarily more intricate and unpredictable.

In order to move beyond the modern notion of a reflexive subject – a concept for which the transition between passive and active participants in art is difficult to assess – it is necessary to consider the issue of time. More specifically, how public time is framed in order that a space of co-production can emerge. This is what Bruno Latour refers to as the need for more 'cohabitation time, the great Complicator', where democratic space is understood as time spent together, publicly, in contradiction with each other.[18] Here in this volume, Hafþór Yngvason describes how a process of self-critique by public art practitioners prompted the shift from 'integrationist' to 'participatory' approaches during the early 1990s.[19] Yet, if we are to think of participation as more than a closed, one-off, relational or social interaction with art, it must take account of duration as a temporal process of cohabitation, in which time can contribute to something that is immeasurable, unquantifiable and unknowable from the outset.

This is most evident when we observe that often a number of the people contributing to durational projects are unaware of exactly what they are taking part in and what the outcome is intended to be; their participation – what has been done, who took part and what was achieved – is not something

—

[15] See Joe Scanlan, 'Culture in Action', in this volume, pp.164–71.

[16] M.J. Jacob, 'Chicago is Culture in Action', in this volume, p.180.

[17] See Simon Grennan, of Grennan & Sperandio, in conversation with Lucy Steeds in this volume, pp.192–201.

[18] Bruno Latour, 'From Realpolitik to Dingpolitik or How to Make Things Public', in B. Latour and Peter Weibel (ed.), *Making Things Public: Atmospheres of Democracy* (exh. cat.), Cambridge, MA: The MIT Press, 2005, p.40.

[19] H. Yngvason, 'The New Public Art: As Opposed to What?', in this volume, p.161.

that can be measured or evaluated in any clear way. As Daniel J. Martinez and Michael Brenson reflect in their conversation here, 'what we actually lived through, what we experienced and what we thought is unrecognisable from the way it's been written about'.[20] Such processes of being together for a period of time with some common objectives, often as a means of constituting a new mode of relational, conversational and participatory practice, tend to offer a multiplicity of modes of interaction between people. Duration also has a destabilising effect because there is no longer a fixed time and place in which to experience, or participate in, the art as event.

As Mary Jane Jacob's contribution to this volume suggests, exhibition-making is a category in need of continual reassessment, a model to be 'expanded, adapted, even transformed, to follow what artists do, and to enable them further'.[21] Although it is an elusive concept, the curatorial speaks to these concerns and offers means by which to understand 'Culture in Action'. The curatorial resists the stasis of the artist-curator-spectator triumvirate and supports more semi-autonomous and self-determined aesthetic and discursive forms of practice that may overlap and intersect, rather than seeking a dialectic (image) or oppositional presentation (form). The concept does not argue either for or against exhibitions as conventionally understood – discursively led curatorial praxis includes such exhibitions among its many productive forms. While the open-endedness of recent discussions around the curatorial is undoubtedly somewhat frustrating at times, this very frustration is, perhaps, the objective. Certain articulations of the curatorial have identified a strand of practice that seeks to resist categorical resolution, preferring to function in the Adornian sense, as a constellation of activities that do not wish to fully reveal themselves.[22] Rather than forcing syntheses, this idea of a curatorial constellation (as an always-emergent praxis) brings together incommensurable social objects, ideas and subject relations in order to demonstrate the structural faults and falsities inherent in the notion of the hermetic exhibition as primary curatorial work.

To the extent that 'Culture in Action' represents a move towards more discursive and duration-specific approaches, it raises the question of access: what happens when the primary outcome of an ongoing project is a more dispersed form of mediation, and when the artwork, the authorial voice and the exhibition site are not easy to locate – in other words, when the project does not result in single autonomous works/exhibitions to be viewed as

—

[20] See D.J. Martinez and M. Brenson in conversation in this volume, p.202.

[21] Where 'the creative, generative, discursive, "exhibit-able" and experiential are all part of what an exhibition affords'. M.J. Jacob, 'Chicago is Culture in Action', in this volume, p.178.

[22] 'As a constellation, theoretical thought circles the concept it would like to unseal, hoping that it will fly open like the lock of a well-guarded safe-deposit box: in response, not to a single key or a single number, but to a combination of numbers.' Theodor W. Adorno, *Negative Dialectics* (1966) (trans. E.B. Ashton), New York: Continuum, 2007, p.163.

one-off experiences? Notably, this is less a problem of access for 'non-art' constituencies than it is for those familiar with museums and galleries, who may restrict themselves to these usual means. For example, as part of 'Culture in Action', Iñigo Manglano-Ovalle and Street-Level Video (S-LV) produced an installation at Chicago's Museum of Contemporary Art, on display at the same time as numerous installations within their own neighbourhood on the West Side; while the project brought many members of S-LV and their neighbours to the MCA for the first time, few of the museum's middle- and upper-class regular attendees visited Manglano-Ovalle and S-LV's culminating block party in their West Town community. If 'Culture in Action' set out to broaden art's connection to the public, indeed to pluralise its publics, then the whole programme also served to problematise what 'public' might mean.

The *Exhibition Histories* project was developed in order to examine art at the moment of its contact with publics, and the present volume – the fifth in the series – is an opportunity to take stock. The first in the series considered two shows, 'Op Losse Schroeven' and 'When Attitudes Become Form' (both 1969), that marked a move by curators to work more closely with artists, in order to test the institutional structures surrounding art's display.[23] The nascent fields of exhibition histories and exhibition studies, analogous to the reflexive processes inherent to their object of analysis, continue to redefine and question their scope and limits – and there is still much work to be done. Michael Warner describes a public as a self-organised relation among strangers,[24] yet to what extent do discursive projects such as those in 'Culture in Action' constitute a public in themselves? Is this a public constituted in a momentary place and time, or is this a form of publicness that is post-produced – after the effect? And if so, might they contribute to emergent concepts of the curatorial, as the co-production of 'public times' rather than public spaces? Furthermore, at what points do they become open to encounter by persons beyond the artists and their collaborative groups – and to us today? For us, these remain open questions.

—

[23] Christian Rattemeyer et al., *Exhibiting the New Art: 'Op Losse Schroeven' and 'When Attitudes Become Form' 1969*, London: Afterall Books, 2010.

[24] Michael Warner describes this relation as being constituted through mere attention, as well as being the social space created through the reflexive circulation of discourse. What this implies, in particular for contemporary public art, is that publics are dependent upon practice and entirely paradoxical, in the sense that a public is neither equivalent to an abstract unity between individuals nor reducible to the actual set of individuals that happen to constitute it at any particular moment. And it is also true that, in many cases, the moment of publicness is never fully revealed. See M. Warner, 'Publics and Counterpublics', *Public Culture*, vol.14, no.1, Winter 2002, pp.49–90.

Culture in Action: Exhibition as Social Redistribution — Joshua Decter

Given the transformations unfolding in the present era of social media – in art, communication, curating, art discourse and just about everything else – how might one re-engage with the specifically *social* dimensions of the 1993 exhibition project 'Culture in Action: A Public Art Program of Sculpture Chicago'?[1] A considerable amount of critical, theoretical and art-historical analysis has been dedicated to this exhibition over the years, yet thorny issues over whether art can operate effectively as an agent of social change – and what sort of criteria we should use for such an evaluation – remain to be navigated. These concerns seem to be at the ideological heart of 'Culture in Action', a show for which curator Mary Jane Jacob worked with eight artist-led groups in order to challenge the parochialisms of public art and the conventions of site specificity: she created an urban platform for artists to research, develop and implement innovative projects that reimagined art as an instrument for new modes of social participation and community engagement.

In her 1991 curatorial project 'Places with a Past: New Site-Specific Art at Charleston's Spoleto Festival', in South Carolina, Jacob had already started rethinking site specificity in relation to place (place thought of as a material embodiment of local, contextual histories), informed by a deep understanding of the legacy of art in public spaces within the US and certain European contexts.[2]

In the US, the National Endowment for the Arts (NEA) began to earmark federal funds for public art in 1967, the year that the organisation established its Art in Public Places programme, and the ensuing outdoor sculptural works included Isamu Noguchi's *Black Sun* in Seattle's Volunteer Park and Alexander Calder's *La Grande Vitesse* in a plaza in Grand Rapids, Michigan (both 1969 and permanent). When funds originating from public taxation are involved in the production and/or siting of works of contemporary art in the public realm, politicisation is inevitable, with disputes compounded by lack of consensus regarding aesthetic value and by an artwork's distinct ideological connotations. This helps us to understand how the controversy and legal case that emerged around Richard Serra's *Tilted Arc*, which was commissioned by the Art in Architecture Program of the US General Services Administration for a plaza in downtown Manhattan in 1979 and removed a decade later, became a watershed situation. A litmus test in regard to popular support for the public funding of contemporary art, Serra's

—

[1] 'Culture in Action: A Public Art Program of Sculpture Chicago', May to September 1993, curated by Mary Jane Jacob.

[2] 'Places with a Past: New Site-Specific Art at Charleston's Spoleto Festival', Charleston, South Carolina, 24 May to 4 August 1991, curated by Mary Jane Jacob and including the artists James Coleman, Kate Ericson and Mel Ziegler, David Hammons, Antony Gormley and Cindy Sherman, for instance.

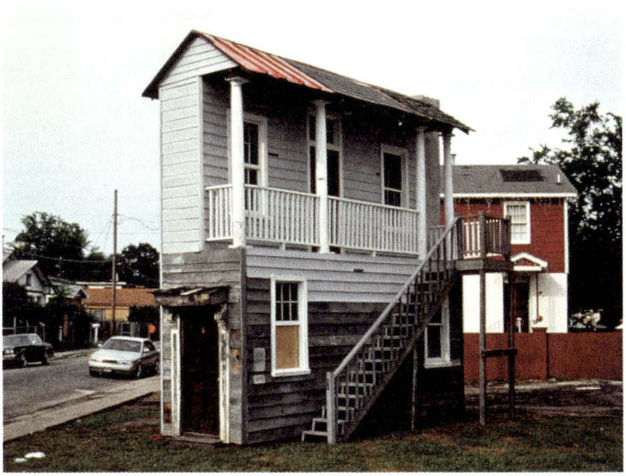

David Hammons,
House of the Future, 1991,
as part of 'Places with a Past',
Charleston, South Carolina, 1991.
© the artist
Photography: John McWilliams
Courtesy the artist and
Jack Tilton Gallery

site-specific outdoor sculpture compelled many to reconsider what it means to situate art within public space, and to understand that the urban social space is a precarious construct, formed out of an interpenetration of various constituencies and interest groups – the government, the private sector, citizens and publics – with disparate and sometimes competing understandings, misunderstandings and value systems.

The twentieth century is rife with examples of artists developing unusual methods for engaging individuals, audiences and communities in the production (and redefinition) of art, wherein forms of co-authorship, collaboration, cooperation and social participation are tested. Modes of aesthetic collectivisation and forms of collaborative authorship can be observed across the ideological spectrum, enunciating a range of aesthetic, political and social agendas. Allan Kaprow and Joseph Beuys are fundamental in this history. By the late 1950s, Kaprow, influenced by John Cage, was already organising Happenings and generating transient, ephemeral, socially participatory events and performative actions to reinvent the terms of art beyond the dominant languages of painting, sculpture and other traditional media, and to challenge the normative institutional parameters of gallery and museum. The development of Beuys's multifaceted practice in the 60s, which included an unusual admixture of object-making, performance, politics, pedagogy and shamanism (among other features), was particularly crucial in terms of a repositioning of the artist as a public figure engaged in broader ideological and political struggles. Beuys's various political activities and statements, as well as his teaching, can be considered elements of an art practice. And his notion of 'social sculpture' was instrumental in unlocking new models of art-making that appeared, at least, to rethink the broader social consequences of aesthetic objects – perhaps even to the extent that certain of Beuys's artworks and/or art activities assumed a post-aesthetic condition, beyond the recognisable precincts or institutional frames of art.

Located along a somewhat different trajectory, a new mode of art activism developed within the context of New York during the 1960s, epitomised by the formation of the Art Workers' Coalition in 1969. The AWC endeavoured to pressure major museums (and New York's Museum of Modern Art in particular) to institute reforms that would guarantee protections for artists' rights and increase the representation of women and artists of colour, and to make public statements against the war in Vietnam. The Coalition would eventually splinter into other art activist groups during the 70s, followed up in the 80s by art collectives such as the Guerrilla Girls and Group Material. The former, an anonymous group of cultural producers committed to feminist activism and costumed in gorilla suits, used a combination of data and cleverly manipulated imagery to bring much needed attention to the under-representation of women artists in museums and galleries; the latter devised a hybrid curatorial/archival model to collate works of art and other cultural materials in the examination of various subjects such as democracy, education and HIV/AIDS. Although such collectives operated from within – and put into representation – the contemporary art community, they also sought a political, social, activist relevance beyond these enclaves. Perhaps most significantly, they were self-organised: these constellations of artists and other cultural workers arose out of a sense of necessity. This history of a more grass-roots, self-organised approach to the work of art – activist or other – within the broader culture was undoubtedly influential in Jacob's thinking for 'Culture in Action', at least as she endeavoured to reimagine the remit of the curator beyond the realm of the museum, gallery or alternative space, and to catalyse or mediate the work of art reconsidered as an instrument of distributed social engagement or intervention within urban communities. Yet, as we will see, 'Culture in Action' was something of a paradoxical undertaking, at once institutional (it had an organisational structure, funding apparatus and curatorial hierarchy) and somewhat post-institutional: it sought to entrench itself and dissipate its top-down institutional identity within the vernacular flows of the city by deploying artists to help facilitate the self-organised empowerment of particular urban residents. Such distinct, if somewhat contradictory, attributes may not be reconcilable at the level of the political, or the socially symbolic.

From sociological, anthropological and certain philosophical perspectives, of course, art is already always imbricated within the social. Art is social even when it claims – or appears – to be turning away from the social. 'Social practice', 'public practice', 'community practice', 'site specificity', 'post-site specificity' and other nuanced discursive-terminological formulations all reflect a desire for the artist and for art to break free from the comforts of circulation among traditional privileged audiences and constituencies of the avant-garde so as to engage with people who inhabit other social domains, class strata and ethnic communities. If art is *always* socially constructed, then art that understands itself as being *socially engaged* transmits a particular desire to connect into broader constituencies, with different values and interests. In other words, a demotic conception of art is envisaged: a repositioning or redistributing of art into the social demos. Participatory and collaborative art practice reflects an amplification and elevation of post-individual (or post-autonomous), group-generated and collectively iterated procedures; these seem more social because they appear to be more directly the product of scaled-up socialised processes *vis-à-vis* autonomous art-making — which, of course, is never fully autonomous, given the elaborately interpersonal network of production, display and socialising that is embedded within art practice. Art is intrinsically biosocial and biopolitical.

Relevant here are the initial generation of Conceptual art practitioners, who emerged in the 1960s and 70s and were engaged in precursor forms of institutional critique that compelled the viewer to think of art in relation to its discursive, linguistic, contextual, social, ideological and other frames – such as Art & Language, Michael Asher, Robert Barry, Marcel Broodthaers, Daniel Buren, Hans Haacke and Douglas Huebler. The younger generation of artists from the 80s who are most closely linked to the nomenclature Institutional Critique – such as Mark Dion (an eventual participant in 'Culture in Action') and Andrea Fraser – had already become fairly well integrated into the contemporary art world by the early 90s. The traditional function of the museum has been to attract various publics to its centralised locus of aesthetic and cultural expertise. Ironically or not, as museums have increasingly begun to operate as zones of cultural tourism at least since the 60s in the US and Europe, they have also managed to re-inscribe their authority as purveyors of enlightenment. Museums, galleries and other types of both non-profit and for-profit cultural spaces comprise the platform for a *social theatrics* of exhibition – and for the exhibition of *socialisations* framed by the institution. Artists such as Asher, Buren, Broodthaers and Haacke had revealed – inadvertently or deliberately – the contradictions, paradoxes, double binds, tautologies and circularities of the critique of art as a system of production, display, circulation, consumption and exchange. And perhaps the younger generation of artists associated with Institutional Critique experienced some degree of anxiety about the aforementioned contradictions; indeed, Fraser seems to have integrated that very anxiety into her practice in rather compelling ways. By the early 90s it was becoming apparent that artists and institutions were producing and managing a feedback loop of reciprocal critique and legitimation. Certain artists and curators began to experience a sense of frustration about this situation – that their work didn't seem to have sufficient impact or relevance for people beyond the professional, specialised and institutional spheres of the art system. This is pertinent to the trajectory of Dion's practice, which, by around 1990, had already shifted away from the discursive space of art history and conservation towards the disciplinary field of ecology and issues of environmental eco-crisis.

In Jürgen Habermas's essay 'Modernity: An Incomplete Project' (1980), the philosopher rebukes the traditional avant-gardist belief that a rupturing of the sphere of culture, as enacted by various aesthetic revolutions, will trigger the disruption (revolutionary or otherwise) of other social spheres, such as those of politics, economy or law. For Habermas, within developed, democratic and rational societies, the 'life-spheres' have been atomised to such an extent that the possibility of radical cross-contamination is remote. At the same time, he invokes the notion of a 're-appropriation of the expert's culture from the standpoint of the life-world', and refers to an example of such re-appropriation within Peter Weiss's novel *The Aesthetics of Resistance* (1975–81), wherein a group of young workers during the late 1930s are described as attending school in order to educate themselves about a part of high European culture from which they have been alienated, and then applying this newly acquired knowledge to their own social context, thereby illuminating both realms.[3] Something about Habermas's argument still resonates. Or rather, it resonates afresh. As much as artists, curators, institutions and other cultural workers and organisations endeavour to have an impact on the fundamental social, economic and other structural conditions of advanced capitalism (or hybrid forms of socialism-capitalism), we may have to acknowledge that change can only happen at the micro-level. And we still lack the evaluative tools to determine what is meant by *social change* – beyond rather basic empirical and statistical modes of analysis. This is an issue that returns again and again in relation to how we reassess 'Culture in Action' as a curatorial model, and in terms of its individual projects. Today it seems that the liberal humanist, cultural-evangelical notion of art as an agent of urban social change may have been repurposed by closet neoliberals such as Richard Florida, who promotes the notion of a 'creative class' positively impacting the economic, cultural and social redevelopment of cities.[4] Although there may be a ring of truth to this argument, many on the cultural left legitimately view it as a pernicious instrumentalisation of art and culture – as a not-so-hidden defence of an urban gentrification process whereby artists often get priced out of the very neighbourhoods they helped to productively transform.

'Culture in Action' is remembered by some as a watershed exhibition project of the early 1990s that embodied – and perhaps inadvertently institutionalised – a convergence of significant conceptual and historical developments from the 60s through to the early 90s. It took up changing notions of art in public space; rethought the potential of art production as a catalyst for (social) activism; experimented with new modes of community-based artistic/cultural engagement; and proposed a new ethos of social and political responsibility as exemplified by artists committed to working with urban citizens in their everyday circumstances of labour, economics, identity, class, ethnicity and so forth. This exhibition sought to expand the limits of what could be identified or recognised *as art* in urban social contexts – beyond the studio, gallery, museum or alternative space; and it probably did so with the understanding that its artists implicitly carried a residue of the discursive, institutional frame of art into every situation, if only in the form of their cultural and intellectual capital.

—

—

[3] Jürgen Habermas, 'Modernity: An Incomplete Project' (1980), in Hal Foster (ed.), *The Anti-Aesthetic: Essays on Postmodern Culture*, New York: The New Press, 2002, p.12.

[4] See Richard Florida, *The Rise of the Creative Class: And How It's Transforming Work, Leisure, Community and Everyday Life*, New York: Basic Books, 2002.

Historically and in the present, a key challenge for those organising exhibitions that engage the environs of a city as a context or platform is how to make the presented works actually available – visible and comprehensible – to diverse potential audiences, constituencies and publics. The difficulty becomes amplified when the curatorial framework seeks to challenge normative approaches by asking artists to collaborate with residents or workers local to areas perhaps unfamiliar to both the artists themselves and the exhibition's visitors, with the overlapping stages of research, development, production and presentation virtually indistinct from each other. When the community involved – or the extended group inhabiting a specific place – becomes, in a sense, the primary audience of a project with an artist, new demands are made of them. Even the secondary and conventional audiences are obliged to move beyond the usual rituals associated with art in public spaces, to navigate into territories that might be rather unfamiliar in terms of the site's, or the neighbourhood's, economic, racial or ethnic make-up. Some of the invited artists had prior experience of working in this way, but the idea of making such methodology the exclusive basis of participation in an exhibition was untested.

Regarding the question of public space in cities, David Harvey has written:

> *The right to the city is not simply about access to what the city contains. The right to the city is a right to change the city, to transform the city, and it has to be also a right that is inherent.* [...] *By claiming space in public, by creating public space, social groups themselves become public.*[5]

Yet it is not only a question of how people claim their place within cities, thereby constituting public social space, but also a question of what types of experiences are generated through the social encounters – and boundary crossings – that occur within public contexts. In their 2001 book, *In Search of New Public Domain*, Maarten Hajer and Arnold Reijndorp go some distance in analysing these social processes, proposing that:

> *The modern city is most easily understood as an archipelago of enclaves, and if the citizen is continuously occupied with maintaining his or her own small network with as little possible friction with other groups, then that does indeed ostensibly spell the demise of any form of public domain. However, that is not how the private space of the archipelago resident looks. The paradoxical fact is that many people are still searching for that experience of intensely felt public places. Public domain is, in our firm opinion, not so much a place as an experience. Public domain experiences occur at the boundary between friction and freedom. On the one hand there is always the tension of a confrontation with the unfamiliar, and on the other the liberation of the experience of a different approach. In the main, our public domain experiences are in fact related to entering the parochial domain of 'others'.*[6]

—

[5] David Harvey, 'Dialogue 1: Liminal Zones / Coursing Flows', *Conversations, inSite_05*, San Diego-Tijuana: inSite, 2004, p.47.

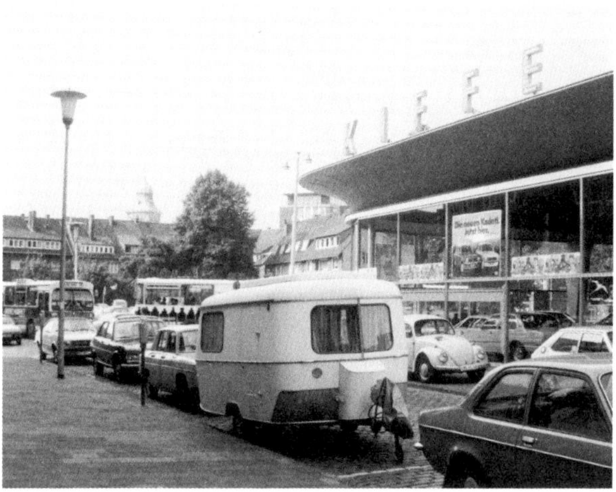

Michael Asher, *Westfälisches Landesmuseum für Kunst und Kulturgeschichte, Münster, Germany, 'Skulptur', July 3 – November 13, 1977*, 1977, 4th week, Alter Steinweg, across from Kiffe Pavilion, parking metre no.274 or 275.
Photography: Rudolf Wakonigg/WLMKuK
Courtesy Michael Asher Foundation

Such frictions and domain crossings are inevitably encountered – if not actively triggered – when the social space of cities becomes the test site for art and curatorial projects.

In relation to the history of exhibitions that engage the question of art in public space, it's productive to consider the extent to which the curatorial framework of 'Culture in Action' evolved out of large-scale, outdoor, city-based exhibitions, and specifically Skulptur Projekte Münster, as initiated by Kasper König in 1977 and taking place in Münster every ten years since. Skulptur Projekte can be read as an important barometer of the changing concepts and practices of art in public space over the decades, ranging from Minimalist sculpture and Conceptual art to variations of site specificity, and increasingly towards relational and socially participatory projects. Yet it seems as if the city of Münster (and its park) primarily functioned as a platform for the introduction of autonomously produced, discrete artworks with stable authorships, albeit with occasionally inspired results.[7] Consider the work of a key artist within the Münster context, Michael Asher, who managed to conceptualise a project for the first edition of Skulptur Projekte that questioned the paradigm of large-scale outdoor sculpture as public art, and sought to rethink art in relation to its urban environment and multiple publics. In 1977, Asher's *Westfälisches Landesmuseum für Kunst und Kulturgeschichte, Münster, Germany, 'Skulptur', July 3 – November 13, 1977* moved an otherwise ordinary travel-trailer to a new location within the city

—

[6] Maarten Hajer and Arnold Reijndorp, *In Search of New Public Domain*, Rotterdam: NAi Publishers, 2001, p.116.

[7] The catalogue for the 2007 edition includes a brief history of the exhibition since 1977. See the editorial 'Preface' to Brigitte Franzen, Kasper König and Carina Plath, *Sculpture Projects Muenster 07* (exh. cat.), Cologne: Walther König, pp.11–18.

weekly, with reiterations using the increasingly vintage model, the Eriba Familia BS, in each successive edition of the exhibition through to the most recent (at the time of writing) in 2007. Asher's mobile work at once appropriated and challenged parochial notions of site specificity, free-standing sculpture, permanency and the aesthetic of the readymade, while ostensibly coaxing visiting art audiences and Münster's citizens to reimagine their urban environs in relation to the vehicle. Although Asher's work was not socially collaborative or participatory in any fundamental sense, it did compel publics to engage in urban space in a different way, and to rethink how a work of art might gain presence, paradoxically, through its fugitive condition.

'Culture in Action', in contrast with Skulptur Projekte Münster – and especially with the second iteration, which most closely preceded it, in 1987 – sought to mobilise artists as interlocutors between particular audiences, entities, individuals and communities in the city of Chicago, and to generate art from these encounters, engagements and cooperations. Jacob invited artists to reactivate the possibilities of culture as a catalyst for education and social transformation, wherein the collaboration between an artist and members of a community somehow generates a social trace or collective memory. This exhibition framework (and curatorial model) undoubtedly influenced later versions of Münster and other large-scale exhibitions: one of the impacts of 'Culture in Action' was not only to help institutionalise and engender forms of socially participatory practice, but also to naturalise models of social participation and localised community engagement as formulae for curating.

—

A general aim of the Chicago project was to produce an exhibition platform through which artists who were already engaged to some extent with concepts and procedures of social collaboration, or modalities of cultural activism, could develop art projects responsive to specific conditions within the urban territories of Chicago. A brief description of the project from the exhibition's programme guide, the primary source of information available to the public during the run of the exhibition, reads:

> *'Culture in Action: New Public Art in Chicago' features eight projects by artists' teams and citizen collaborators sited throughout Chicago from May to September 1993. Over the past year, the invited artists have developed partnerships through a process of public exchange that has extended the role of audience beyond spectator to that of participant. Forging a fundamental link between art and education, this process of local engagement has led to artworks that reflect a shared voice.*[8]

And:

> *'Culture in Action: New Public Art in Chicago' reflects the social concerns which fuel artists working in the public arena today, while serving as an urban laboratory to actively involve diverse audiences in the creation of innovative public art projects.*[9]

The guide communicated that this was not a conventional group exhibition, but rather an extra-institutional show, taking place beyond the precincts of museum, gallery or alternative space, while retaining the vestiges of specialised art discourse; and that the project desired to follow neither the traditional form of a community-based art initiative nor a conventional public art endeavour. Yet 'Culture in Action' does not belong in the category of what would traditionally be considered a grass-roots social movement, since there was a hierarchical institutional structure guiding the production of the artists' localised urban engagements (even in regard to those Chicago-based artists who were already engaged in art projects specific to the city). The project was from start to finish a construction, a constructed situation, however much the desired engagement with traditionally overlooked precincts sought an organic, community-driven ethos. Yet the show also demonstrated that these conditions are not mutually exclusive – and specifically that in creating an exhibition infrastructure to nurture potential relationships among artists, citizens and communities in the production of new forms of art practice, innovative forms of curatorial organisation need to be simultaneously developed. The viewing publics for 'Culture in Action' were asked to commit to more active forms of encounter – even if it was just the act of navigating the environs of Chicago, entering into a variety of neighbourhoods and social environments – in what constituted a shift from the usual rituals of cultural tourism, and aimed towards a reimagining of art's impact on the city. It was not only that the participating artists were developing what might today be considered various forms of community-based practice, but that this was accompanied by the belief that audiences and publics might also become agents of social exploration – or, at the very least, able and willing to experience unfamiliar social realms.

In order to assess whether the artists' extended processes of research, collaboration and engagement with local Chicagoans – lasting at least a year in each case – actually led to what Sculpture Chicago characterised as 'artworks that reflect a shared voice', it is necessary to do some unpacking, both ideologically and in material, pragmatic terms. 'Culture in Action' might be characterised as a liberal humanist initiative, and 'sharing' would suggest a relatively conflict- or friction-free environment, masking the internal struggles that must have taken place as the exhibition came into being. The organisers' promotional language was designed to attract new audiences and publics, perhaps as a way to offer an alternative type of cultural tourism. For example, the programme guide communicated that 'Culture in Action' was distributed across a variety of urban areas by including a map of Chicago with a legend indicating the location of the artists' projects, with brief descriptions.[10]

—

[8] 'Culture in Action' programme guide, Center for Curatorial Studies (CCS), Bard College, Archives: Mary Jane Jacob Papers, Series II: 'Culture in Action' 1987–96, box 04, folder 75.

[9] *Ibid.*

[10] Extracts from the project descriptions in the programme guide are reproduced in the following sections of this book. See pp.67–157.

In February 1995, Sculpture Chicago filed a 'Final Descriptive Report' to the NEA (mandatory for all NEA grant recipients) that provided a summation of the overall project, including descriptions of all the individual projects. Its 'Narrative Summary' reads:

> *'Culture in Action' consisted of eight artist groups who collaborated with Chicago residents, groups that numbered from six to hundreds of individuals. The artists selected for this programme addressed within their projects such pressing urban issues as public housing, HIV/AIDS caregiving, labour/management relations, minority youth leadership, ecology, volunteer activism and women's achievements over the last century, and directed their art to take the forms of collaborative public programmes, performances, installations and other innovative genre[s]. Conversations taking place over months with cooperating institutions such as The Bakery, Confectionery & Tobacco Workers' Union Local 552, Chicago Housing Authority, Chicago Botanic Gardens, Community Television Network, Emerson House Chicago Commons and the City of Chicago Departments of the Environment, Planning and Economic Development and Transportation opened the way for artists to root their projects in diverse places. These multiple liaisons enabled the artists to establish themselves within communities, understand the concerns of their targeted constituencies and define works that speak to a new union of artistic and community interests.*[11]

The research and social-outreach processes engaged in by the participating artists and their collaborators resulted in a rather diverse range of project-based works, wherein notions and strategies of sustainability, intervention, deep collaboration and cooperation, pedagogy and activism were reinvented and tested. The social, cultural and political repercussions of these projects beyond the contemporary art world were open to question in 1993, and perhaps to a large extent remain unknown today. While one may identify how aspects of artistic and curatorial practice were transformed within the framework of 'Culture in Action', it is trickier to discern the impact of the exhibition upon the lives of those individuals who participated in or lived alongside the eight projects. The narrative of the NEA report refers to a 'new union of artistic and community interests', which is perhaps a somewhat inflated claim, designed for consumption by one of the exhibition's funders. It might be more accurate to use the term 'temporary' before 'union' – or, 'social constellations' might replace 'union', since this is what Jacob and Sculpture Chicago did end up cultivating and, to a certain extent, engineering.

(Simon) Grennan & (Christopher) Sperandio's contribution to 'Culture in Action',[12] *We Got It! The Workforce Makes the Candy of Their Dreams* (1992–93) was generated in collaboration with twelve members of Local 552 of fig.17-26

—

[11] 'Culture in Action' Final Descriptive Report to the National Endowment for the Arts, Art in Public Places grant, 27 February 1995, CCS Bard Archives: Mary Jane Jacob Papers, Series II: 'Culture in Action' 1987–96, box 04, folder 82.
[12] Almost immediately following the exhibition the artists assumed the moniker Grennan & Sperandio.

The Bakery, Confectionery and Tobacco Workers' International Union of America, who worked at a Nestlé Corporation manufacturing plant in Chicago. The artists and union members developed and branded a new chocolate bar, as well as its advertising campaign. The bar's bright yellow wrappers with fetching 'We Got It!' logos, framed by the US flag on the left and the union's logo on the right, featured in stores in central Chicago during the summer of 1993; promotional billboards appeared in predominantly working-class areas, for the most part, in the south of the city.[13] This hybrid item – at once conceptual art object and food product – and its attendant campaigns, involving billboards that were themselves hybrid entities that doubled as artworks, alluded to the interrelationship between labour and corporations, or to normative modes of product distribution and consumerism, perhaps with a desire to inflect the material conditions of how workers are connected to – or divorced from – what they produce within the factory context. The store-display carton, emblazoned with the catchphrase 'Now You Get It!', also provided basic information on the project, along with a group portrait of the two artists and collaborating union workers holding an outsized version of the wrapper. The grass-roots, even populist, visual style suggested the collective processes intrinsic to unions, as well as reflecting something of the collaborative methodology utilised by Grennan & Sperandio. The graphics of the chocolate-bar wrapper and display carton anticipated the artists' ongoing reworking of the visual language of comics, a language that is at once underground and countercultural, yet also accessible to diverse audiences.

fig.19, 20
fig.22, 23
fig.21

As it turns out, this is the only project in the 'Culture in Action' exhibition that I actually experienced in 1993, and not in its Chicago context, but in the form of a display carton perched atop the front desk of Andrea Rosen's former gallery space in New York's SoHo district. At the time, I was already familiar with Grennan & Sperandio's socially collaborative work (they met in art school at the University of Illinois at Chicago (UIC), and their artistic partnership had been developing since 1990), but the *We Got It!* project especially caught my attention, as well as that of many people in the contemporary art world. Indeed, the chocolate bar was the lead illustration for Michael Kimmelman's extensive review of 'Culture in Action' for *The New York Times*.[14]

The *We Got It!* chocolate bar can be understood as a conceptual-political (art) object predicated upon – and declarative of – processes of deep collaboration. An edible product distributed in various locations to make evident the extent to which artistic labour and other modes of specialised labour are not that far apart, and thereby not only symbolising but also actualising a momentary breakdown in traditional modernist hierarchies. The bars indexed

—

[13] A map indicating the position of the billboards is reproduced in this volume, see p.99.
[14] See Michael Kimmelman, 'Of Candy Bars and Public Art', *The New York Times*, 26 September 1993, section 2 (Arts and Leisure), pp.1 and 43–44. Online at http://www.nytimes.com/1993/09/26/arts/art-view-of-candy-bars-and-public-art.html?pagewanted=all&src=pm (last accessed on 14 April 2014).

a redistribution of authorial power in relation to both the production of artworks and other kinds of cultural things: a delicious counter-commodity emblematic of 'disalienated' labour. *The Workforce Makes the Candy of Their Dreams* remains a very important project for the two artists, by their own assessment.[15] What long-term impact the project has had on their collaborators, or co-authors, is not easy to determine, although even a temporary transformative effect upon these individuals' relationships to labour, production and creative processes might have engendered a new sense of social or political agency in the world.

Already by the late 1980s, New York artist Mark Dion had begun to shift his attention away from a critical focus on the institutional frame of art and art history towards the broader frame of urban ecologies and environmental conditions. At the same time, he was beginning to rethink the potential of research-based processes, as well as new concepts for art in public space. Reflecting on the early 90s, Dion has recently indicated that he and Jacob had engaged in discussions early in the process of 'Culture in Action' about how to 'reshape the idea of public art'; they agreed 'that public art wasn't simply art outside of the museum, but that it could be responsive to and responsible to what a broader public means'.[16]

In the project that Dion initiated under the umbrella of Jacob's exhibition and remained committed to for one year, the artist worked with a group of fourteen high school students from Chicago's inner city, establishing a kind of pedagogical framework to co-investigate urban ecologies in relation to tropical ecosystems. The students – who were to become known as the Chicago Urban Ecology Action Group (CUEAG) with Dion, and credited with the artist as co-producers of the art project – met regularly with him,[17] eventually in an experimental ecological field station established in Lincoln Park. The students were also led by Dion on an expedition and research trip to Belize, thereby establishing a comparative analysis between distinct contexts, and suggesting a kind of global translocalism.

fig.1–13

fig.2–5

Iñigo Manglano-Ovalle's *Tele-Vecindario: A Street-Level Video Project* (1992–93) was produced in collaboration with a group that came together under the name of the Westtown Vecinos Video Channel and its youth division, Street-Level Video. It led to the establishment, in 1995, of a non-profit organisation, Street-Level Youth Media, that still exists in West Town, the neighbourhood where Manglano-Ovalle has lived since 1991. For *Tele-Vecindario*, the artist collaborated with a core group of fifteen youths to produce video portraits of and for the community, which took the form of

fig.45–56

—

[15] Conversation with Christopher Sperandio, of Grennan & Sperandio, 17 February 2013.
[16] Conversation with Mark Dion, 21 May 2012.
[17] There were meetings every Saturday during the school year, a two-week trip over December 1992 to January 1993 and then an ongoing presence in the course of the exhibition in the summer of 1993. For more on the project narrative, see pp.72–83 in this volume.

fig.49 street installations, television programming and a work titled *Cul-de-Sac: A Street-Level Video Installation*, sited at the Museum of Contemporary Art in Chicago from 3 July to 8 August 1993. The artist and his collaborators referred to the project as 'video mapping', designed to generate discussions fig.52–56 about community and place. A day-long block party on 28 August 1993 signalled the end of the project within 'Culture in Action'; however, the technical equipment used for *Tele-Vecindario* then became the material infrastructure for the emergence of Street-Level Youth Media. There is further discussion of Manglano-Ovalle's project later in this essay,[18] but it's important to stress here that the transformation of *Tele-Vecindario* into a sustainable non-profit organisation in West Town seems to have been a relatively organic, self-organised and community-generated process; that it was not imposed on local residents by the artist; and that Manglano-Ovalle was a member of this community.

Of course, that which appears to be a spontaneous grass-roots articulation or eruption is always contingent to a certain degree upon some thing, event or person to galvanise it – a political match to help light the fire of local activism or reaffirm community solidarity. Artists can play the role of urban agents occasionally, and it seems that Jacob was counting, in least in part, upon artists to reignite the social activism of citizens and communities. This fig.57–67 and p.*203* approach is clearly evident within Daniel J. Martinez's *Consequences of a Gesture* and *100 Victories/10,000 Tears* (1992–93), a two-part project by the Los Angeles-based artist: an installation and a parade that he developed with VinZula Kara and a group that took on the name West Side Three-Point Marchers / Los Desfiladores Tres Puntos del West Side. The project was conceived as a way to reflect upon the demographic, ethnic and economic transformations and social displacements that had taken place within various Mexican American and African American urban neighbourhoods of the city (around Maxwell Street, Garfield Park and Harrison Park). The parade, fig.57–63 which proceeded through the aforementioned areas, involved participation from hundreds of people from schools, community centres and other local organisations, and apparently attracted more than one thousand additional fig.65–67 and p.*203* locals. The other element of the project, *100 Victories/10,000 Tears*, comprised forty granite slabs sourced from demolished structures at the University of Illinois at Chicago and reinstalled in a lot within the historic Maxwell Street Market, the locus of contestation surrounding the expansion of UIC, along with a sequence of 24 signs that referenced, among other things, significant events in the labour history of Chicago.[19] Martinez's work was taken down in November 1993. The next year UIC began its expansion, eventually replacing the market with athletic fields, retails and housing – rethinking it in a new location, several blocks away, in 2008.

—

[18] For an extended description of Manglano-Ovalle's project, see pp.122–35 in this volume.

[19] The signs are reproduced in the exhibition catalogue that was published subsequently: see Mary Jane Jacob (ed.), *Culture in Action: A Public Art Program of Sculpture Chicago* (exh. cat.), Seattle: Bay Press, 1995, pp.140–41.

The installation *100 Victories/10,000 Tears* highlighted and dovetailed with work underway by community activists who sought to keep the market at its original location. Martinez's project not only pointed to a controversial site of urban redevelopment – emphasising tensions dividing community residents, small entrepreneurs, UIC and the municipal government in terms of who had the right to the city's land and the power to determine how it is used – but it also provided a forum for protest around an ongoing issue. This multifaceted work – at once interventionist, participatory, activist, pedagogical and performative – worked in solidarity with community action, yet could not effectively forestall the urban transformation of its site. To the extent that the university and the city were unshakably resolute in their course of urban redevelopment, *100 Victories/10,000 Tears* verged on being a work in memoriam. Ironically, given the pedagogical dimension of the project, it is possible that it played directly into the hands of this public university's interests – that in desublimating the historical, ideological, political and economic elements of the contested site in the public sphere of debate, Martinez might have inadvertently given the government an opening through which to move forward with its redevelopment of the site. Yet this is always a risk when art – even art that is socially activist or interventionist – enters into the complex politics of contested urban place. At the same time, Martinez's project highlighted the fundamental question of whether the city and the university were actually serving the public good, for instance by working on behalf of local communities.

Like Manglano-Ovalle's project, Haha and Flood's *Flood: A Volunteer Network for Active Participation in Healthcare* (1992–95) was generated by local Chicagoans. Haha was an artists' collaborative – whose members were Richard House, Wendy Jacob, Laurie Palmer and John Ploof – established in Chicago in 1988 and active until 2008. Flood refers to a group of twenty to thirty people Haha originally assembled as A Volunteer Network for Active Participation in Healthcare, to build a hydroponic garden in a storefront on Chicago's North Side. They grew vegetables such as kale, collards and Swiss chard as well as therapeutic herbs for distribution to people with HIV. The storefront / walk-in garden also functioned as a platform for various educational and community-based activities – for example, public discussions or the distribution of information on HIV/AIDS, hydroponics and nutrition. The project continued to operate for two years after the official closing of 'Culture in Action', and planted the seeds for the establishment of an HIV/AIDS facility in Rogers Park that opened in 1997 and continues to serve the community today. Flood participants subsequently engaged with communities in Dekalb, Illinois, and Cedar Rapids, Iowa,[20] which suggests that the original model that Haha and Flood developed for an alternative space and network in response to a health care crisis perhaps has been sustained, albeit transformed, in other local contexts. Although the Flood project, or something very much like it, might have emerged even without the 'Culture in Action'

fig.27–36

—

[20] See Haha's website: http://www.hahahaha.org/projFlood.html (last accessed on 14 April 2014). For more information on the project for 'Culture in Action', see this volume, pp.100–09.

context, there appears to have been a symbiotic relationship between Haha's artistic language, structure and working methods, on the one hand, and Jacob's goals in responding to this and related practices, on the other, such that collaborative art practice became distributed into various local networks (in turn producing additional community and social networks) – offering evidence that art just might actually be able to play a role as a useful, pragmatic thing in materialising progressive social change.

Kate Ericson and Mel Ziegler worked as a collaborative team from 1985 to 1995 (until Ericson's death at age 39), and contributed *Camouflaged History* to Jacob's 1991 exhibition project 'Places with a Past', which took place within the context of the Spoleto Festival in Charleston, South Carolina. *Camouflaged History* involved painting a house in a military camouflage pattern using 72 commercial paint colours approved for use on historic
fig.14–16 homes. For 'Culture in Action', Ericson and Ziegler's *Eminent Domain* (1992–93) was developed with a group of tenants from Ogden Courts, a Chicago Housing Authority residence. As with other public housing in Chicago (and elsewhere in the US), these large architectural structures had originally been conceived and built in the 1960s to help provide people on low incomes with affordable housing in urban centres, and they bore the influence of Le Corbusier's vision of the building itself functioning as a city within a city. Many of these mid-century housing projects in Chicago have since been demolished (including Ogden Courts in 2005) because the buildings further ghettoised their populations and were poorly maintained by their municipalities, leading to unsanitary living conditions. On the other hand, public housing projects have often generated well-established communities, and this is the reality that Ericson and Ziegler discovered in the early 90s. Their research and consultation with a group at Ogden Courts resulted in the design of a paint chart that indexed the history of public housing in the US through a system of colours, texts and names. An educational project, a related objective was to market and distribute the chart, along with corresponding paint colours, through the Tru-Test Manufacturing Company, but budgetary constraints halted *Eminent Domain* at its prototype stage.

fig.37–42 Suzanne Lacy's *Full Circle* (1992–93) was one of the more ambitious projects in terms of budget, scale and scope of organisation. Lacy had, since the late 1970s, established herself as an important figure in the development of socially engaged, participatory, activist, feminist and pedagogically-inflected art practices – a legacy of work that may have influenced Jacob as she developed her curatorial framework. Shortly after 'Culture in Action', Lacy would publish *Mapping the Terrain: New Genre Public Art* (1995), a book that compiled the work of artists pushing the boundaries of public art and the political agency of art in relation to activism through various approaches to social engagement, non-permanency and event-based situations. Lacy worked on *Full Circle* in collaboration with a coalition of Chicago women, invoking the legacy of Jane Addams, who won the Nobel Peace Prize in 1931 for her groundbreaking social work and feminist activism in Chicago and internationally. From that starting point, the project intended to explore

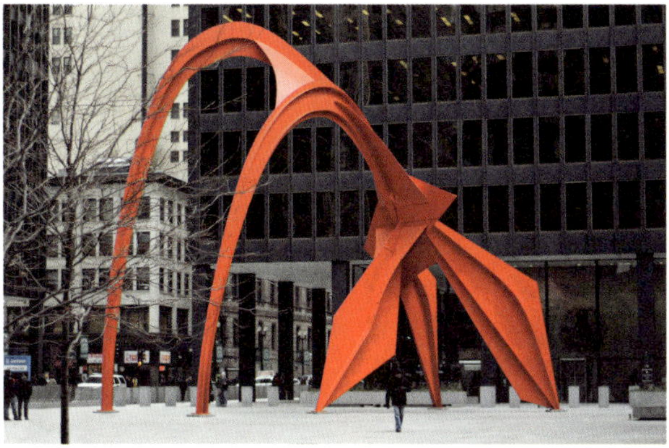

Alexander Calder, *Flamingo*, Chicago Federal Center Plaza, 1974.
© 2013 Calder Foundation, New York / DACS London
Photography: Sarah Mendelsohn.

the history and present situation of women's accomplishments and contributions to the city. Playing with then-prevalent conventions of public art – its outdoor site, its sculptural presence – the artist embarked on an extensive research process and developed individual limestone monuments honouring one hundred women who had been selected through community nominations. These rocks with small bronze plaques were sited in various locations within the Loop, Chicago's busy downtown zone, frequented by tourists, shoppers, museum-goers, businesspeople and locals; though Lacy's original conception later developed into a call to establish permanent sites for the monuments, the city did not approve.[21] If Chicago already had its share of apparently eternal, extra-large outdoor sculptures by primarily male modernists such as Alexander Calder, Pablo Picasso and Claes Oldenburg, Lacy's was a political-cultural intervention indicating a desire to seek a form of civil social justice – that is, to apply pressure on the city to recognise the contributions of women who were important to specific communities – as a central element of an activist art project. And one element of this effort involved the mimicking of tropes of traditional public art by which permanence seems the only way to vouchsafe collective public memory. On 22 May 1993, 'Culture in Action' was inaugurated with a public ceremony for the ninety women honourees (ten historic women were simultaneously honoured); and the concluding event of the project, on 30 September at the Jane Addams Hull-House Museum at UIC, was a dinner-as-performance and discussion featuring fourteen global women leaders, among them Gloria Steinem, Anita Hill, Susan Faludi and Dolores Huerta, who met with the Chicago honourees the next morning. In organising events and situations that function as issue-oriented social activism and political protest, often framed as discursive events and situations of exchange in an informal pedagogical style, Lacy's art has involved a social theatricality (or, theatre of the social) that some may find uncomfortably close to a form of event-engineering.

fig.40–42
fig.39
fig.43, 44

—
[21] The 'Culture in Action' Final Descriptive Report to the National Endowment for the Arts (27 February 1995) mentions negotiations with the City's Public Art Fund. CCS Bard Archives, *ibid.*

Yet *Full Circle* seemed to exemplify the curatorial-organisational ethos of 'Culture in Action' in engendering an unusual meeting of individuals outside the mainstream of the contemporary art world in order to shape a social tribute to empowered women.

fig.68–74 Rounding out the eight projects was Robert Peters's *Naming Others: Manufacturing Yourself* (1992–93), produced with what the artist described as 'Mushroom Pickers, Ghosts, Frogs and other Others' – a quirky reference to the semantic-linguistic and participatory character of this work. Troubled by the ways in which classificatory language can be deployed as an abusive weapon in everyday social communication and as a means of reinforcing one's putative normativity by relying upon stereotypes regarding class, ethnicity and other conditions, the Chicago-based artist set out to study *how* language constructs social identities. Peters, an artist who trained as a fig.69, 70 biometrician, developed a written survey that was distributed to thousands of city residents, asking respondents to list the names they used to designate other individuals, and compiled the research into an audio piece that could be reached by calling a toll-free telephone number: 1-800-808-THEM. For the weekly *Chicago Reader*, a journalist summed up Peters's project:

> *Peters wove the terms he collected into an interactive ear play that sounds like market research on drugs. Call the number to become part of it: 'If you are one of us, press U; religious, press P-R-A-Y; uncertain of your sex, press X.' At the tape's conclusion, each auditor is asked to leave a self-description, using terms they've heard.*[22]

There is a subtle link between Manglano-Ovalle's use of video technology to create the conditions for community members to represent themselves through documentary language to the world beyond their neighbourhoods, and Peters's use of telephonic communication and audio recording to give Chicago's citizens an opportunity to enunciate their real or imagined identity constructions as a database. However, Peters apparently remixed the public's responses into what might be understood as an avant-garde sound composition, with participation as only one step in the overall process of making the work, and so Roberts seems to have sought a balance of social engagement and authorial control.

—

Among the broader issues at stake within 'Culture in Action', we might consider how a specific curatorial approach reframed and sought to catalyse redefinitions of art-making in relation to notions and material conditions of the social. The participating artists were invited to test their cultural or intellectual capital (their knowledge expertise) to see just what sort of art projects might be produced at different levels of collaboration with citizens

—

[22] Deanna Isaacs, 'Art People: Robert Peters has a name for people like you', *Chicago Reader*, Arts & Culture Calendar, 1 July 1993, available at http://www.chicagoreader.com/chicago/art-people-robert-peters-has-a-name-for-people-like-you/Content?oid=882286 (last accessed on 14 April 2014).

on the micro-level of the neighbourhood, the work place, the domicile and other urban contexts and situations. It could be argued that 'Culture in Action' helped to both foment and facilitate a critical discussion around project-based art practices – projects-as-works or works-as-projects that are conceptualised, developed, implemented and orchestrated by artists with organisational support. These practices call upon a skill set that requires effective conversation and negotiation with individuals and groups who are not necessarily versed in the discourses of contemporary art, and for whom community-based art may have an entirely different set of associations. 'Culture in Action' countered the apparent hegemony of the museum paradigm in an attempt to reverse the normative flow of power radiating from the centralised institution and to generate a material and symbolic decentralisation of cultural authority and knowledge, so that the cultural, intellectual and political capital of artists, curators and organisers might be strategically re-embedded into communities. The discourse that frames this exhibition project explores the notion that in order for art to be socially responsible, its first duty is to engage in a more direct manner – that is, not mediated by traditional institutional frames – with urban communities that have been historically neglected by traditional art and museum cultures.[23]

So how and where can this exhibition be *located*? Does the project reside somewhere in the space between the public presentation of the actual art projects within a relatively compressed period of time in Chicago's urban zones, from spring through autumn 1993, and the 1995 publication that functions as both document of the project and (retrospective) discursive frame? 'Culture in Action' was a platform for testing the critical possibilities of the exhibition form so as to generate a constellation of ephemeral artworks and projects, and discursive processes of conversation and discussion among artists, curators, art organisations and the city of Chicago's distinct communities. It provided a unique context for a group of artists who were already testing the possibilities of cultural decentralisation and social redistribution in quite distinct ways, whether in terms of the real or perceived needs of citizens and communities. The exhibition reconsidered interrelationships between art and activism, redefining art in relation to public space on material terms, exploring new forms of collaborative authorship and investigating class divisions.

Sculpture Chicago had been commissioning public art in Chicago for ten years, yet by the start of the 1990s the organisation – egged on by the critique offered by Jacob, who was then a board member, and by others more generally – was open to questioning the disconnection between public art and the various urban communities and audiences who were supposedly served by this art. 'Culture in Action' problematised how conventional public art's often monumental works seemed remote from the economic conditions, social realities and cultural values of many communities and

—

[23] The primary source for this discourse is the publication-as-document that was released in 1995, two years after the project itself: M.J. Jacob (ed.), *Culture in Action*, *op. cit.*

citizens, since traditionally much art in public space had been centralised in downtown hubs of cultural tourism.

The funding structure of 'Culture in Action' is instructive here, as it reflects the successful outcome of private-sector and public-sector partnerships, although with a larger percentage garnered from the former. The exhibition received an Art in Public Spaces grant from the NEA, as well as the NEA's much larger Challenge Grant.[24] But the majority of funding came from a range of private foundations,[25] some corporate support and considerable in-kind support from various local organisations.[26] So an exhibition project that was ostensibly devoted to generating new audiences and publics and to engaging other communities was very much the result of private-sector support, illuminating the extent to which, at least in the US, public culture has largely been underwritten by private interests. Did 'Culture in Action' deliberately or inadvertently mask these conditions? I think not, but it does testify to these contradictions.

In terms of the critical reception of 'Culture in Action', it is not outlandish to suggest that most people gained access to the exhibition through the discursive framework of the catalogue. While catalogues often function as the primary sources for the transmission of exhibition information to publics not present at the exhibition (allowing mediated, vicarious experiences), because of the unique way in which 'Culture in Action' was articulated – as a constellation of relatively discrete, temporary, transitional and transitive engagements with citizens in particular communities across the urban environs of Chicago – the exhibition demanded a publication that would forcefully (re)represent a geographically distributed project that emphasised the social underpinnings of art in public, private and interstitial spaces.

The titles of the essays reveal the hopes and aspirations of an exhibition project that sought to expand concepts and practices of public art in relation to community-based cultural activism predicated upon processes of collaboration and participation. In the opening essay, 'New Art, New Audiences: Experiments in Public Art', Eva Olson, then Executive Director of Sculpture Chicago, focuses on the extent to which the organisation was seeking to support a new way of thinking about the interrelationships connecting artists, artworks, audiences, communities and publics.[27] She concludes that

—

[24] The former amounted to $20,000 and the latter $200,000. Sculpture Chicago Funding Plan, February 1994, CCS Bard Archives: Mary Jane Jacob Papers, Series II: 'Culture in Action' 1987–96, box 04, folder 85.

[25] The major source of financial support, alongside the NEA, was the Lila Wallace–Reader's Digest Fund, which donated $250,000. The other significant contributors were the MacArthur Foundation and Rockefeller Foundation, which gave $100,000 and $75,000 respectively towards the exhibition. See *ibid.*

[26] The corporate sponsor named in the catalogue, along with additional contributors, is AT&T, which gave $50,000, with half of that sum apparently dedicated to the catalogue. See *ibid.*

[27] Eva M. Olson, 'New Art, New Audiences: Experiments in Public Art', in M.J. Jacob (ed.), *Culture in Action*, *op. cit.*, pp.10–14.

'Culture in Action' ultimately functioned effectively as a discursive platform to pose questions and initiate dialogues about issues grounded in the urban realities of Chicago. In 'Outside the Loop', Jacob reflects on the evolution of public art practices and modes of governmental and organisational sponsorship in the US during the 1960s and 70s in relation to activist, site-specific and community-oriented practices,[28] and carefully positions 'Culture in Action' within the evolution of municipally sanctioned public art since those decades. She refers to the emergence in 1967 of the NEA's Art in Public Places programme, and to 'percent-for-art' programmes developed in various US cities during the 70s.[29] According to Jacob, by 1974 the NEA had begun to modify the discourse and parameters of their Art in Public Places programme, moving steadily away from the paradigm of the large-scale modernist sculptural object sitting on the urban plaza – an aesthetic replacement of the earlier model of the monument-memorial – towards an increasing embrace of 'art in public situations', involving site-specific methods, procedures and experimental media.[30]

Critic Michael Brenson, who had written an appreciative review of Jacob's 'Places with a Past' for *The New York Times* in 1991[31] – authored what is probably the most probing text in *Culture in Action*, 'Healing in Time'.[32] The essay presents an eloquent critical analysis of the primary issues at stake, emphasising that activist, community-based, collaborative art projects demand an elevated degree of responsibility from all parties (artist, curator, citizen, audience, etc.) and generate a distinct temporality as engagements, events and processes unfolding through time both quantitatively and qualitatively – distinct from how audiences encounter traditional art objects. Brenson also suggests that the projects in 'Culture in Action' invited audiences into another kind of space, or to experience space differently – the space of social materiality within the lived city. Brenson appears to support the overall goals of 'Culture in Action', yet he also provides a candid assessment of the strengths and weaknesses of individual art projects within it. His observations and admonitions regarding activist and community-based practices are germane beyond 'Culture in Action':

—

[28] M.J. Jacob, 'Outside the Loop', in *ibid.*, pp.50–61. The title plays on Chicago's Loop district, a commercial and business area significantly redeveloped in the 1990s, anchored by art institutions such as the Art Institute of Chicago.

[29] Percent-for-art was established as a mechanism by which local governments in the US could require private developers to set aside a small percentage of large architectural/building budgets to support the inclusion of art on site.

[30] This phrase was used by the NEA in 1974. See http://www.nea.gov/pub/nea-history-1965-2008.pdf (last accessed on 14 April 2014). The term 'earthworks' was also used by the NEA in 1974 to refer to alternative modes of context-specific art-making.

[31] Michael Brenson, 'Visual Arts Join Spoleto Festival USA', *The New York Times*, 27 May 1991, and online at http://www.nytimes.com/1991/05/27/arts/review-art-visual-arts-join-spoleto-festival-usa.html?pagewanted=all&src=pm (last accessed on 14 April 2014).

[32] M. Brenson, 'Healing in Time', in M.J. Jacob (ed.), *Culture in Action*, *op. cit.*, pp.16–49.

Community-based art is shaped by a particular place and particular conditions and a particular political and artistic moment. It is designed to respond to very particular situations. Unless those situations are grasped or experienced to some degree, it is very hard for any evaluation of a project to be responsible or just. [...] *In any consideration of art for public places, it is important to make a distinction between projects that result from collaborations between artists and communities and projects conceived by artists to call attention to communities.*[33]

Brenson's comments allude to certain contradictions evident within the 'Culture in Action' situation. He argues that in order for the art critic or art historian to 'responsibly' evaluate community-based art practices, some experience with, or understanding of, that community is an important prerequisite.

It is in the art world where the efforts of these artists will be recorded and discussed and where the thinking will evolve that will enable other artists to engage communities as well as or better than they have done here. In serious discussions of community-based projects, however, the effect of the art on the communities must not be forgotten. And, ideally, not just the effect at the time of the project or immediately thereafter.[34]

But what criteria do we utilise to determine if or when the critic or historian is adequately knowledgeable in this regard? Are we talking about first- or second-hand experience? For instance, although I have visited Chicago on numerous occasions, I am not directly familiar with many of the neighbourhoods and communities engaged by the 'Culture in Action' artists. With sufficient research, however, I would argue that anyone can probably gain a sufficient understanding of these contexts.

Brenson further suggests that there are two distinct trajectories in operation here: the discursive frame of contemporary art on the one hand, and the effect of art on a community on the other. The former is largely the purview of experts who share a specialised discourse; the latter is to be uncovered typically through the testimonies of citizens within specific communities who collaborated with an artist or group of artists or who experienced the project at the time. There is also some overlap between these trajectories; for example, an expert might be well positioned in terms of sociological research to gather together the experiences and recollections of community members, but potentially culpable of generating frictions and misunderstandings. We can understand 'Culture in Action', in retrospect, as an embodiment and representation of these overlaps and contradictions.

—

In his review of 'Culture in Action' for *The New York Times*, Michael Kimmelman refers to two potential downsides of the type of artistic practice made possible by the show. First, he warns against the possibility of making

—

[33] *Ibid.*, pp.40 and 42.
[34] *Ibid.*, p.46.

socially engaged public art the only type of art accessible to economically or politically marginalised communities, revealing, for better or for worse, his own cosmopolitan perspective. Second, he indicates concern that the exhibition model and practices of 'Culture in Action' might become 'trendy', and its paradigms recycled and applied to multiple situations.[35] But the dynamic of the avant-garde itself could be characterised as a logical progression (and interplay) of aesthetic ruptures, and as the gradual assimilation of these ruptures into trends. And why would there be an ethical problem with the 'Culture in Action' curatorial framework being reproduced in other cities (or again in Chicago for that matter)? That Jacob *did not* produce subsequent iterations of 'Culture in Action' in Chicago suggests that she was reluctant to further institutionalise its curatorial framework and models of socially collaborative art practice.

Kimmelman's scepticism is echoed, and intensified, in artist and writer Joe Scanlan's review for *frieze*, specially directed towards some of what he believes are the exhibition's underlying assumptions about Chicago, communities and art:

> *But what happens when communities and their residents become the subjects of art? Prospects to be mined by underwriters on a social mission in the form of culture? … Sadly, the most telling aspect of 'Culture in Action' was the disparity between what Sculpture Chicago and its sponsors claimed to accomplish through these projects and what most of the artists knew was really possible, and the subsequent scepticism about whom the culture was really for.*[36]

Scanlan writes eloquently about Dion's project, which he appreciates for its 'indefiniteness' and avoidance of normative structures of science and notions of 'art as social betterment'.[37] Scanlan reserves his most significant praise for Haha's *Flood*, but also has generally supportive words for the Manglano-Ovalle and Martinez projects. However, despite his overall respect for Jacob's commitment, he asserts that 'Culture in Action' was, essentially, superfluous:

> *It is to Mary Jane Jacob's credit that all of the artists in 'Culture in Action' were already personally involved in alternative art forms, politics and community activism. But did Sculpture Chicago's more sophisticated relationships with cultural funding institutions necessarily translate into more intelligent and effective public artworks? Or would these projects have happened anyway – on smaller scales definitely, perhaps in different places and over longer periods of time – just minus all the hoopla and hype? I think so. And if that's the case, Sculpture Chicago was only responsible for making them happen on a massive scale, together, adding*

—

[35] M. Kimmelman, 'Of Candy Bars and Public Art', *op. cit.*

[36] Joe Scanlan, 'Culture in Action', *frieze*, no.13, November–December 1993, pp.22–27; and reproduced in this publication, pp.164–71.

[37] *Ibid.*

little to the projects themselves, but certainly following recent (government) guidelines that art be useful and have immediate, measurable effects.[38]

What appears to underlie Scanlan's critique is a belief that somehow a funded, large-scale exhibition project, emanating as 'Culture in Action' did from the contemporary art world, is a corruption of an *authentic* scene of community-based art, and therefore a disqualifier. This critique is misplaced, since the participating artists were not all self-defined as community arts practitioners, but were in the main testing out various modes of vanguard production in art as such. So while it's conceivable that one or two of the artist's projects might have evolved in some related way independently of the 'Culture in Action' frame, the fact remains that the exhibition was the principal incubator. Furthermore, art is always sponsored or supported in some way, which means that culture, indirectly and directly, is also made possible through forms of sponsorship – popular, high or any other type of cultural production. And it is incumbent upon us to analyse cultural production in relation to a whole set of economic, social and ideological conditions.

'Culture in Action' reminds us that art is never an utterly autonomous endeavour: it is caught up in an array of societal relations, some of which are messy, and some bureaucratic. And, what are the criteria for belonging to a specific community? An individual who was once a so-called outsider can develop a sense of belonging to a community, and may be embraced by that community even if he or she does not necessarily live within the community or neighbourhood. 'Culture in Action' reveals that community is not a monolithic thing, that it is sometimes surprisingly porous and that artists can create the conditions of becoming at least temporary members of a group, which may be sufficient for generating meaningful art and producing new cultural forms. Scanlan also suggests that the best public art is generated by artists who have a genuine interest in a particular community (i.e. with an a priori familiarity and commitment to that local context), yet this is both naïve and parochial, as it constructs a monolithic idea of community and establishes an aesthetic criteria of evaluation that can be easily contradicted by an art project that later inspires those who collaborated on it. At the base of his critique, there is a suspicion of what appeared to be a top-down, institutionally generated project, rather than a bottom-up, grass-roots process. Life and culture, however, are not always so clear-cut in their polarisations and divisions of labour. In the case of 'Culture in Action', it would be tenable to suggest that vanguard art culture endeavoured to meet local communities at least halfway.

An in-depth analytical examination of 'Culture in Action' is to be found in 'From Site to Community in New Genre Public Art: The Case of "Culture in Action"', a chapter within Miwon Kwon's 2002 book of revisionist contemporary art history, *One Place after Another: Site-Specific Art and Locational Identity*.[39] Actually, Kwon references 'Culture in Action' earlier,

—

[38] *Ibid.*

in the essay published in *October* in 1997, 'One Place after Another: Notes on Site Specificity', which anticipates the book, locating a shift from the more insular critique of the institutional spheres of art to social engagements beyond that frame:

> *Deeming the focus on the social nature of* art's *production and reception to be too exclusive, even elitist, this expanded engagement with culture favours 'public' sites outside the traditional confines of art in physical and intellectual terms.*[40]

The footnote to this statement suggests that such developments

> *coincide with developments in public art, which has reprogrammed site-specific art to be synonymous with community-based art. As exemplified in projects such as 'Culture in Action' in Chicago (1992–93) and 'Points of Entry' in Pittsburgh (1996), site-specific public art in the 1990s marks a convergence between cultural practices grounded in leftist political activism, community-based aesthetic traditions, conceptually driven art borne out of institutional critique and identity politics.*[41]

Here Kwon effectively identifies the confluence of tendencies embodied within 'Culture in Action', and it seems that there is a degree of suspicion regarding the aims of public art during this period; it is possible to read into her use of the term 'reprogrammed' an insinuation of opportunism and bad faith *vis-à-vis* certain public art initiatives. Also in this footnote, Kwon refers to Grant Kester's essay in the January 1995 issue of *Afterimage*, 'Aesthetic Evangelists: Conversion and Empowerment in Contemporary Community Art', an analysis of the redemptive underpinnings of community-based public art in this period, wherein Kester argues that there is a tendency to assume a relationship to communities by which art and culture are instrumentalised to perform something analogous to social work.

In the chapter on 'Culture in Action' within Kwon's *One Place After Another*, the author leads off with a discussion of Lacy's project for the exhibition, while also referencing the artist's *Mapping the Terrain: New Genre Public Art* book. Kwon proposes that 'Culture in Action' is basically a large-scale embodiment of Lacy's rethinking of art in public space, in which processes of social engagement with audiences, publics and communities are paramount in terms of methodology and outcome, and constitute the 'new genre'. Kwon reflects upon how, when a mode of art practice is endowed with a genre appellation, it is also inscribed in that moment within the disciplinary field as a newly minted, institutionalised, historical category.

—

[39] Miwon Kwon, 'From Site to Community in New Genre Public Art: The Case of "Culture in Action"', *One Place after Another: Site-Specific Art and Locational Identity*, Cambridge, MA: The MIT Press, 2002, pp.100–37.
[40] M. Kwon, 'One Place after Another: Notes on Site Specificity', *October*, no.80, Spring 1997, p.91.
[41] *Ibid.*, fn.13.

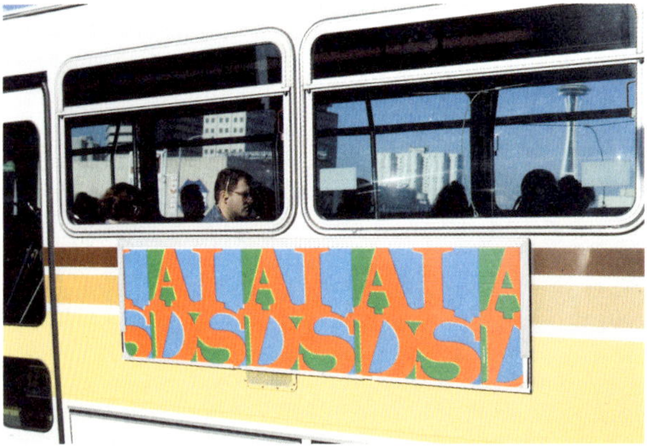

General Idea, *AIDS (Project for Seattle Arts Commission)*, as part of 'In Public: Seattle 1991', 1991, screenprint on adhesive-backed vinyl: 610 x 2235 mm, edition of approximately 100, unsigned and unnumbered, published by Seattle Arts Commission, Seattle. © the artists
Photography:
Seattle Arts Commission
Courtesy the artists and Esther Schipper, Berlin

That an artist – Lacy – should be engaged in this process might seem self-serving to some, yet it is continuous with the avant-garde tradition of manifestos and other such platforms.

Elsewhere in her essay, Kwon references the role played in 1986 by the percent-for-art programme in relation to the expansion of the Seattle Art Museum, where funding was generated for artists to 'address, intervene in and engage the public life of the city', and how these funds apparently formed the basis for a subsequent exhibition by curator Diane Shamash.[42] The exhibition, 'In Public: Seattle 1991', consisted of projects by eighteen artists, all 'sited', to use Kwon's term, throughout the city.[43] Kwon then proceeds to offer a superb analysis of how 'Culture in Action' operated as a frame to both foster and index transitions in modes of site specificity, public art and community-based, activist practice, yet her most significant contribution is a nuanced assessment of the meaning of 'community', and how distinctions and differences in that term (linguistically and in a social sense) need to be scrutinised and honoured. In other words: that community is never a homogeneous thing, and therefore cannot be engaged –

—

[42] Diane Shamash was at that time the manager of the Public Arts Program of the Seattle Arts Commission, and would subsequently found the public art organisation Minetta Brook in New York. 'In Public: Seattle 1991' commissioned 25 public artworks to take place in Seattle during 1991 including temporary projects by, for instance, Daniel J. Martinez, Group Material, Martha Rosler and General Idea, and two permanent projects, a sculpture by Jonathan Borofsky and a collaborative architectural installation at Pier 62/63, 1951 Alaskan Way, Seattle. At the time of the official end of the programme twelve projects remained unrealised, and seven of these were cancelled altogether, including those proposed by David Hammons and Louise Lawler. See Delores Tarzan Ament, 'Public Art, Civil Disappointment – Many Blemishes, Only a Few Bright Spots for SAC's "In Public" Project', *The Seattle Times*, 31 December, 1991. Online at http://community.seattletimes.nwsource.com/archive/?date=19911231&slug=1325846 (last accessed on 14 April 2014). See also *In Public: Seattle 1991* (exh. cat.), Seattle: Seattle Arts Commission, 1988.
[43] M. Kwon, *One Place After Another*, *op. cit.*, p.103.

or represented – as such. Kwon discusses problems and frictions that occurred during the organisation of the exhibition, which she gained knowledge of through conversations with certain artists, notably those who ultimately did not take part. This may be evidence of an investigative methodology using primary sources, and with such accounts Kwon does illuminate the challenges and problems specific to this ambitious exhibition project, but such disagreements are not exclusive to exhibitions with a social or participatory focus, and are rather common within curator-artist relations.

It is unclear whether Kwon, by disclosing disagreements between artists and the curator, intends to offer a cautionary tale with specific criteria for how to go about organising such endeavours in the future. In chapter five of her book, 'The (Un)Sitings of Community', she writes of two projects, by Elaine Reichek and Renée Green, that were supposed to be part of 'Culture in Action' but did not materialise. Kwon's analysis of Green's project draws upon Hal Foster's take on the putative anthropological methodologies of certain contemporary art practices that employ collaboration with communities[44] and Kester's critique of the 'evangelical' dimension of some community-based practices (in relation to Pierre Bourdieu's analysis of community *vis-à-vis* identity)[45] to argue that the institution itself (Jacob and Sculpture Chicago) contributes to the 'fashioning of the artist' by producing over-determined representations (or misrepresentions) of the artist through the promulgation of particular identity codes.[46] In Green's case, it was the codes of African American identity and the communities that Green, as an African American artist, would supposedly be interested in engaging with. The artist had made a preliminary visit to the city to explore her possible participation in 'Culture in Action'; in advance of this, Jacob generated and distributed a biographical note and a project outline to community organisations in order to explore possible collaborations – apparently without consulting the artist.[47] Green was taken to an African American neighbourhood to meet with representatives of local cultural organisations, the itinerary apparently based upon a book titled *Passports to Chicago*. According to Kwon, Green was interested in the possibility of developing a project dealing with Frank Lloyd Wright's architectural legacy, and this factor, along with Green's discomfort at the cultural, ideological and racial projections made in relation to her (i.e. apparent stereotyping) by Jacob and Sculpture Chicago, led to the artist not developing a project for 'Culture in Action'.

—

[44] See H. Foster, 'The Artist as Ethnographer', *The Return of the Real*, Cambridge, MA: The MIT Press, 1996, pp.171–204.
[45] See G. H. Kester, 'Aesthetic Evangelists: Conversion and Empowerment in Contemporary Community Art', *Afterimage*, January 1995, pp.5–11.
[46] M. Kwon, *One Place After Another*, *op. cit.*, p.140.
[47] *Ibid.*, p.202. In a footnote, the author indicates that Green, as expressed in an interview on 28 April 1997, was 'somewhat confounded by the ways in which she and her work were described ... by Sculpture Chicago'.

This narrative may need some unpacking. The early 1990s were a particularly heated period for the always complex politics of the representation of race and ethnicity in the contemporary art world, and while there were some viable concepts of community as a differenced, heterogeneous construction *vis-à-vis* postcolonial cultural studies at the time, artists of colour were significantly under-represented in exhibitions, the market and critical and historical discourses. Reconsidering that earlier context today, at a distance of two decades, is Jacob's idea that Green might be interested in the economics and social and cultural situations of black communities in Chicago an illegitimate projection? By 1993, Green had produced works that critically examined identity, systems of representation and cultural histories; for example, p.55 *Import / Export Funk Office* (1992) traced the genealogies of hip-hop music, and *Mise-en-Scène: Commemorative Toile* (1992) slyly reimagined the visual codes of the Atlantic slave trade.[48] While Kwon's contribution to the critical art-historical literature on 'Culture in Action' cannot be underestimated, her delving into the nitty-gritty of the curatorial interactions of the organiser, institution and artist arguably distracts somewhat from the more trenchant aspects of her discussion.

In 2011, perhaps as a retrospective response to Kwon (and others), Jacob reflected upon her curatorial evolution and process in relation to 'Culture in Action':

> *In the beginning I was critiquing sculpture in urban spaces, but as time went on notions of collaboration came to the forefront, along with co-authorship among a segment of the population that, before or for this occasion, could be thought of as a community. Some artists came and went in that evolutionary process. My way of working on a group show always involves starting the conversation with a few artists, bringing them on board to think with me, and not waiting till I have settled on a final list before beginning on the ground.*[49]

—

Manglano-Ovalle's *Tele-Vecindario* has generated a verifiable, long-term impact and legacy, although sustainability was not an a priori goal for the artists, curator or Sculpture Chicago. Manglano-Ovalle had a familiarity with the ethnically diverse West Town neighbourhood of the city through living there (the artist continues to be based in West Town). In the early 1990s, a significant proportion of residents of Mexican descent settled in the neighbourhood, joining communities of Latin American and Eastern European descent, and the area faced economic challenges and crime,

—

[48] For a discussion of these and other projects by Green engaging in racial and identity issues, see, for example, Joshua Decter, 'Renée Green: Re-Mapping Narratives of History and Identity', *Forum International,* vol.4, no.16, January–February 1993, pp.49–53.

[49] M.J. Jacob interviewed by Daniel Tucker (July 2011), *Never the Same: Conversations About Art Transforming Politics & Community in Chicago & Beyond*, http://never-the-same.org/interviews/mary-jane-jacob/ (last accessed on 14 April 2014).

particularly gang-related violence. However, West Town was starting to feel the effects of gentrification, and its lower-income residents were concerned about losing their homes as rents went up or they were forced to vacate – this was one of the subjects taken up in the youths' videos. Manglano-Ovalle's *Tele-Vecindario* also gave at-risk youth, many of whom were involved in gangs, an opportunity to produce video-based works that might help facilitate critical self-understanding of their lives and circumstances, in a process that could be creatively, socially, economically and politically transformative, even emancipatory. And, the project led to the establishment of a community-based, non-profit organisation that still exists: Street-Level Youth Media (Manglano-Ovalle is not involved in the organisation today). While Haha today stresses the legacy of the Flood initiative,[50] and one of the teenagers in Dion's project went on to become a professional curator, the social effects or reverberations of the majority of the 'Culture in Action' projects are difficult to trace. We might imagine Dion's project having led to the creation of a new kind of school, Martinez's to galvanising a more progressive urban redevelopment approach or Grennan & Sperandio's to inspiring unionised workers to form their own company. However, we should be cautious to apply sustainability as the primary criterion of evaluation here, since this outcome was not a precondition of Jacob's curatorial framework.

Notwithstanding the various historical and contemporary efforts by artists, organisations, curators, writers and others to demonstrate that art has applied utility in contemporary life, it is probably misguided to imagine that art operates in the world and can be evaluated in the same way as, say, investigative journalism, political activism or hard science (or even theoretical science). Yes, there are some artists who claim that their practices – collaborative, participatory or otherwise – not only provide some sort of critical commentary on a context, situation, issue or place, but also function to induce verifiable forms of political or social transformation. This begs for proof of these outcomes, but the proof is not easy to find; it is somewhat easier to trace effects and reverberations in relation to one's peers within the same disciplinary sphere or professional field, since there are systems of communication – and criteria of evaluation – already established to help facilitate these enquiries. Besides, artists, critics, historians, curators, editors and other interested parties have a greater stake in persuading others (and perhaps themselves) that modes of socially based, collaborative and participatory art actually have an effect. But when it comes to people whose primary mode of participation with art still takes place within museums and in the form of cultural tourism, one would need to think rather deeply about how to evaluate the impact of extra-museum encounters that take place between audiences, constituencies, publics and art projects – particularly those projects conceived by artists to engender amplified modes of participation. We are not yet able to adequately assess, in terms of social effects, even those participative art projects that are staged *within* the public-private spaces of museums and other cultural

—

[50] As already noted, see Haha's website: http://www.hahahaha.org/projFlood.html (last accessed on 14 April 2014).

institutions, given outmoded museum education discourses and parochial strategies of audience outreach.

It is the case that modes of socially engaged, participatory, collaborative art-making that were shaped, in part, within the framework of 'Culture in Action' have now become institutionalised as genres and methods of 'public practice' or 'social practice' within art academies and schools,[51] something that Jacob sees as an encouraging sign in widening the options for younger artists today.[52] As history demonstrates, communities seeking remedies to their economic and social problems or political marginalisation often produce activists, educators and spokespeople from their own midst. There is a long and well-documented history of community activism in the US, and also a history of art and cultural production that has emerged from specific communities in the mode of activism or protest. In the face of this history, the fundamental task is to ascertain the ways in which art, artists, curators and arts and cultural organisations may actually help to facilitate social, economic and political justice for citizens and communities, and to measure these effects *vis-à-vis* various urban publics. Further, there is a need to analyse how the definitions of art and aesthetics are always undergoing transformation in relation to these processes.

It is fair to ask whether Jacob and Sculpture Chicago were making the liberal-humanist assumption that certain citizens or communities were unconsciously waiting for the assistance of agents from the contemporary art world to provide instruments of emancipation from their economic, political, social or cultural circumstances. But it is equally important to emphasise that those involved made a great effort to organise meetings between artists, community members, organisers, funders and other stakeholders throughout the exhibition's development, reflecting a commitment to the possibilities of forming new kinds of affiliations and solidarities across class, ethnic, cultural and other lines without a predetermined outcome in mind.

In the 'Culture in Action' publication, Manglano-Ovalle reminds us of the stakes involved in his project, regarding the importance of tangible change within a Chicago community that was afflicted by gang activity: 'The meeting of local residents could create a sense of place, ownership and home; not just a "site of critique", but a "site of possibility", where productive change might be initiated.'[53] Street-Level Youth Media has had more than twenty years of self-sustained success as an organisation that emerged out of his project – success in utilising the instruments of art and culture to help members of a community come to terms with the precarity of their lives in the early 1990s. Is it a mistake, then, to postulate that in curating 'Culture in Action' Jacob made a general assumption that the apparently more

—

[51] In the US, for example, Lacy launched an MFA-degree programme in Public Practice at Otis College of Art and Design in Los Angeles in 2007. See http://www.otis.edu/academics/graduate-public-practice/index.html (last accessed on 14 April 2014).

[52] M.J. Jacob interviewed by D. Tucker, *op. cit.*

democratically open procedures of artistic collaboration and participation – with their intrinsic contestation of the autonomy of the artist – could result in some form of social empowerment and political enfranchisement for these residents, citizens and communities? At the same time, is it tenable to suggest that all forms of collaboration, cooperation, participation or intervention inevitably involve some degree of subtle coercion – whether from artists, curators, institutions, citizens or peers? Did Jacob inadvertently instrumentalise residents, citizens, communities, publics and maybe even the participating artists, somehow repurposing them as *subjects* of her curatorial-political agenda? Or, did she actually empower them as subjects with an amplified level of sovereignty? Did the various forms of collaboration between artists and people trouble – or inadvertently reproduce – a neo-Enlightenment condition wherein high culture is deemed to be beneficent in relation to the broader society? Did 'Culture in Action' generate a 'cultural commons' wherein creative exchanges coaxed even uninterested audiences and distracted publics into being committed stakeholders? Or did these citizens and communities already understand themselves to be committed stakeholders in their own lives and circumstances – did they really require the intercession of art to induce critical consciousness, or some form of material change to their lives?

In lieu of the implementation of a rigorous sociological research process that would require us to interview those citizens of Chicago who encountered aspects of 'Culture in Action' to determine the impact of this curatorial project upon their lives, one can hope that people came away with an appreciation of the expanded language of art and of the desire of certain artists to operate as agents of broader progressive change. At the very least, there was an attempt made within the expanded framework of 'Culture in Action' to galvanise an ethos of ethical cooperation between specialised producers of culture and people more broadly – people who might never have imagined that some within the contemporary art world aspire to foment economic and social justice.

—

[53] Entry on Iñigo Manglano-Ovalle's project in M.J. Jacob (ed.), *Culture in Action* (exh. cat.), *op. cit.*, p.83.

The Turn from the Turns: An Avant-Garde Moving Out of the Centre (1986–93)
—Helmut Draxler

Which Narrative?

Claiming one's own artistic trajectory as belonging to the avant-garde involves making intrinsic as well as extrinsic assumptions. Intrinsic in the sense Theodor W. Adorno invoked when describing the material state or developmental condition of art,[1] and which – to follow this logic – has to be assessed with the benefit of hindsight, historically, and expressed in each new artistic production. The avant-garde, in its intrinsic newness, escapes social determination and thus – collapsing intrinsic into extrinsic qualities – indicates a path for social change. Today, many claims continue to be made on the basis of such an idea of the avant-garde, whether in relation to art understood as research, as technology, as social service or as political activism. However, for the most part, the crucial problem of how to relate an artistic practice to its material (intrinsic) and social (extrinsic) conditions seems no longer to be considered relevant; such practices imagine themselves in a post-historical situation, where they can exist and circulate without restriction from the moment they are accepted within the art field. A historical perspective, understood more as the unfolding of a problem than as the propagation of a solution, is hardly anywhere recognisable, and not acknowledged in terms of either intrinsic or extrinsic factors.

Of course, Adorno's argument is itself historical. Incorporating the 'advanced world spirit' (*Weltgeist*) from the Hegelian tradition, it is deeply rooted in an idealist understanding of a philosophy of history and its universalist and progressivist implications. As such, it does not readily function with the postmodern, postcolonial and feminist discourses that have gained widespread currency since the 1980s precisely in rejecting such assumptions. Despite this limitation, however, Adorno's argument is still valuable in posing the challenging question of how to relate contemporary art practices to certain artistic traditions as well as to changing social conditions. Only within this double set of relations can the actual commitment of a specific art practice be grasped.

—

[1] Adorno defines the intrinsic and irreversible conditions of any artistic practice as the material or technical state of art; any substantial artistic contribution has to address that state, and therefore its historical moment. The argument is directed against any idea of 'free' artistic creation, as well as against unconditional appropriations of historical materials. The category of the new is precisely articulated in this way, through material (intrinsic) form, and as such simultaneously reveals its extrinsic qualities (those determined by apparently external, non-intrinsic conditions – for instance, social context): 'The more the [compositional materials] bear historical necessity in themselves, the less they are immediately legible as historical traits. In the moment when the historical expression of a chord can no longer be discerned, the chord demands that the sounds surrounding it do justice to its historical implications.' Theodor W. Adorno, *Philosophy of New Music* (trans. Robert Hullot-Kentor), Minneapolis: University of Minnesota Press, 2006, p.31.

What has changed since Adorno's times? In the first place, the development of an ever more global art field, which, as a social condition, has meant the emergence of a differentiated social sphere within which art is essentially negotiated in terms of specific discursive and institutional conditions. For Adorno, individual artistic achievement (his notable example being Arnold Schoenberg's) is what bears immediate social consequence; nowadays, however, there is always a mediated social space that must be acknowledged. Artistic practices are always already framed by the specific conditions of the art field, which at the same time enable and obstruct them in their specific productivity. Even the most direct or immediate attempts to engage with the world are symbolically, culturally and economically marked by these conditions. Therefore, extrinsic reasons do not just refer to the world as it is or should be, but to a specific social sphere allowing individual access to that world, and shaping the perspectives, the speaking positions and the phantasmatic visions of one's own role within it. To me, the insistence on finding solutions instead of posing problems, which we witness today, has to do with the flourishing of a system of differentiated social spheres, with the art field constituting only one amongst many – amongst, for instance, the specific social spheres relating to the fields of science, politics or law, to name just a few. Particular to the field of art seems to be that ideologically it tends to overlook its own specificity in taking itself still as a representation of the world as such; therefore everything seems possible within its confines except the questioning of these conditions.[2]

What about the intrinsic reasons? For an artist to see herself or himself following a clear line of artistic succession, or to draw a logical (positive or negative) conclusion from the genealogical essence of a series of works, has undoubtedly become difficult. The postmodern condition implies the absence of direct tradition; it must be understood as a rupture which distances us from history altogether. This has resulted in an obsession in contemporary art with historical content, materialised in re-enactments, retro fashions and recollections of past events that merely reveal an absence of its own historicity. However, Europe in the eighteenth century had already reflected on the experience of the thread of tradition being torn apart.[3] Modernism and the notion of the avant-garde can be understood as attempts to overcome that experience and to build a tradition of the new to essentially negate the problem – the problem that there is no inner logic, no reason or founding principle for history, which is the constitutive condition of history itself. History as a symbolic form emerged precisely when the absence of a guiding principle became palpable. That is, history is not

—

[2] For a more detailed discussion of the relationships between the fields of science and art, see my essay 'A Culture of Division – Artistic Research as a Problem', in metroZones (ed.), *Faith is the Place: The Urban Cultures of Global Prayers*, Berlin: b_books, 2012, pp.124–29.

[3] This is essentially the argument in Werner Busch, *Das Sentimentalische Bild, Die Krise der Kunst im 18. Jahrhundert und die Geburt der Moderne*, Munich: C.H. Beck, 1993.

identical with tradition; it is the imagined loss of tradition that is the reason for history. And, because of this, it constantly demands a reflection and a reinvention of its own historicity.

The story I want to tell in this essay is a story about these changing conditions for artistic practices since the 1980s, exploring in particular the intrinsic and extrinsic reasons for these changes as well as the relations between the two. These conditions include the historical narratives and the social imaginaries of those practices, and their art historical or art critical accounts. Hence, the guiding question will concern why it has become so difficult to narrate art history since the 80s – art history in its entirety as well as specific developments in art since that decade. As a narrowly woven bond between art and history, certain ideas about the intrinsic and extrinsic reasons for art's development have always been embedded in the academic discipline of art history. Precisely those ideas are considered suspect today, and art history is seen as a narrative form slithering into an ongoing crisis. Raising an art-historical claim might only be possible today after separating art and history as symbolic categories – to a certain degree in order to envision their specific historical and social character. Their relation can be conceived only within a loose connection, and not as a direct entanglement.

For contemporary art practices that means there is an imperative not to embody the most advanced state of art history (in a Hegelian and Adornian tradition), and instead to explore the space in between art and history, between the intrinsic and the extrinsic. This is precisely a call to work on their difference and to create situations and historical references, and thus to link what I will identify as the main categories of the time: the *discursive* and the *exhibitionary*. The history that can be extracted from this will be a history not of heroic achievements, but one concerning a series of intense investigations around ruptures and discrepancies, which will engage the ethos of the avant-garde, even as a post-modern or post-mortem avant-garde.[4]

—

The Discursive and the Exhibitionary

In 1983, the art historian Serge Guilbaut published a study on the origins of New York modernism under the title *How New York Stole the Idea of Modern Art*. He described a series of largely successful cultural, political and financial manoeuvres aiming to develop a 'vital centre' that shaped a hegemonic, liberal and commercial 'art world' immediately after World War II. Framed by a formalist discourse and operating from the institutional battleship of the Museum of Modern Art, New York would provide the rest of the world with rhythmically changing new waves of avant-garde art for several decades.[5] When Guilbaut's book was published, his description of New York

—

[4] See Thomas Elsaesser, 'Film als Möglichkeitsform: Vom "post mortem" – Kino zu mindgame movies', *Hollywood heute. Geschichte, Gender und Nation im postklassischen Kino*, Berlin: Bertz+Fischer 2009, pp.237–63.

[5] See Serge Guilbaut, *How New York Stole the Idea of Modern Art*, Chicago: University of Chicago Press, 1983.

as the hegemonic centre of art's production and commerce was still convincingly apt. Of course, modernist and avant-garde inspired movements were continuing around the globe, but they remained dependent on New York for recognition. Just as Brancusi had to move to Paris from Romania at the beginning of the twentieth century in order to become Brancusi, during the 1960s and 70s moving to New York was thought a wise career step.

Yet only a few years after Guilbaut's publication, things had changed dramatically, charting a direction that could be described as 'how New York lost the idea of modern art'. New York today may still be an important marketplace for ideas and works, but it is definitely not the hegemonic centre of a hierarchically structured 'art world'. Today's globalised contemporary *art field* might rather be described as a combination of multiple and highly diverse – if often overlapping – spheres of interest, uniting academic research and political activism with a world market based on project culture and regular art fairs and biennials, deeply involved in the neoliberal competition between cities and regions, and hence representing cultural economics on a global scale.

To narrate the transition, it might be useful to start with an exhibition that was perhaps the last to fit within the New York-based hegemonic model of the avant-garde, according to which a coherent historical reading traced the artworks back linearly, especially to the readymade via its different forms of adaption in postwar American art. 'Art and its Double: A New York Persective' opened in late 1986 in Barcelona and early 1987 in Madrid, at the respective Caixa de Pensiones in these two cities.[6] It was curated by Dan Cameron and included work by artists from the Pictures Generation, such as Louise Lawler, Sherrie Levine and Cindy Sherman, assembled alongside the latest 'object-oriented ontologies', from artists such as Jeff Koons, Haim Steinbach and Robert Gober. New York was, however, already a 'perspective' rather than a self-evident climax, and the focus was more on repetition than newness; or rather, repetition was supposed to be the new thing within the context of simulative and affirmative strategies drawn from French postmodern theory.

Only a few months earlier, New York's New Museum hosted a show with largely the same (local) artists – including Koons, Lawler and Steinbach – but the 'perspective' was completely different. Curated by Brian Wallis, the exhibition 'Damaged Goods: Desire and the Economy of the Object'[7]

—

[6] 'Art and its Double: A New York Perspective', Fundació Caixa de Pensions, Barcelona, 27 November to 11 January 1987, and Madrid, 6 February to 22 March 1987. The exhibition featured Ashley Bickerton, Sarah Charlesworth, Robert Gober, Peter Halley, Jenny Holzer, Jeff Koons, Barbara Kruger, Louise Lawler, Sherrie Levine, Matt Mullican, Tim Rollins and K.O.S., Peter Schuyff, Cindy Sherman, Haim Steinbach and Philip Taaffe.
[7] 'Damaged Goods: Desire and the Economy of the Object', New Museum, New York, 21 June to 10 August 1986. The exhibition included Judith Barry, Barbara Bloom, Gretchen Bender, Andrea Fraser, Jeff Koons, Justen Ladda, Louise Lawler, Ken Lum, Allan McCollum and Haim Steinbach.

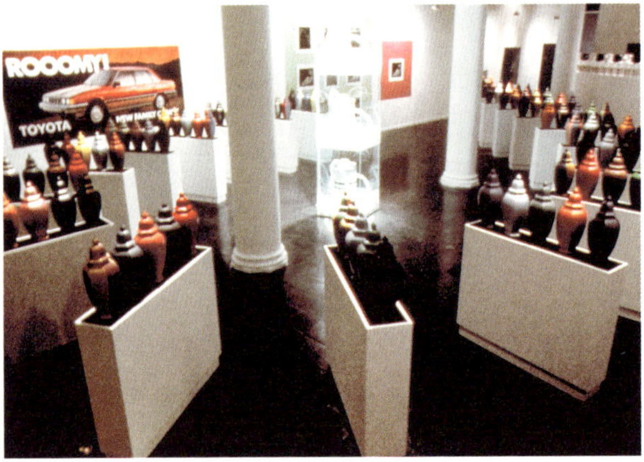

'Damaged Goods: Desire and the Economy of the Object', New Museum, 1986. Clockwise from left: Allan McCollum, *Perfect Vehicles*, 1986; Jeff Koons, *New Rooomy Toyota Family Camry*, 1983; *New Shelton Wet/Drys Tripledecker*, 1981; Louise Lawler, *Two Editions*, 1986; Haim Steinbach, *announcing something*, 1986. Exhibition design as artist contribution by Judith Barry. © the artists
Courtesy the artists and Rosamund Felsen Gallery, Los Angeles

borrowed its title from a song by the British post-punk band Gang of Four, and through them invoked a Situationist-inspired critique of consumer culture. Against the simulative interpretation highlighted in the Barcelona/Madrid show, 'Damaged Goods' maintained a *representative* approach, indicating a very different attitude towards the historical and social conditions of individual works. Two contributions worked on a paratextual level rather than delivering objects to the exhibition: Judith Barry's exhibition design and Andrea Fraser's exhibition tour. Working in close cooperation with the curator and the participating artists, Barry created a *parcours* through the show, relating individual works and interfering with their alleged autonomy. Using the artworks in an eccentric way, Barry's design highlighted possible relations among the diverse representative, theatrical or functional forms of presentation.[8] Fraser's tour in the guise of museum educator Jane Castleton was the first such performance in her career.[9] She guided her audience through the New Museum's lobby and discussed the building's security system, gift shop and restrooms, but allowed only a glimpse into the actual show. Thus, in referring to the actual infrastructural, social and economic conditions of the institution as well as to the more-or-less individual desire of a professional subject (the docent educator who is 'supposed to know'), Fraser was enacting a discursive intersection rather than an individual character, merging feminist, socio-analytical and psychoanalytical aspects.

Besides demonstrating two different and 'new' approaches to the production of contemporary art, these two examples of practice refer to two specific analytical categories, the *discursive* and the *exhibitionary*, which can readily be extended to other practices as well. I would maintain that these two

---

[8] For a detailed analysis, see my 'Ambivalence and Actualization: Exhibition Design as Artistic Practice', *Texte zur Kunst*, no.72, December 2008, pp.126–31.
[9] The script for *Damaged Goods Gallery Talk Starts Here* (1986) is included in Yilmaz Dziewior (ed.), *Andrea Fraser, Works 1984–2003* (exh. cat.), Cologne: DuMont, 2003, pp.240–43.

notions are more useful in understanding the specific transformations of practice in the late 1980s and early 90s than more commonly discussed concepts from the late 60s and early 70s, such as 'site specificity' or 'institutional critique'. In contrast to the structuralist idea of language as the basic symbolic condition of any culture, the discursive is concerned with a way of speaking: language within the social arena, indicating the performative aspect of language itself. Discourse is also how theory has established itself as a major symbolic form since the 80s, when theory became understood not as the only way of 'truth speaking', as in Adorno, but as performing precisely the absence of that possibility. Discourse always already implies a plurality of theoretical positions. Likewise, for artistic practice the perceived lack of historical necessity seemed to demand discursive references. By the 80s it was no longer enough to turn elements of language into art – as in the high times of Conceptual art – but a script might nonetheless be produced and performed, either in an actual performance or enacted through another mediated or exhibited form.

The exhibitionary does not just refer to the 'white cube' exhibition space as it was addressed in installation art after Minimalism, but to the different cultural practices engaged by exhibition-making, with design being just one. These cultural practices include ways of arranging and presenting objects or displaying information; ways of addressing, assembling and guiding people; and ways of interacting symbolically with those objects or information via conversation, education, marketing or critique. They concern the production and distribution of specific public values in an ongoing exchange between the institution and its audience, and thus constitute one of the key elements of contemporary cultural economics. What Walter Benjamin called 'exhibition value'[10] can be grasped in those cultural practices of the exhibitionary: instead of indicating a general public sphere automatically regulating individual access to a common world, these imply a loose network of competing, increasingly culturally specific and at best semi-public spheres, which buffer individual ambitions and social demands. The contemporary art field generates plenty of these spheres, contributing involuntarily to social segmentation and differentiation, and thus turning the exhibitionary into its own essential condition.[11] It is this condition which is addressed in artistic practices like Barry's or Fraser's.

Yet not only in theirs. The period of the late 1980s and early 90s is specifically interesting, in retrospect, for how modes of artistic practice developed in order to explore the discursive and the exhibitionary as two separate categories, and also to relate them. For example, Fareed Armaly's early magazine projects

—

[10] See Walter Benjamin, 'The Work of Art in the Age of Mechanical Reproduction' (1936), *Illuminations: Essays and Reflections* (ed. Hannah Arendt, trans. Harry Zohn), London: Jonathan Cape, 1970, pp.211–44.

[11] I have extracted the term 'exhibitionary' from Tony Bennett's notion of 'the exhibitionary complex' as first articulated in his essay of that title in *New Formations*, no.4, Spring 1988, pp.73–102, and later developed in his book *The Birth of the Museum: History, Theory, Politics*, London: Routledge, 1995.

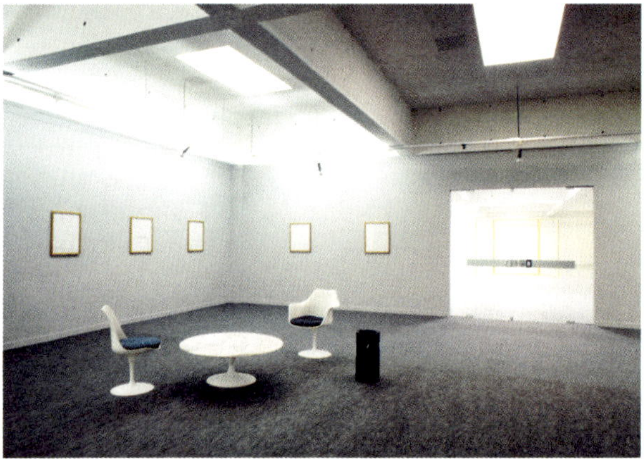

Fareed Armaly, 'Orphée 1990', installation view, Maison de la Culture et de la Communication (MCC), Saint-Étienne, 1990. Photograph: Cyrille Sabatier/ Jean-Pierre Thien
© and courtesy the artist

Terminal Zone in 1987 and *R.O.O.M.* in 1989, or his exhibitions '(re)Orient' in Paris in 1989 and 'Orphée 1990' in Saint-Étienne in 1990,[12] were based in a certain mode of producing and presenting discourse, referring to cultural- or postcolonial-studies methods and transforming them into a presentational, or exhibitionary, format.[13] Rather than reproducing existing discourses pedagogically, in a purely illustrative manner, Armaly's work directed research tools towards the exhibition situation itself, and vice versa. Questions concerning the historicity of presentational forms and institutional exhibition formats were raised to address their implicit political meaning (or the 'political unconscious', according to Fredric Jameson).[14] For example, the fact that art museums and academies might be grounded in colonial and nation-building fantasies was brought to the fore, with such ideological foundations shown to underwrite social exclusion and violence as problems reaching far into the artworks presented in such institutions. The question of how an artistic practice could and should function within those material and symbolic conditions became crucial; how to work within those conditions and reflect on them at the same time? Articulating that kind of ambivalence was not possible through new, discrete works that would be displayed within the given framework (which is why the door to the main exhibition space in 'Orphée 1990' was locked),[15] nor through an academic text

—

[12] Fareed Armaly, '(re)Orient', Gallery Sylvana Lorenz, Paris, 7 October to 4 November 1989, and 'Orphée 1990', Maison de la Culture et de la Communication (MCC), Saint-Étienne, 13 July to 18 August 1990.

[13] For a detailed analysis of those works see my essay, 'Die Gewalt des Zusammenhangs. Raum, Referenz und Repräsentation bei Fareed Armaly' ('Coercing Constellations: Space, Reference and Representation') in Helmut Draxler (ed.) *Fareed Armaly*, Berlin: b_books, 2007.

[14] See Fredric Jameson, *The Political Unconscious: Narrative as a Socially Symbolic Act*, Ithaca, NY: Cornell University Press, 1982.

[15] Armaly's project restored the MCC foyer to its original 1970s form, reinstalling the furniture, carpet, light fixtures and glass doors leading to the exhibition space (which were locked for the duration of the exhibition). A full-size model of the

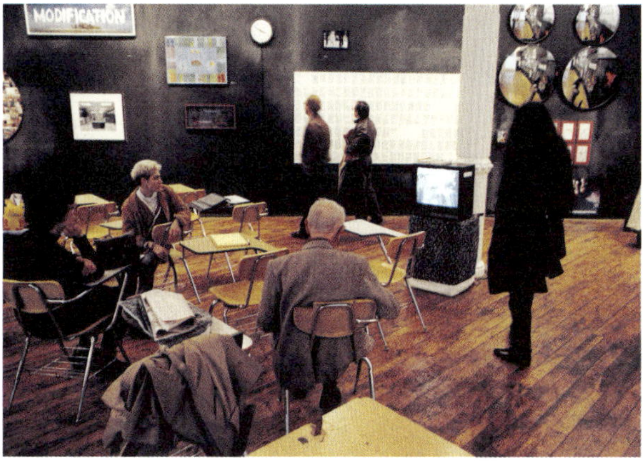

Group Material,
'Democracy: Education'
at Dia Art Foundation, 1988.
© the artists
Courtesy the artists and
Four Corners Books

describing the representational sphere of an institution's visual and textual culture. Armaly opted instead to link a 'script' to a constellation of institutional conditions, and vice versa. Through installation art, exhibition design and montage methodologies, the exhibition became the real medium for visualising the discursive and also for showing the exhibitionary itself as both the limiting and enabling condition of his own institutional performance.

Similar approaches are evident in the work of other artists who gained prominence in the late 1980s and early 90s, including Renée Green, Mark Dion, Fred Wilson, Christian Philipp Müller, Stephen Prina and Tom Burr.[16] Works such as *Case I–IV* (1990) and *Color Paintings* (1990), by Green and Dion respectively, took up Marcel Broodthaers's critical museum investigations of the 70s, shifting his installation strategies involving archival order and metaphors of power towards the implicit imperialist and racist narratives of scientific and artistic display. Wilson 'mined the museum' with

—

mirror seen in Jean Cocteau's film *Orphée* (1950) was installed in the exhibition space, visible through the doors, and on the foyer walls were hung children's drawings produced in a MCC workshop led by the artist, based on imagining and then drawing a door in the MCC; a doorway leading to the MCC's framing workshop, normally closed to the public, was also opened up and led to a further audiovisual installation.

[16] This is not only a generational history. You can find the discursive in Dan Graham's essays, which became highly influential during this period and refer to a broad array of cultural, architectural, urbanist and design practices. Moreover, those discursive elements are kept strictly in tension in the exhibitionary and almost formalist agenda he was pursuing in his pavilions at the time. The so-called 'site reflexivity' of John Knight's 1980s projects – from the *Museotypes* (1983) to *The Right to be Lazy* (1986) and *Une Vue Culturelle* (1987–88), the latter also at the MCC, Saint-Étienne – were also shifting the exhibition site towards its discursive conditions. And even Joseph Kosuth, in his turn towards Ludwig Wittgenstein's language games, was shifting interchangeably between language and exhibitionary registers (see, especially, the show curated by Kosuth 'Ludwig Wittgenstein, Das Spiel des Unsagbaren', Secession, Vienna, 13 September to 29 October 1989).

the ghostly presence of slavery (1992–93),[17] and Müller, Prina and Burr queered modernist and avant-garde strategies by reconstructing them in their underlying ambiguity. Müller's show 'porte bonheur' in Saint-Étienne in 1989 had a programmatic stance that referenced and parodied a purely spatial intervention in the manner of Michael Asher's early 70s projects: he added flower boxes planted with lucky clovers to cement structures he had built to mirror those on the ceiling above.[18]

Most significantly, however, the relation between the discursive and the exhibitionary can be seen in two extraordinarily influential projects that arguably inaugurated the very format known today as the 'project
p.51
exhibition':[19] Group Material's 'Democracy' (1988–89) and Martha Rosler's 'If you lived here...' (1989), both commissioned by Dia Art Foundation. These projects referred neither to discourse in a strict theoretical sense, nor to the exhibitionary in a purely artistic sense. Rather, they were directed towards activist and alternative practices. Both involved so-called 'town meetings' – open public discussions on issues such as homelessness or sexual politics in light of the AIDS crisis. The exhibitions, despite including actual displays of imagery, did not exhibit 'social aesthetics' in the model of the productivist tradition, but they were certainly exhibitions, and as such became influential beyond the '(imagined) age of unalienated exhibition', as Yvonne Rainer phrases it in her introduction to the two publications resulting from the projects.[20] It is precisely the social within the exhibitionary that is at stake: assembling artists and 'neighbours', or just people more generally, in order to discuss social issues; providing those discussions with information beyond mainstream media and artistic practices; and arranging, designing, qualifying and performing that information. The discursive lies in the background, pointing the questions posed towards specific content; and the discursive sits in the foreground, in the voiced debates, interfering with the exhibitionary situation, turning one of New York's leading art institutions, the Dia Art Foundation, into an 'alternative project space'.[21] By gathering people, information and objects in defiance of the exclusionary and elitist logics of the established art world, the 'project' came into being as the defining exhibition category of the time.[22]

—

[17] 'Mining the Museum: An Installation by Fred Wilson', The Contemporary and Maryland Historical Society, Baltimore, 3 April 1992 to 28 February 1993.
[18] Christian Philipp Müller, *The Ceiling on the Floor*, in 'porte bonheur', Maison de la Culture et de la Communication, Saint-Étienne, 8 June to 13 July 1989.
[19] Examples of the 'project exhibition' are: Marion von Osten and Kathrin Rhomberg's 'Projekt Migration' (Cologne, 2005); von Osten's 'In the Desert of Modernity' (Berlin, 2008); Alice Creischer, Andreas Sieckmann and Max Jorge Hinderer's 'The Potosí Principle' (Madrid, Berlin and Bogota, 2011); and Anselm Franke's 'Animism' (Antwerp, Bern, Vienna and Berlin, 2010–12) and 'Global Prayers' (Berlin and Graz, 2012).
[20] Yvonne Rainer, 'Preface: The Work of Art in the (Imagined) Age of Unalienated Exhibition', in Brian Wallis (ed.), *Democracy: A Project by Group Material*, Seattle: Bay Press, 1990, pp.xvii–xix.
[21] Julie Ault (ed.), *Alternative Art New York, 1965–1985: A Cultural Politics Book for the Social Text Collective*, Minneapolis: University of Minnesota Press, 2003.

Since the 1990s a real *project culture* has emerged, usually emphasising and focusing one of these crucial aspects – the exhibitionary, the discursive – and not as a new wave of avant-gardism but through a social network. We might consider, for example, the sociality of the artists' communities at work in the highly influential constellation known as the Berlin 'Zusammenhänge', seen in particular in the programme for the Shedhalle in Zürich from 1994 under the curatorial responsibility of Renate Lorenz and Marion von Osten.[23] For me, however, the more interesting and promising projects are those that try to combine different layers of the discursive and the exhibitionary: for example by investing in questions of how discourse can be performed and exhibited; how the academic conference format is adapted within art contexts; how individual and collective ambitions can relate; or how the different roles of artist, curator, activist and administrator can commingle without losing the intrinsic specificities of each. At the core of all these questions is the development of artistic practice itself, alongside the self-conception of theoretical, curatorial or critical practice. In project culture, reflecting on the possible fusion of differences, rather than allowing their total confusion, has become decisive. Is there still something recognisable as an artistic practice distinct from critical, curatorial, activist and administrative approaches, and can its history be told? Or, to borrow a euphemism of the 90s, is it all just 'cultural production' in different shades?

—

Exodus from the Centre

My enquiry here is only tangentially about the history of project exhibitions. My primary concern is how such history relates to the changing conditions of the art field as evident in the global dimension of contemporary art today. For example, have individual artists' practices been able to reflect that change in productive ways? Between a universalist and linear conception of the historical necessity of artistic practice, on the one hand, and a global scene filled with apparent singularity, on the other, it has become necessary to insist on the specificities of historical moments, locational conditions and artistic practices, understood mainly as symbolic procedures merging the historical and the locational, the discursive and the exhibitionary, and performative and reflexive moments within their own understanding of practice.

Doubtless, there are many discrepancies between the different approaches, productions and intentions concerning the self-understanding of historical moments, locations and practical agencies, but a common element –

—

[22] Of course, there were projects already in the 1970s, but as of the 80s the term seems to have acquired a new and specific meaning.

[23] Project groups like WochenKlausur in Vienna tried at the same time to loosen the ties with with the exhibitionary altogether. Their aim was to intervene 'directly' into the social sphere by turning artists into social activists; but precisely in wanting to overcome the art world they remained symbolically embedded within the cultural and economic conditions of the art field in a wider sense. And even if they had succeeded in cutting off all symbolic and economic connections with the art field, they probably would not have found themselves in reality as such, but rather within the regime of another field – the social field.

with attention turned precisely towards moments, locations and practices – may be identified in 1980s New York, where there were specific relations between intrinsic and extrinsic factors in the consideration of art practice. This is the case with the work made by a group of former students from the Whitney Independent Study Program (Gregg Bordowitz, Joshua Decter, Mark Dion, Andrea Fraser, Jason Simon and Renée Green, as agitated by teachers such as Craig Owens, Benjamin Buchloh, Simone Forti and Yvonne Rainer) and by others, as already mentioned above. But why did this history stray from becoming just another New York-based wave of the avant-garde? These artists were taking up issues from previous waves of avant-gardism – largely those of the late 1960s to the mid-70s, and specifically of the ensuing Pictures Generation – and perceived themselves to be working in such a tradition, producing a new aesthetic turn. It just happened to be a turn away from such turns in avant-garde history. Ever since, and especially within the global contemporary today, there seems to be no longer any place for turns.

This shift beyond turns has to do with the concurrent de-legitimisation of New York as the hegemonic site – as the centre of the art world. Perhaps in historicising New York's approach to modern art in 1983, Guilbaut's book was already questioning the city's naturalised position and the idea of a hierarchical art world altogether. And, in 1984, on the occasion of '"Primitivism" in 20th Century Art: Affinity of the Tribal and the Modern' at New York's Museum of Modern Art, critique intensified concerning one of the core myths maintaining the hegemony; namely, that modern art is somehow releasing 'primitive' or provincial art towards a universal destiny, which is incorporated into the museum's own prerogatives.[24] In the ensuing years, it is possible to identify a sort of 'self-provincialisation' within New York itself. Group Material's and Martha Rosler's town meetings helped to transform the image of New York away from its being the 'hyperreal'[25] centre of the world and into its being an urban setting devastated by disastrous neoliberal politics. The New Museum made efforts to reach beyond the established art world, working against its marginalising tendencies and focusing instead on the minority politics of an 'invisible centre'.[26] Postmodern, postcolonial, queer and feminist readings developed beyond the purely deconstructive critique of formalist modernism and addressed the avant-garde's own entanglement in progressive and universal narratives. A fundamental contradiction became palpable in almost all of these emerging practices and projects: between an artist's advanced discourse and practical ambitions in search of a new avant-garde, on the one hand, and the implicit

—

[24] See James Clifford, 'Histories of the Tribal and the Modern', *The Predicament of Culture: Twentieth-Century Ethnography, Literature, and Art*, Cambridge, MA: Harvard University Press, 1988, pp.189–214.

[25] Dipesh Chakrabarty speaks of a 'hyperreal Europe' in D. Chakrabarty, *Provincializing Europe: Postcolonial Thought and Historical Difference*, Princeton, NJ: Princeton University Press, 1994, p.27.

[26] Russell Ferguson, 'Introduction: Invisible Center', in R. Ferguson, Martha Gever, Trinh T. Minh-ha and Cornel West (ed.), *Out There: Marginalization and Contemporary Cultures*, Cambridge, MA: The MIT Press, 1990, pp.9–14.

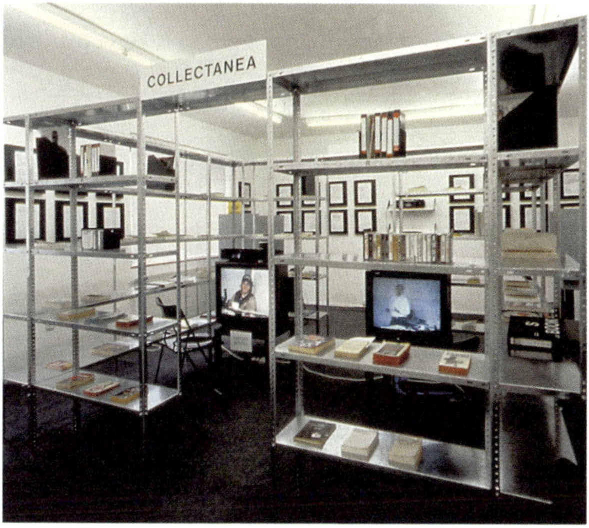

Renée Green, *Import/Export Funk Office*, 1992, installation view, Galerie Christian Nagel, Cologne.
© the artist
Courtesy the artist and Free Agent Media

consequences of this discourse on the other – the questioning of those progressive ambitions was always also part of the hegemonic narrative.[27]

Moreover, the expanding art field of the 1980s increasingly demanded that artists travel from one site to the next, and some artists made constant travel their way of life. New sites emerged through the newly funded biennials, and in Europe this frequently meant an emphasis on festivals and spaces for contemporary art in small towns.[28] At the same time, SoHo, which had been embraced as the spiritual centre of the New York avant-garde at least since the 1960s, began to lose its 'alternative' quality, with lessening claims to be a site of intense intellectual, artistic and political exchange, becoming more and more dominated by market logic and gentrification.[29] Consequently, in the minds of some younger artists it became mandatory to leave New York in order to maintain the ethos of the avant-garde. Within the European

—

[27] Further indicators of a loss of New York's control over the idea of the avant-garde might also be seen in Rasheed Araeen's journal *Third Text*, started in 1987 for the purpose of programmatically questioning the hierarchical relation of centres to peripheries, or Boris Groys's 1988 book *Gesamtkunstwerk Stalin. Die gespaltene Kultur in der Sowjetunion*, which narrates an uncanny history of the classical avant-garde movements of the 1910s and 20s in terms of their entanglement in phantasies of total power and control. See B. Groys, *The Total Art of Stalinism: Avant-Garde, Aesthetic Dictatorship, and Beyond* (trans. Charles Rougle), London: Verso, 2011.

[28] The Bienal de La Habana began in 1984, with the Istanbul Biennial starting three years later. The 90s saw the inauguration of biennials in Dakar, Gwangju, Johannesburg, Montreal, Porto Alegre, Sante Fe, Shanghai and Taipei, among other places, with equivalent events established simultaneously in Europe in Lyon and Liverpool.

context, traditional cultural centres did not profit from the changing contemporary art situation. Most significantly, modern art did not return to Paris. Even in the 1950s, the European avant-garde had been thriving in highly 'provincial' contexts: between Krefeld and Nice, Arnhem and Kassel, and on to Wiesbaden, where Fluxus had its first festival. The decentralised cultural politics of Germany, France, Belgium, the Netherlands and Scandinavia were spreading throughout the continent, and perhaps Manifesta, the itinerant, pan-European biennial that first took place in 1996, is its logical outcome.

Europe, however, was not completely and productively lost in provinciality. In the mid-1980s, Cologne began creating its own model of a centre, at least for a short time: a centre mainly for social and discursive exchange. With the foundation of the Cologne Art Fair in 1967, the city gained increasing importance as a marketplace for contemporary art, hitting its peak with the success of painting's revival in the late 1970s and early 80s. Cologne became a magnet for artists and gallery owners from all over Germany and beyond; and a different idea of the avant-garde emerged, focused more on integrating painting into an avant-garde narrative than on rejecting it. History painting became the crucial field of struggle, enabling references to disastrous German history in general, as well as to its representation in media campaigns and art world politics. From Gerhard Richter, Anselm Kiefer and Joerg Immendorff, to Martin Kippenberger and Albert Oehlen, different formal approaches towards history painting developed, indicating a variety of political ambitions and positions at the same time. During the mid-1980s, Kippenberger and Oehlen cultivated an aggressive post-punk attitude, embracing the unorthodox Situationist Asger Jorn as their hero, and acting against the previous generation's pacifying acceptance of both history and a smooth-functioning art world.[30]

In 1990, with artists like Fareed Armaly moving to Cologne,[31] Christian Nagel opening his gallery there and *Texte zur Kunst* being founded locally by Isabelle Graw and Stefan Germer, the city became a meeting point between New York and German ideas of the avant-garde. What seemed to be radically different trajectories became highly productive in a specific network of exchange, with the exhibitionary and the discursive shaping the dispersed

—

[29] Colin de Land and his American Fine Arts gallery perhaps represents the last outpost of the old spirit.

[30] In 1984, the collaborative exhibition of Kippenberger, Oehlen and Werner Büttner 'Wahrheit ist Arbeit' ('Truth is Work') exemplified their almost anarchist position (which Diedrich Diederichsen has called a 'virtual Maoism') and developed their otherwise exclusive interest in painting and collage even further in the direction of the exhibitionary and of projects. Kippenberger's 1987 exhibition 'Peter' at Galerie Max Hetzler emphasised that development, integrating a network of assistants into a sort of collective authorship. Artists like Michael Krebber and later Merlin Carpenter emerged out of this context.

[31] And there meeting artists such as Josef Strau, Michael Krebber, Jutta Köther, Michael Clegg, Cosima von Bonin and many others moving in and out of the city, including John Miller, Stephen Prina and Heimo Zobernig, to name just a few.

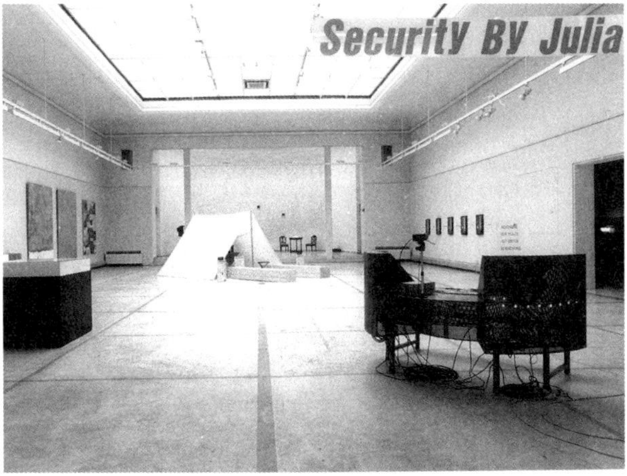

'Kontext Kunst', Graz, 1993: Kunstlerhaus, installation view: Clockwise from left: Stephen Prina, *Galerie Max Hetzler*, 1991; Rudolf Stingel, *Instructions*, 1989, *Untitled*, 1992, *Untitled*, 1992; Renée Green, *The Pigskin Library*, 1991; Kasimir Malevich, *Three Suprematist Icons*, 1985; Louise Lawler, *Bought in Paris, New York, Switzerland or Tokyo*, 1986; Julia Scher, *Superdesk*, 1993.
© the artists
Courtesy the artists and Neue Galerie Graz – Universalmuseum Joanneum/Archiv
Photography: Neue Galerie Graz – Universalmuseum Joanneum

debate. Andrea Fraser's first exhibition at Galerie Christian Nagel in November 1990 contained a black binder that assembled research materials about American-German economic and cultural politics after World War II, inscribing her own individual approach to cultural production within those historical conditions.[32] Renée Green's 'Import/Export Funk Office', also at p.55 Christian Nagel, in 1992, required that the gallery function as a project space, where she arranged Diedrich Diederichsen's collection of black American popular culture in order to highlight overlaps with her own collection – thus emphasising cross-cultural traffic at the heart of a critical self-assertion.[33]

Among German artists the exchange is also clearly notable, but, in comparison with those from the US, it was mostly directed towards a self-reflexivity of artistic means and codes of subjectivity. Michael Krebber's cultivation of a hyper-referential, appropriationist, fan-like approach became increasingly concerned with painting, while exploring exhibitionary modes – involving the presentation of, for example, empty vitrines, or the work of other artists – thus aspiring to a position beyond medium specificity, reacting to the social demands of the art field in a dialectical way. Similar moves towards the discursive and the exhibitionary can be found in the work made by Cosima von Bonin, Jutta Köther and Heimo Zobernig at this time.[34]

—

[32] This material was nicely represented, spreading over a wall, in Fraser's recent retrospective at the Museum Ludwig, 21 April to 21 July 2013, where it directly opposed 'masterpieces' of the New York avant-garde, from Robert Rauschenberg and Jasper Johns to Andy Warhol and Tom Wesselmann.

[33] See Kobena Mercer, 'Archive and Dépaysement in the Art of Renée Green', in *Renée Green, Ongoing Becomings: Retrospective 1989 – 2009* (exh. cat.), Catalogue Musée cantonal des Beaux-Arts, Lausanne and Zürich: JRP-Ringier, 2009, pp.21–26.

[34] Especially in Zobernig's show at Villa Arson in Nice early in 1991, the exhibitionary and the discursive were intrinsically tied to each other. See my 'Constructivism as Allegory: Sculptural Discourse, Methodology and Aesthetic Practice in the Work of Heimo Zobernig', in *Heimo Zobernig* (exh. cat.), Cologne:

The project space Friesenwall, inaugurated by Stephan Dillemuth and Josef Strau in 1990 in Cologne, also integrated discursive and exhibitionary moments. But, in contrast to New York precedents, and although there were projects directed towards audiences beyond the art world's typical purview (for example, providing a venue for the Gray Panthers, an elderly persons' activist group), the main focus, as for the whole Cologne scene, remained an artists' community that lived a romantic and bohemian lifestyle that levelled the differences between (commercial) gallery and (public) project cultures.

My own project, 'The Message as Medium',[35] which consisted of monthly contributions by ten artists to the Viennese newspaper *Der Standard* and to the financial magazine *Cash Flow* between October 1990 and June 1991, is perhaps the first group 'exhibition' that endeavoured to cover this Cologne scene. In bringing together the practices of artists coming from the US (including Armaly, Clegg & Guttman, Dion, Fraser and Prina) with those of European artists (Werner Büttner, Krebber, Thomas Locher, Müller and Zobernig), it attempted to unite US and European avant-garde ideas. The project was conceived as an 'exhibition' in two media formats – the newspaper and the financial magazine – rather than as 'direct' media interventions. Through its durational aspect, it also emphasised competition between artists as to how far the limits of the two media could be pushed in controlling content and form.[36]

Times of productive exchange, however, did not last long. Again, there are intrinsic and extrinsic reasons for this. The huge differences within existing understandings of artistic practice and the importance given to critical discourse and ideas of communality did not disappear in Cologne's shabby beer bars. And, as with every avant-garde claim, its social attractiveness produced immediate counter-reactions, generating social dynamics far beyond individual intention or control. Although the whole 'movement' had some level of institutional success, the crisis of the art market since November 1989 was felt more and more directly, limiting possibilities and enforcing competition. Already in 1991, the Basel Art Fair decided to withdraw from promoting experimental work while favouring a strategy of 'classifying' the heroes of the 1960s, mainly Minimalist and Pop artists, and ever since it has defined the contemporary through similarity with and confirmation of those historical avant-gardes. Another external reason might be that the de-legitimisation of New York as a centre concerned Cologne also – in the moment it perceived itself as a centre. Increasingly, the political ambitions of the Cologne scene's participants (especially the specific form in which critical discourse and bohemian attitudes had merged so productively

—

Verlag der Buchhandlung Walter König, pp.394–400. Regarding von Bonin and Köther, see Isabelle Graw, *Die bessere Hälfte. Künstlerinnen des 20. und 21. Jahrhunderts*, Cologne: Dumont, 2003, pp.92–144.

[35] See http://www.mip.at/projects/botschaft-als-medium (last accessed on the 14 April 2014).

[36] See my 'Articulatory Practices (The Message as Medium)', *Parkett*, no.29, 1991, pp.160–62.

within *Texte zur Kunst*) were questioned again. As early as 1992, Armaly's invitation card for his show 'Contact' at Christian Nagel announced: 'No opening!'. In listing other non-Germanic names from the local telephone book, selected from around his own name, a completely different kind of community from the bohemian art crowd was at least evoked. And within the post-unification context of spreading German nationalism, from 1993 a more direct and locally based idea of political activism, directed mainly towards migrational and refugee politics, seemed for many to be more urgent than avant-garde problems.

In 1993, multiple projects and events in keeping with this spirit took place on a much wider European art stage, among them 'Kontext Kunst' at the p.57 Neue Galerie in Graz, 'Sonsbeek 93' in Arnhem, 'On taking a normal situation...' at the Museum van Hedendaagse Kunst in Antwerp, the Austrian pavilion at the Venice Biennale and 'PROJECT UNITE' in Firminy, France.[37] Simultaneousy, a small critical event named 'Trap' took place in Berlin, attacking the specific Cologne mix of art and politics.[38] 'PROJECT UNITE' was curated by Yves Aupetitallot in a Unité d'habitation designed by Le Corbusier and built in 1967 in Firminy, a small industrial town next to Saint-Étienne. 'PROJECT UNITE' can be taken up as exemplary in its integration of discursive and exhibitionary elements – in addressing the limits and possibilities of any avant-garde approach concerning its intrinsic historical and extrinsic locational or contextual reasons. Perhaps because of this, the project was received negatively.[39]

At the time of 'PROJECT UNITE', the Unité had long been established as a paradigmatic location for poor, migrant and working-class cultures across Europe, and only half of the Firminy building was still inhabited, with its

—

[37] 'Kontext Kunst. Kunst der 90er Jahre' ('Kontext Kunst: The Art of the 90s'), Neue Galerie im Künstlerhaus, Graz, 2 October to 7 November 1993, was curated by Peter Weibel and featured over thirty artists, among them Fareed Armaly, Andrea Fraser, Stephen Prina and Heimo Zobernig. 'Sonsbeek 93', Arnhem, 5 June to 26 September 1993, was curated by Valerie Smith and included Michael Asher, Alighiero e Boetti, Stephan Dillemuth and Mike Kelley, for instance. 'On taking a normal situation and retranslating it into overlapping and multiple readings of conditions past and present' was curated by Yves Aupetitallot, Iwona Blazwick and Carolyn Christov-Bakargiev within the framework of 'Antwerp 93'; described in its accompanying literature as 'An Exhibition on Exhibiting', it included installations by Judith Barry, Mark Dion and Renée Green as well as a historical overview of 'artistic events that took place in the progressive Antwerp between the years 1958 and 1969'. The Austrian pavilion at the 45th Venice Biennale, 13 June to 10 October 1993, was commissioned by Peter Weibel and featured Fraser, Christian Philipp Müller and Gerwald Rockenschaub. 'PROJECT UNITE', Firminy, 1993, was curated by Yves Aupetitallot and featured over thirty artists.

[38] See Buero Bert (ed.), *Copyshop: Kunstpraxis und politische Oeffentlichkeit*, Berlin: edition ID-Archiv, 1993, pp.214–15.

[39] See, for example, Hal Foster, *Return of the Real*, Cambridge, MA: The MIT Press, 1996, pp.196–97 (from his essay 'The Artist as Ethnographer'), and Claire Bishop, *Artificial Hells: Participatory Art and the Politics of Spectatorship*, London: Verso, 2012, pp.195–206.

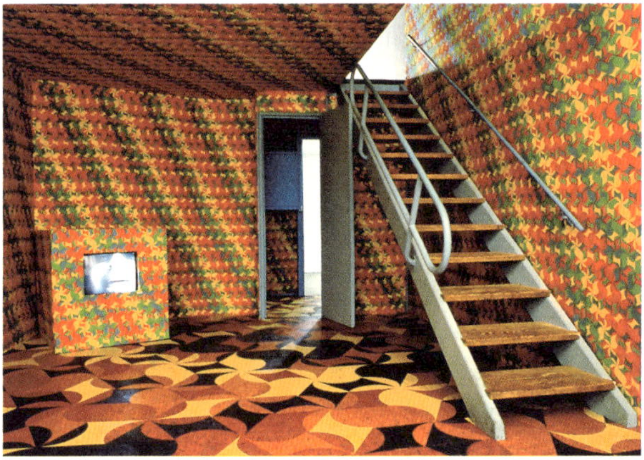

Jim Isermann, *Project Unité*, 1993, screen-printed cotton and laser-cut linoleum. Installation view showing apartment interior, 'PROJECT UNITE', Firminy, 1993. © and courtesy the artist

infrastructural features – such as shops and educational and sports facilities – slowly falling out of use. Taking place on one floor of the empty half of the building, most of the projects in 'PROJECT UNITE' were presented in individual residential apartments, which therefore maintained their 'autonomy' and communicated, in their communal appearance, the character of a group show; the building was thus utilised as a temporary 'exhibitionary complex'. All the invited artists, architects and designers – mainly from the US, Germany and France – were encouraged to reflect on those architectural, urban or social conditions, and to seek collaborations with each other or local inhabitants.

Aupetitallot rejected a direct public or social art approach, insisting instead on the fact that Le Corbusier's housing development claimed to generate a micro-society by architectural means and therefore offered an allegorical framework for reflection – not so much on the utopian dimension of modernist aesthetics but on how social difference can be negotiated by artistic practices within a wider historical and cultural context. Thus, both Le Corbusier's formal and conceptual allure, on the one hand, and his patronising attitude towards the inhabitants of his designs, on the other, were still haunting the building and challenging the exhibition project. In close exchange with some of the artists, mainly Armaly, Aupetitallot conceived a project which focused not on finding solutions 'out there' (meaning outside the art field), but on posing problems concerning the social contact, moral legitimacy and artistic possibilities on the heels of a highly ambitious modernist project. The exhibition overall made no claim for a community between artists and local inhabitants, and adopted no utopian stance towards a new formal totality: it didn't pretend to overcome differences of any sort. Instead it offered a subtle exploration of differences and common grounds between modernism and the contemporary, as well as between the harsh local living conditions of the residents of the Firminy Unité and those of the internationally travelling artists, as two very different forms of migrational identities.

Some of the artists' projects were focused on the problems of the architecture itself, as 'commanding' a certain way of living (in the work of Thomas Locher, for example, by means of a linguistic analysis of architecture's discursive tropes) or for its lack of privacy owing to the thin walls (Christian Philipp Müller) and insufficient number of closets (Tom Burr). The strongly visual exchange between the inside and the outside of the building, its imaginary role as a socially coherent 'machine' within a natural environment, became the starting point for Mark Dion's collaborative project with Art Orienté Objet, examining the decayed part of the building as an ecological system on its own, recuperating the utopian space through nature once more. Other projects focused on the social functions of the building, such as Martha Rosler's series of video interviews with the inhabitants, *How Do We Know What Home Looks Like?*, or Regina Möller's *Doll's House*, which turned Le Corbusier's rooms for children into miniature models for more flexible use. Kate Ericson and Mel Ziegler focused on domestic cleaning, producing a household cleanser with a scent of 'monumentality'. Pointing out the early 'misuse' of the apartments through appropriation, Jim Isermann commented on the inhabitants' use of wallpaper by creating his own modernist version to cover the walls, while Renée Green reflected on the artist's status as an alienated 'intruder' by transforming one apartment into a highly private space full of references to her own family's living situation. Dominique Gonzalez-Foerster and Anne Frémy changed their apartment into a very transitory living environment referencing temporary and migrational forms of architecture.

Aupetitallot was interested in media intersections rather than 'direct' social work. The exhibition included a television environment in one apartment, featuring an artist's video programme curated by Jason Simon. Posters were produced by artists, mostly painters (John Currin, Peter Doig, Michael Krebber and Cosima von Bonin), who reacted with emblematic signs to the significance of Le Corbusier's purist approach. Against the implicit total control over design in that approach, aspects of decoration, design, media and their appropriation by artists and residents alike were courted curatorially, especially in a section devoted to Victor Vasarely's devices for self-made artworks; but also in projects such as Jasper Morrison's *The World Slide Show*, Judith Barry and Ken Sayler's *(Home)icide: House of the Present*, which focused mainly on constantly morphing, computer-animated models of the apartment displayed on several computer stations in addition to a magazine documenting domestic fantasies and concepts of home, and Philippe Parreno's fiction film *La Nuit des héros* (*Night of the Heroes*), about an eccentric art historian living inside the Unité. Fareed Armaly's collaboration with Radio Ondaine, a station based in the Unité building, integrated social and media elements with artistic and cultural media, and was inspired by a common interest in Rai Music. Clegg & Guttmann's trading platform for music cassettes could be read as a highly allegorised model for alternative means of exchange; similarly, Heimo Zobernig's conversion of an apartment into a café could be understood as purely functional, but the exhibitionary context allowed for the functional to be perceived as something allegorical in itself. And Stephan Dillemuth's documentary on curator Valerie Smith's

'Sonsbeek 93', of the same year, linked 'PROJECT UNITE' to that exhibition. In all these projects it was impossible to separate issues of architecture (Nigel Coates and Stewart Helm took part), design (Tony Arefin and ABR Stuttgart were contributors) and media from social entanglements.

On the whole, the works in 'PROJECT UNITE' indicated neither a pure 'othering' from a universal ethnographic point of view – making local inhabitants into informants about difficult living conditions (and extracting symbolic surplus from that) – nor the business-as-usual attitude of an international art world. From a curatorial perspective, it was anchored in the local so as to focus on its intersections with the global, the modern and the contemporary; it prioritised interdisciplinarity and the coexistence of varying exhibition formats (group show and thematic show, intervention and programme). 'PROJECT UNITE' did so while performing and reflecting its own conditions, localising and historicising itself, not through a 'unifying' strategy, but in posing 'unity' as a still-haunting question in and through negotiating difference. As a case study for what was called 'Context art' (*Kontext Kunst*), at the time it indeed may have failed. But precisely in p.57 comparison with Peter Weibel's 'Kontext Kunst' exhibition at the Neue Galerie in Graz – which has become notorious as an attempt to label the whole scene under that title and to establish it as a new 'turn' (and, in so doing, designating the works almost exclusively as a sort of sculpture) – the difference made by 'PROJECT UNITE' becomes obvious. It was precisely not about a new art form being aware and in control of its context as its specific symbolic capital, but rather a project integrating different generations, disciplines and localities and thus creating a meaningful constellation directly out of a multiplicity of contradictions. Insisting on the problematic conditions of its own appearance in terms of social difference as well as its dependencies on the quickly changing economic and cultural relations of the expanding art field, 'UNITE' did not represent a movement but rather staged an ongoing conflict of artistic self-assertion in terms of its projects' discursive and exhibitionary potentials.

Therefore, the discursive and the exhibitionary should not be understood in terms of style – as available and recognisable patterns that can be easily followed or opposed in the name of pure practice, materiality or process. Rather, they function as a kind of horizon for all kinds of practice. The difference I want to stress here lies in the capacity to address that horizon and to reflect it within one's own practice, whether as artist, curator or critic. Within those practices we can recognise specific forms of a post-avant-garde methodology, based not so much on models of transgression, but on forms of displacement and condensation. As such, they are neither interested in the specificity of a medium nor in a complete overcoming of all traditional forms, but in specific ways of shifting and relating media to form, and situations to references, in all their historic, social and local dimensions.[40]

—

[40] I have tried to describe that methodology in many articles dedicated to the works of particular artists. See, for example, 'Coercing Constellations: Space, Reference and Representation', *op. cit.*; 'Displaying Design: Situation and

These methodologies can only keep their peculiar tensions and critical potential if they neither get lost in the *mise en abyme* of discursive referentiality nor disappear within the seductions of a purely spatial presence. This means there cannot be any reconciliation between the discursive and the exhibitionary in terms of a universal truth moment. Only as particular and conflicting moments, localities and agencies do they make sense.[41]

—

Coda

I will end my story here, at the moment when 'Culture in Action' simultaneously staged the exhibitionary and the discursive, in its own way, in the American Midwest. A lot could be said about the exodus from Cologne after 1993, about people moving from there again to New York (Müller, Köther, Charline von Heyl), and even more so on to London or Berlin.

Decisive, however, seems to be that no new centre has emerged so far, no more Chicago than Cologne. Is this for good or bad? In 1994 Pat Hearn opened the first gallery in Chelsea and a new, previously unimaginable success story of New York's commercial world emerged, while London and Berlin became discursively influential yet highly decentralised centres, dispersing artistic productivity in many different directions. Similar conglomerations are nowadays present around the globe, and of course it is to be celebrated that the Central and Eastern European, Latin American, African and Asian avant-gardes have appeared on the art-historical map. But still, something seems to be lacking – a specific way of integrating ambitious art and critical projects, of focusing on the reflection of historic and social conditions on one's own speaking position, of providing the contemporary and the global with a conceptual, aesthetic and allegorical moment. We require a situation of approving and validating such efforts and not just replacing them with every new biennial.

—

Reference in the Work of Angela Bulloch', in *Prime Numbers: Angela Bulloch* (exh. cat.), Vienna, Oxford, Tilburg and Toronto: Secession, Modern Art Oxford, De Pont Museum voor Hedendaagse Kunst and the Power Plant, 2006, pp.9–26; 'Modernity as a Modality: The Condition of Photography According to Christopher Williams', in *Christopher Williams, Program* (exh. cat.), Braunschweig: Kunstverein Braunschweig, 2006; and 'Or: The Last Bourgeois', in *Michael Krebber* (exh. cat.), Vienna: Secession, 2005, pp.5–7.

[41] My own curatorial work at the Kunstverein in Munich (1992–95) tried to explore the conflicting moments of history, locality and agency in 'solo' shows (by Andrea Fraser, Christian Philipp Müller, Adrian Piper, Martin Kippenberger / Albert Oehlen / Werner Büttner, Christopher Williams and Louise Lawler), as well as in project exhibitions including 'Die Arena des Privaten' ('The Arena of the Private', 1993), 'Die Utopie des Designs' ('The Utopia of Design', 1994), Stephan Dillemuth's 'Sommerakademie' ('Summer Academy', 1994), Renate Lorenz and Stephan Geene's 'Game Grrrl' (1994) and Group Material's 'Market' (1995). The idea of a 'discursive exhibition' is still haunting me – see my recent exhibitions 'Shandyism: Authorship as Genre' at the Secession in Vienna (2007) and 'The Content of Form' at the Generali Foundation in Vienna (2013).

This is not, however, supposed to be another story that moves into endgame. The question remains, do we really need the avant-garde or require a centre? And anyway, how do these two concepts relate to each other, especially if the avant-garde is understood as historically and socially coherent, a sort of 'supreme fiction' stating its own importance?[42] Precisely within the global conditions of the contemporary, the question of what an avant-garde could be becomes crucial, not in rejecting the local and the particular once more, but as a sort of regulative idea about the meaning of any locality, its implicit potential to become an imaginary centre, perhaps among multiple centres. Between the spreading of a 'bad' pluralism and the insistence on one's own phantasmatic claims, the avant-garde only makes sense as a reflection of its own intrinsic as well as extrinsic criteria. As such, it needs history. Because only in history can its main agenda become visible: not in repeating the radical moments and reiterating art's implicit hegemonic codes, but in reinventing itself constantly as an ongoing reflection on and performance of the moment – the locality and its own agency as artistic practice – in order to grasp and question the changing living conditions within today's art field.

—

[42] See Simon Critchley, *The Faith of the Faithless: Experiments in Political Theology*, London: Verso, 2012.

‘Culture in Action: A Public Art Program of Sculpture Chicago’

Multiple sites and venues in Chicago
May–September 1993

Mark Dion and the Chicago Urban Ecology Action Group

Kate Ericson, Mel Ziegler and a resident group of Ogden Courts

Simon Grennan, Christopher Sperandio and Local 552 of the Bakery, Confectionery and Tobacco Workers’ International Union of America

Haha (Richard House, Wendy Jacob, Laurie Palmer and John Ploof) and Flood: A Volunteer Network for Active Participation in Healthcare

Suzanne Lacy and a coalition of Chicago women

Iñigo Manglano-Ovalle and Street-Level Video

Daniel J. Martinez, VinZula Kara and the West Side Three-Point Marchers / Los Desfiladores Tres Puntos del West Side

Robert Peters with Mushroom Pickers, Ghosts, Frogs and other Others

A guide was produced to provide an overview of each of the eight collaborative art projects in 'Culture in Action'. This was produced and disseminated as an insert in the *Chicago Reader*, a free weekly newspaper, on Friday 21 May 1993. Additional copies from this print run, which totalled approximately 175,000, were subsequently distributed through the project sites, cultural institutions and major tourist attractions in Chicago.

Program Guide May-September 1993

Second Edition

CULTURE IN ACTION

A PUBLIC ART PROGRAM OF SCULPTURE CHICAGO

"Culture in Action: New Public Art in Chicago"

"Culture in Action" features eight projects by artist teams and citizen collaborators sited throughout Chicago from May to September 1993. Over the past year, the invited artists have developed partnerships through a process of public exchange that has extended the role of audience beyond spectator to that of participant. Forging a fundamental link between art and education, this process of local engagement has led to artworks that reflect a shared voice.

Sculpture Chicago

A unique visual arts organization not defined by a single established location, Sculpture Chicago acts as a catalyst for artists to create new works for the public. In its ten-year history, it has established an impressive track record, most recently with the commissioning of artist Ronald Jones to design Pritzker Park, permanently sited in the Loop on the corner of State Street and Van Buren. Its current program, "Culture in Action: New Public Art in Chicago," reflects the social concerns which fuel artists working in the public arena today, while serving as an urban laboratory to actively involve diverse audiences in the creation of innovative public art projects.

Table of Contents

This 12-page program guide features events for "Culture in Action: New Public Art in Chicago."
The following pages will give you an overview of the activities and philosophies of each of the eight collaborative public art projects.
Keep this program guide to follow each project as it unfolds over the summer.

Chicago, USA: City Centre North

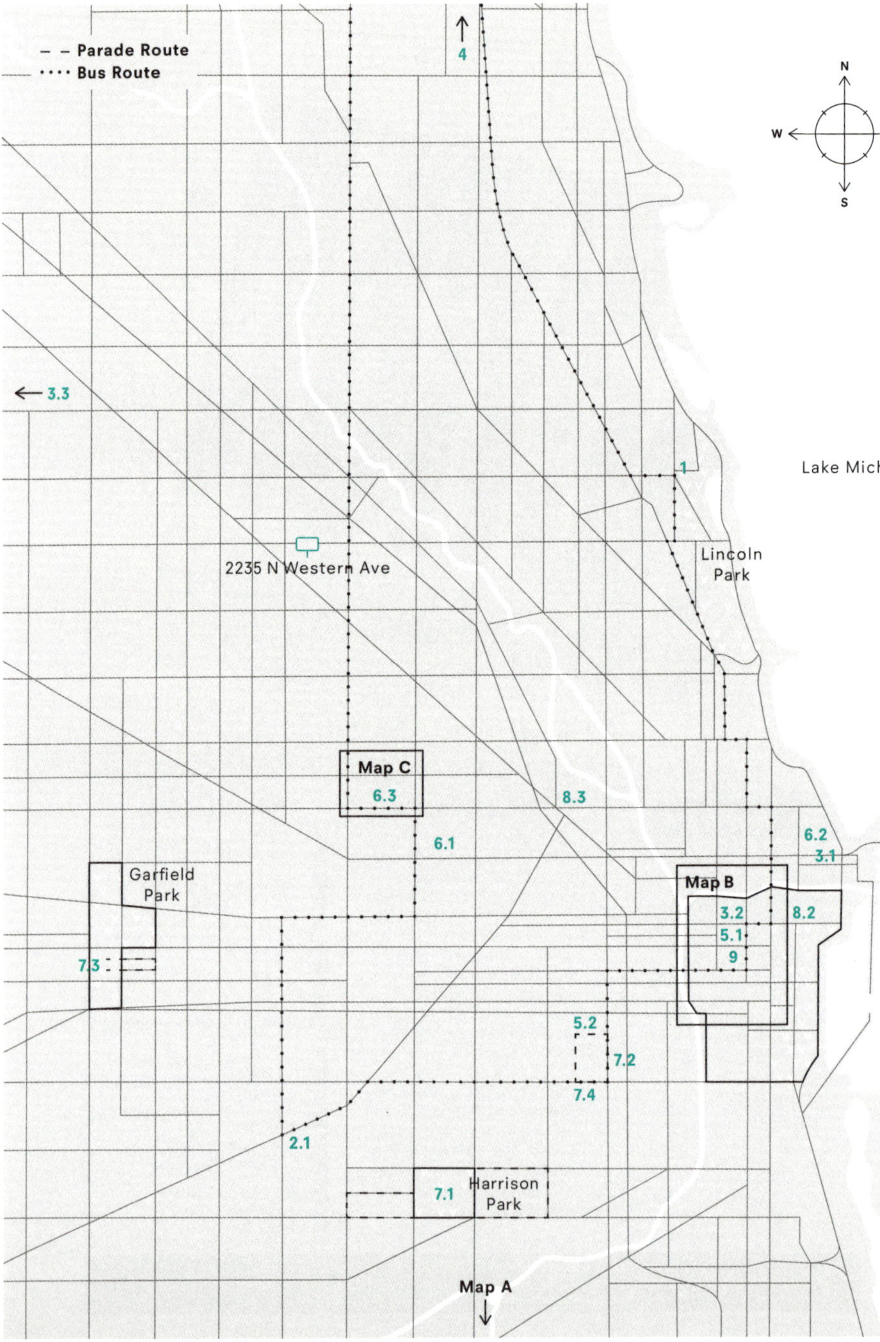

Mark Dion and the Chicago Urban Ecology Action Group (CUEAG)

1 CUEAG headquarters (clubhouse and field station) in Lincoln Park

Kate Ericson, Mel Ziegler and a resident group of Ogden Courts

2.1 Ogden Courts, Chicago Housing Authority apartments

2.2 *Eminent Domain*, a paint chart, distributed through the exhibition in Chicago*

Simon Grennan, Christopher Sperandio and Local 552 of the Bakery, Confectionery and Tobacco Workers' International Union of America

3.1 *We Got It!* chocolate bars available at The Market Place Foodstore

3.2 *We Got It!* chocolate bars available at Eastern Lobby shops within the Loop

3.3 Nestlé Factory, 3401 Mount Prospect Road

We Got It! billboard (see Map A on p.99 for further locations)

Haha (Richard House, Wendy Jacob, Laurie Palmer and John Ploof) and Flood: A Volunteer Network for Active Participation in Healthcare

4 *Flood: A Volunteer Network for Active Participation in Healthcare* at 1769 West Greenleaf Avenue

Suzanne Lacy and a coalition of Chicago women

5.1 A hundred monuments honouring women associated with the Chicago area and located within the Loop (see Map B on p.120 for greater detail)

5.2 Dinner for fourteen women, leaders from around the world, at the Jane Addams Hull-House Museum, part of the University of Illinois at Chicago

Iñigo Manglano-Ovalle and Street-Level Video

6.1 *This is My Stuff: A Street-Level Video Installation*, Emerson House Community Center

6.2 *Cul-de-Sac: A Street-Level Video Installation*, Museum of Contemporary Art, Chicago

6.3 *Tele-Vecindario: A Street-Level Video Block Party* on Erie Street, West Town (see Map C on p.135 for greater detail)

Daniel J. Martinez, VinZula Kara and the West Side Three-Point Marchers / Los Desfiladores Tres Puntos del West Side

7.1 *Consequences of a Gesture* parade around Harrison Park

7.2 *Consequences of a Gesture* parade in the Maxwell Street Market area

7.3 *Consequences of a Gesture* parade through Garfield Park

7.4 *100 Victories / 10,000 Tears* installation at the junction of West 14th Place and South Peoria Street

Robert Peters with Mushroom Pickers, Ghosts, Frogs and other Others

8.1 *Naming Others: Manufacturing Yourself* cards on Chicago Transit Authority bus routes*

8.2 'Meeting Grounds' symposium organised with Randolph Street Gallery at the Chicago Cultural Center

8.3 Randolph Street Gallery

Bus tours

9 Start of the bus tour for exhibition visitors: route lasting four to five hours, including lunch, on specified Fridays and Saturdays in June, July and August, costing $10, led by artist and educator Rebecca Keller

* Not indicated on the map

The Chicago Urban Ecology Action Group (1992–93)

Mark Dion and the Chicago Urban Ecology Action Group (CUEAG): Naomi Beckwith, Sharmaine Hendrix, Nynier Hodge, Tresnita Ivy, Catherine Mach, Dionne Emiko Mason, Charmaine Morgan, Muneerah Muhammad, Claudia Travis, Karlyn Westover, Jerry Winners, Kazumi Yoshinaga and others. Also Lisa Langken, art teacher, and Paul Adams, Principal, Providence St Mel High School; and Cheryl McWorter, Director, Lincoln Park High School Dance Program.

—

As described in the 'Culture in Action' programme guide
'A year-long collaboration between the artist and fourteen inner-city high school students which focused on tropical ecosystems and urban environments has resulted in an experimental ecological field station that bridges the realms of art and nature.'

—

General point(s) of access
CUEAG headquarters, a field station established in a clubhouse formerly used by anglers in Lincoln Park, with environmental projects taking place in Chicago more widely. The premises were open to the public with members of the CUEAG present, 1 July to 27 August 1993, Wednesday to Sunday 11am to 5pm.

—

More than a dozen pupils attending one of two schools (one public, one private) on the basis of scholarships or magnet programmes were selected by their teachers to participate in the project. Aged fifteen to seventeen, the students had applied to take part in activities, lectures and discussions addressing art, science and ecology, with the opportunity to join a two-week study trip to Belize, where Dion had recently been working.

A project proposal from January 1992 gives Lincoln Park Zoo and other natural history and environmental organisations as key sites and bases for collaboration. Dion envisaged making an installation at the zoo with students (exactly whom had yet to be established) following the trip to Belize, with the students employed as zoo guides. While collaboration of this particular nature did not come about as such, the group ultimately founded their headquarters in Lincoln Park nonetheless.

Initially calling themselves the Chicago Tropical Ecology Study Group, there were more or less weekly meetings on Saturday mornings at Providence St Mel School, taking place over an eight-month period, from 3 October 1992 to 19 June 1993. Dion led classes on tropical ecosystems and urban environments, with visiting speakers – such as Alexis Rockman and a number of professional tropical biologists – and local teaching staff involved in his stead a third of the time. Field trips to environmental education sites

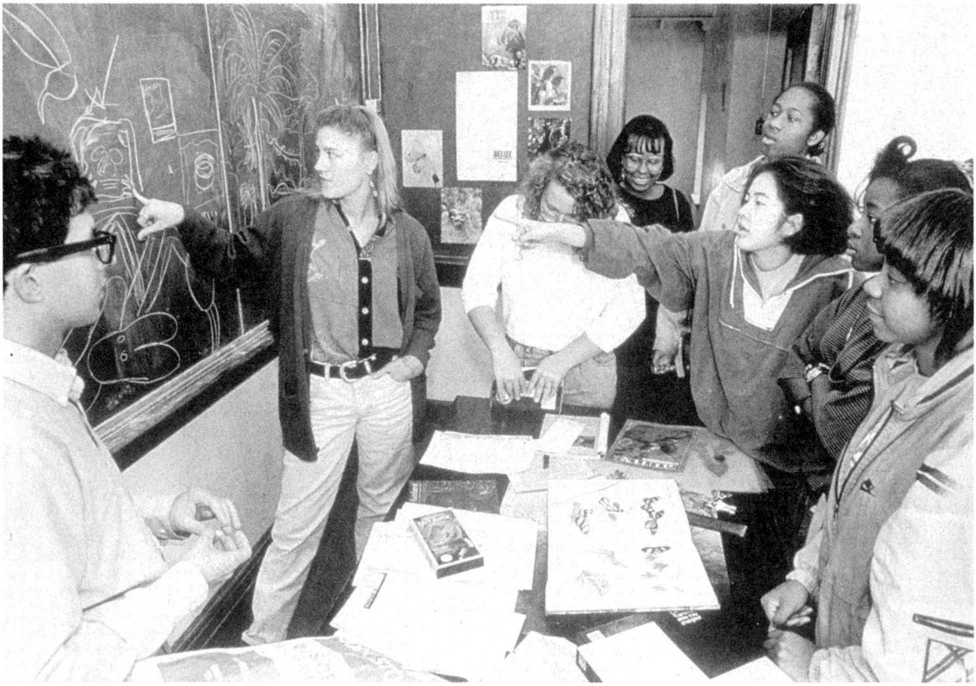

fig.1

Providence St Mel School, Chicago, 1992.
From left: Mark Dion, art teacher Lisa Langken
and a group of students.

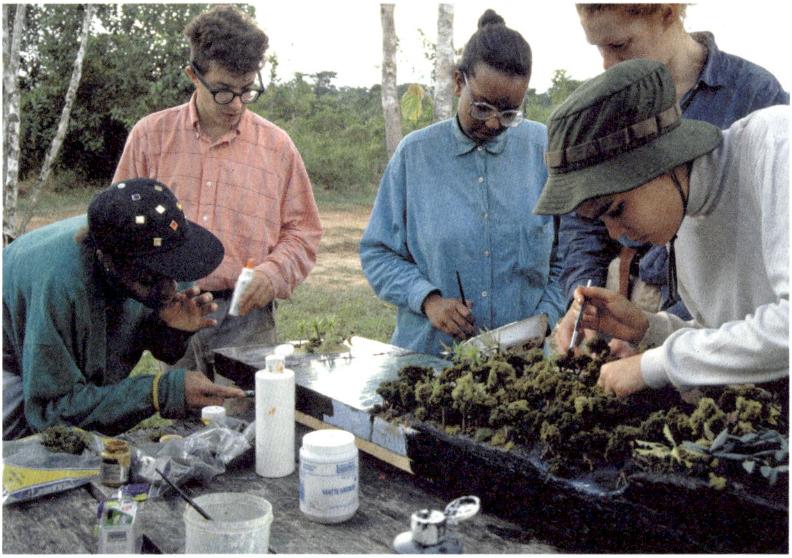

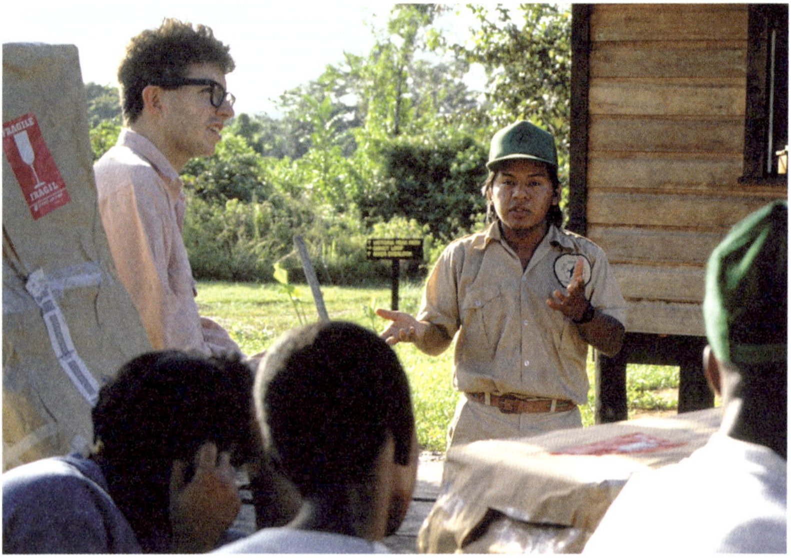

fig.2 and 3

Dion and members of the CUEAG in Belize.

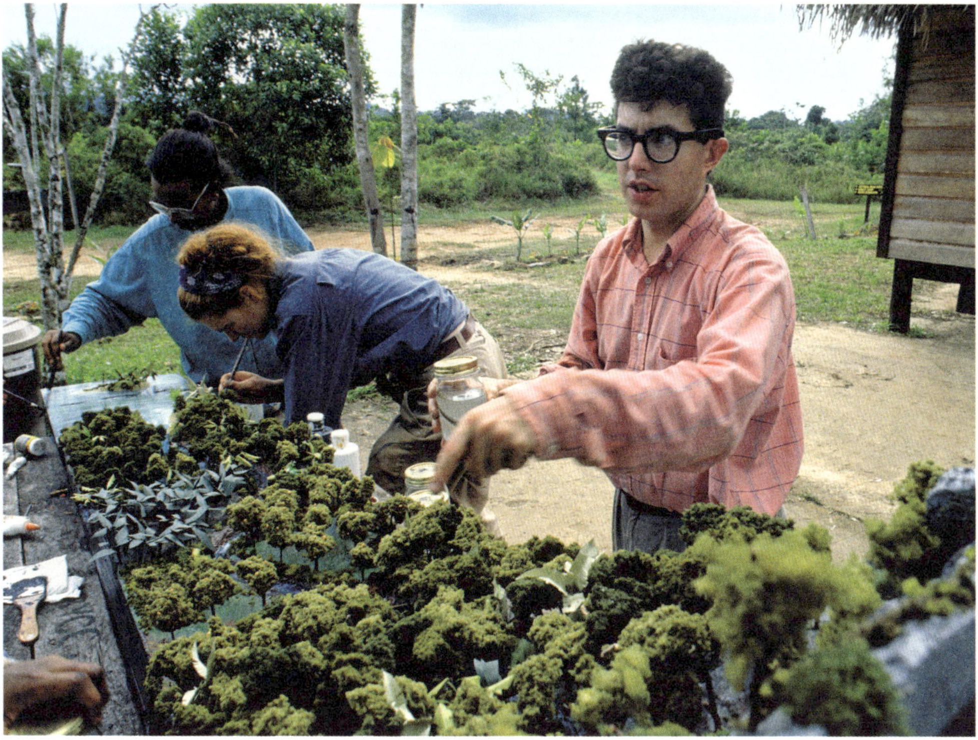

fig.4

within Chicago were also organised. Until December 1992, they worked collectively on creating a three-dimensional representation of territory along part of the Belize River, later taking this model with them to install at a visitor and education centre along the actual river. They also, for instance, designed a team logo and screen-printed their own T-shirts promoting the group.

From late December 1992 to early January 1993, Dion and fourteen students travelled to Belize, visiting the Cockscomb Basin Wildlife Sanctuary (where they installed their model), the Monkey Bay Biological Research Station and the Belize Zoo in particular. From their base in the rainforest, at the Cockscomb Basin Wildlife Sanctuary, they were taken by local experts on guided walks and introduced to further sites of ecological interest.

Back in Chicago, meetings resumed on Saturday mornings, newly informed by the group's deepened understanding of tropical ecosystems, and this fuelled the establishment of their headquarters to act as an experimental eco-field station and drop-in centre or clubhouse. The artists, conservationists and environmental activists invited to the meetings continued to contribute their perspectives, with social change and community agency under ongoing discussion. The collective name was changed to the Chicago Urban Ecology Action Group, and individual projects included assignments given by Dion and sculptural installations for the field station in Lincoln Park. The latter was established in the spring, in the clubhouse previously used by local anglers.

From May to August, concurrent with the exhibition period of 'Culture in Action', the CUEAG students were involved in environmental projects around Chicago, such as clean-up programmes, community gardening, tree planting and restoration ecology projects. The clubhouse was opened to visitors a month after the official launch date for the show, and closed a month before its end. The 'Culture in Action' programme guide invited people along for July and August during given times, forewarning that they might find themselves put to work. The student members of the CEUAG were paid $5 an hour to be present during opening hours, discussing the installation as art, workshop space and ecology information centre.

The secluded location of the clubhouse did not particularly lend itself to visits from passers-by, however it was the final destination (prior to the return to Pritzker Park) for a weekly 'Culture in Action' bus tour, and interested parties were taken round on request. Chicago residents also encountered the CUEAG when the latter were at work in various local neighbourhoods.

Following the end of their school year and summer employment at the clubhouse, the student members of the CUEAG continued to meet on an informal basis for another year.

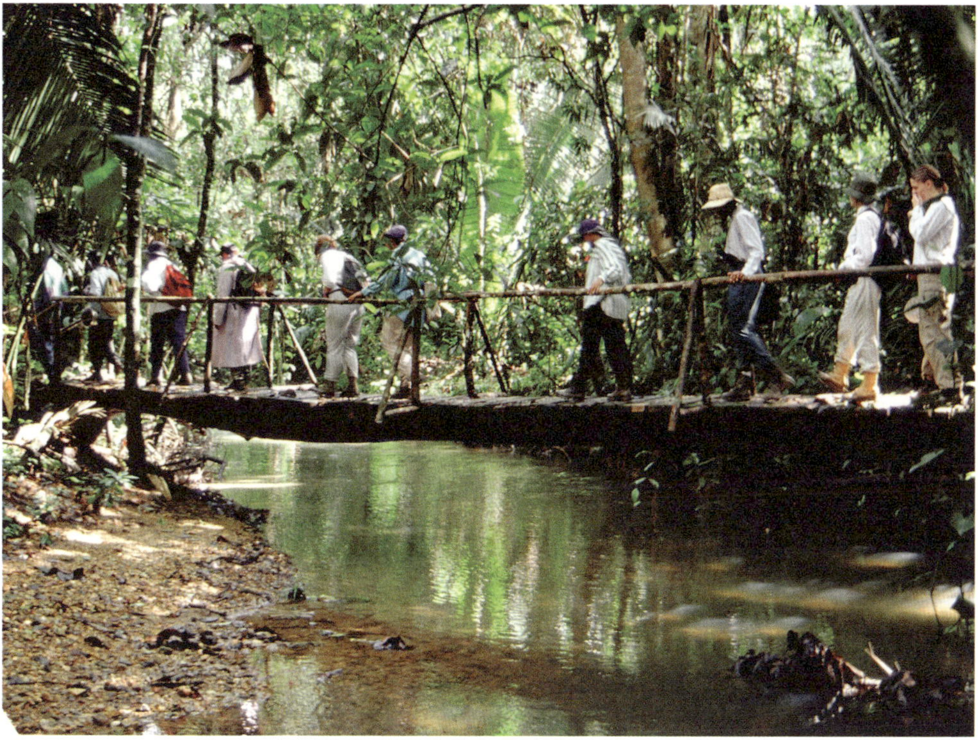

fig.5

Dion and members of the CUEAG in Belize.

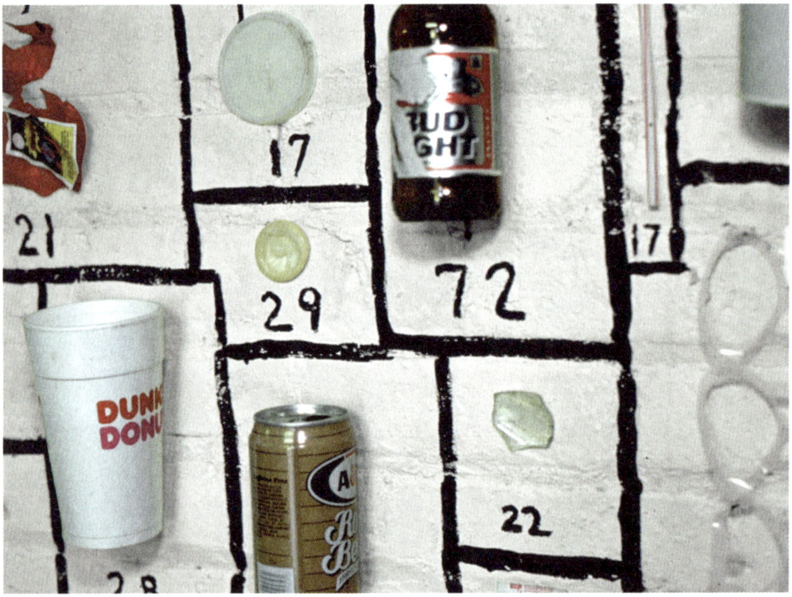

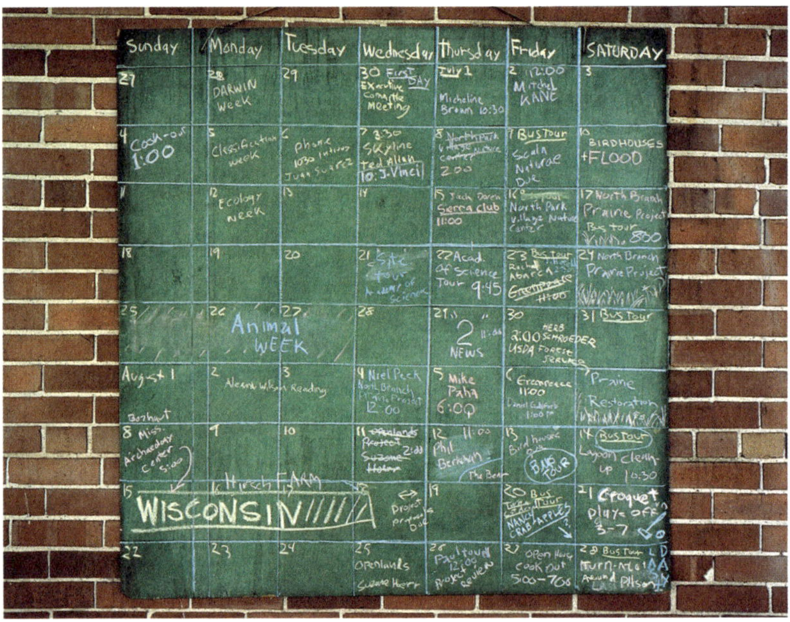

fig.6 and 7

Inside the CUEAG headquarters.

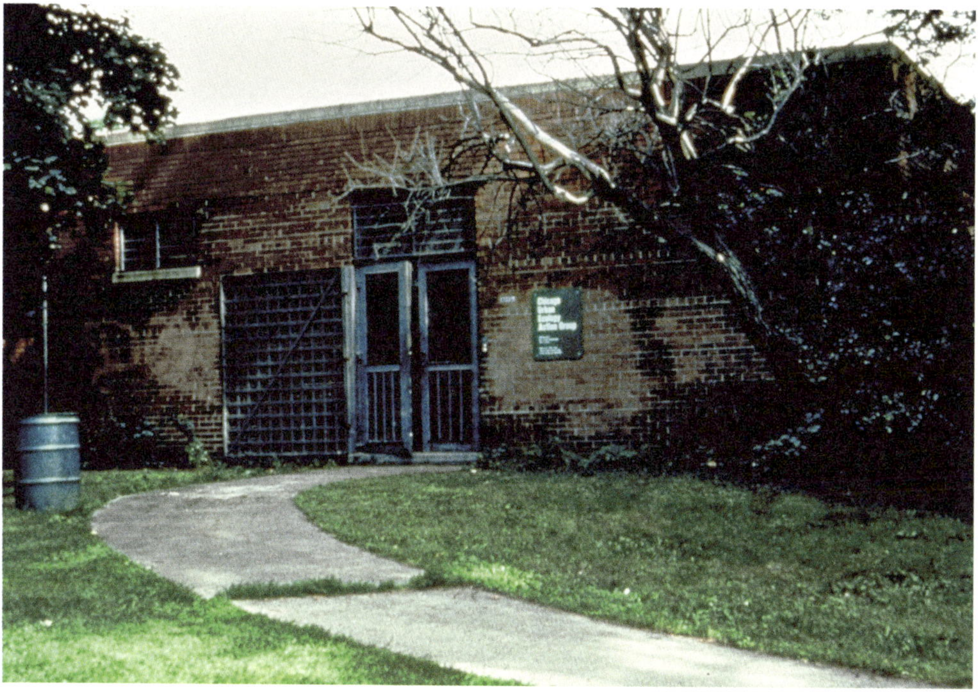

fig.8

Exterior of the CUEAG headquarters, Lincoln Park.

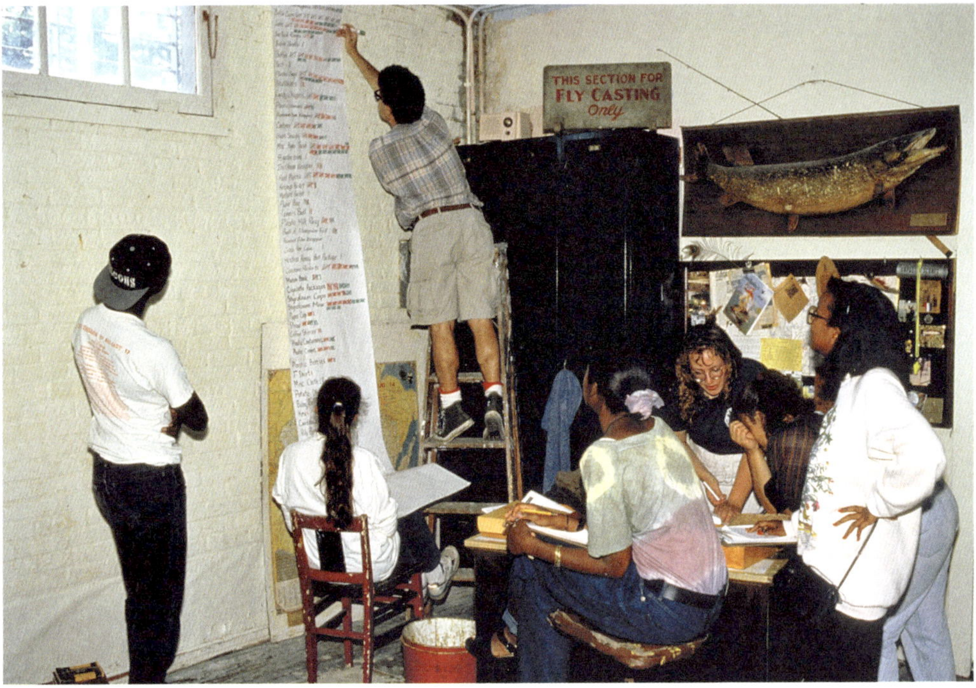

fig.9

Inside the CUEAG headquarters.
Clockwise from centre: Mark Dion, Catherine Mach, Kazumi Yoshinaga, Charmaine Morgan, Naomi Beckwith, Karlyn Westover and Jerry Winners.

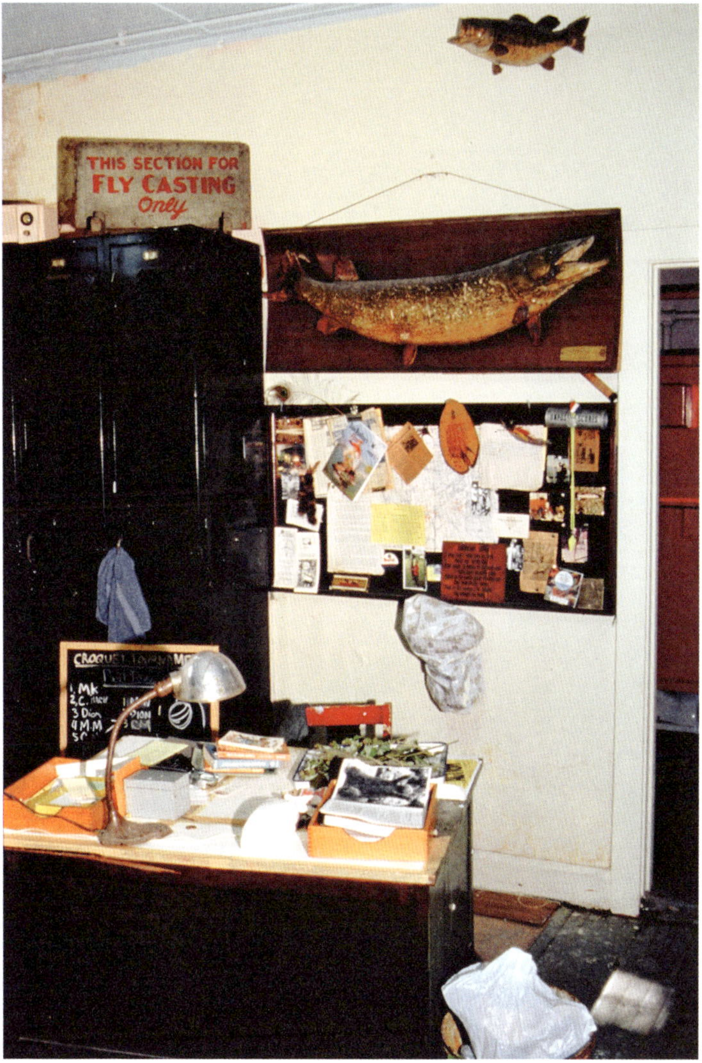

fig.10

The CUEAG clearing up a vacant lot for a community garden.

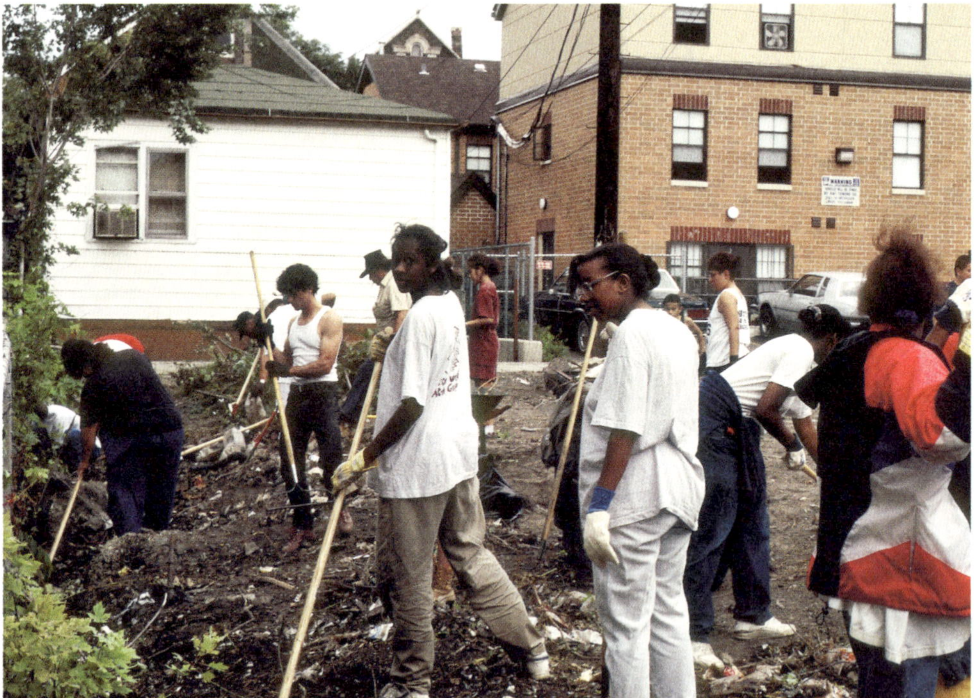

fig.11

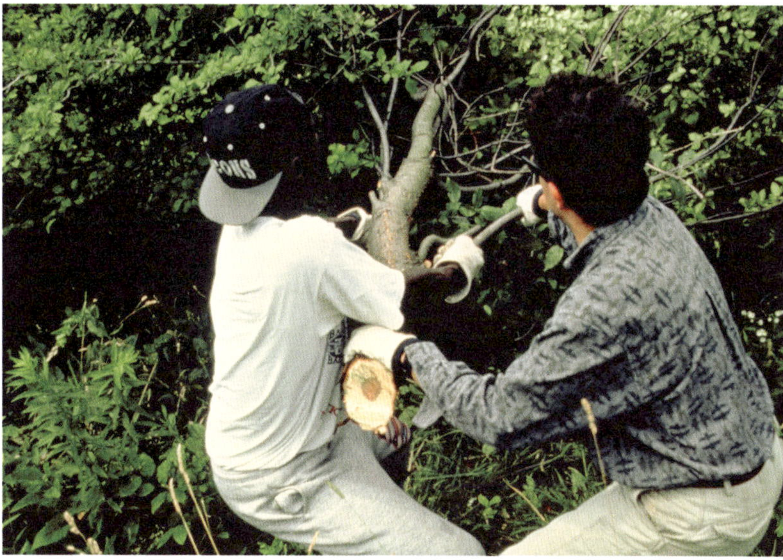

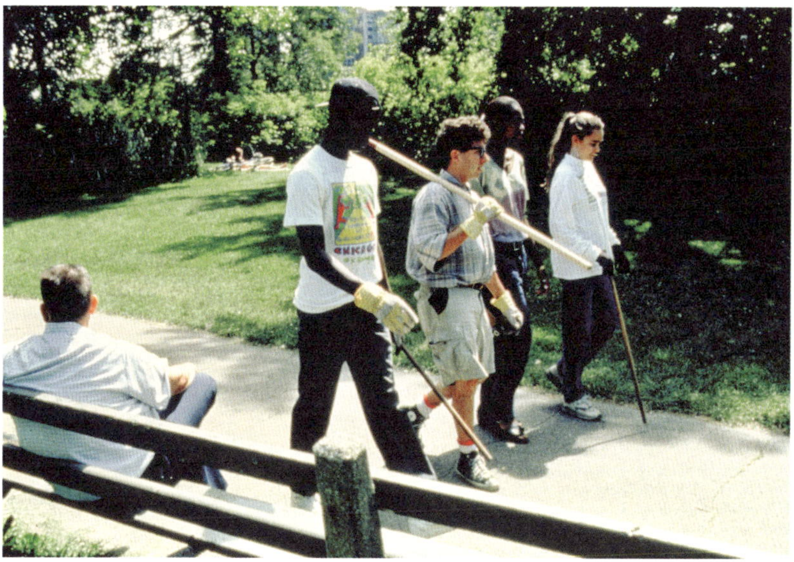

fig.12 and 13

The CUEAG in Lincoln Park: Jerry Winners and Mark Dion (fig.12) and (walking, from left) Winners, Dion, Naomi Beckwith and Karlyn Westover (fig.13).

Eminent Domain (1992–93)

Kate Ericson, Mel Ziegler and a resident group of Ogden Courts, Chicago Housing Authority apartments, led by Arrie Martin and Elois Smith, together with Brenda Bolden, Iretha Ford and Loretta Lacy.

—

As described in the 'Culture in Action' programme guide
'Tenants and artists created an artwork in the form of a paint chart whose design, text, colours and their names are based on an American heritage of public housing.'

—

General point(s) of access
Paint charts distributed to those attending the 'Culture in Action' bus tour, which passed by Ogden Courts.

—

Ericson and Ziegler had a long-established interest in the social and architectural signification of domestic paint, visible in works such as Ziegler's *Red House* (1979) and Ericson and Ziegler's *If Landscapes Were Sold* (1987). Although by 1991 the artists had begun working directly with commercial-paint colour charts, as seen in two projects from that year, *Exported Pallet* and *Camouflaged History* (the latter as part of 'Places with a Past', curated by Mary Jane Jacob in Charleston, South Carolina), this model did not form part of their initial proposal for 'Culture in Action'. The artists' first written proposal described a multi-site installation based on 'the fiction of the American home' and the lived realities of public housing, that would incorporate geographical and biographical details of the buildings' occupants in collaboration with Chicago Housing Association (CHA) and resident groups.

Through research and discussions with CHA and other public housing officials, and with the goal of developing a close relationship with tenants, the artists opted to work within a single housing complex. Following a CHA tour of four possible locations, the artists chose Ogden Courts, which had an established tenants' organisation committed to improving conditions. Built on the West Side of Chicago in 1950, Ogden Courts comprised two buildings, each with seven storeys and ten apartments per floor. Perceived as an early success, it led to similar developments elsewhere within the city. However, by 1992 living conditions in the blocks had deteriorated, with residents facing a high incidence of crime, among other issues.

Ericson and Ziegler's first formal presentation of the paint-chart concept in 1992 met with both interest and scepticism from members of the tenants' council, but by the end of the year a number of them had agreed to engage with the project. The artists are quoted in the exhibition catalogue as stating: 'We will act solely as the catalyst for the project to occur; the point of view will be that of the group, and all design, colour and names their choice … it will be

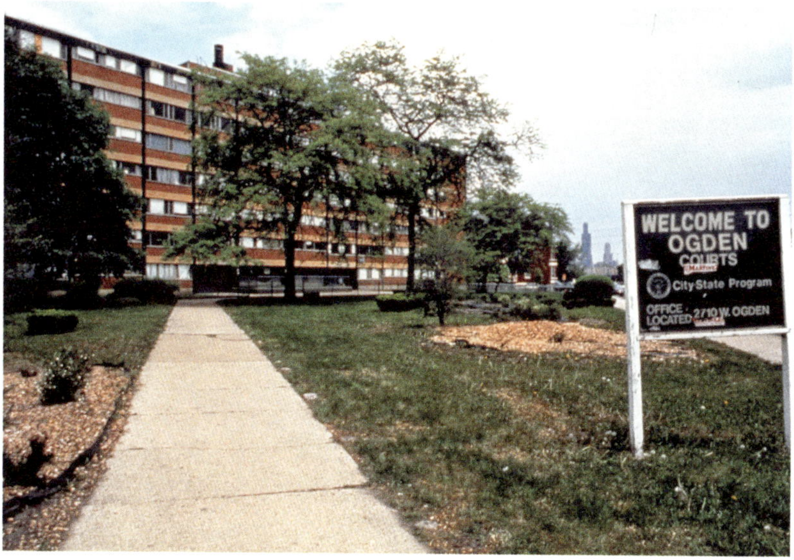
WELCOME TO
OGDEN
COURTS
City State Program
OFFICE
LOCATED 2710 W. OGDEN

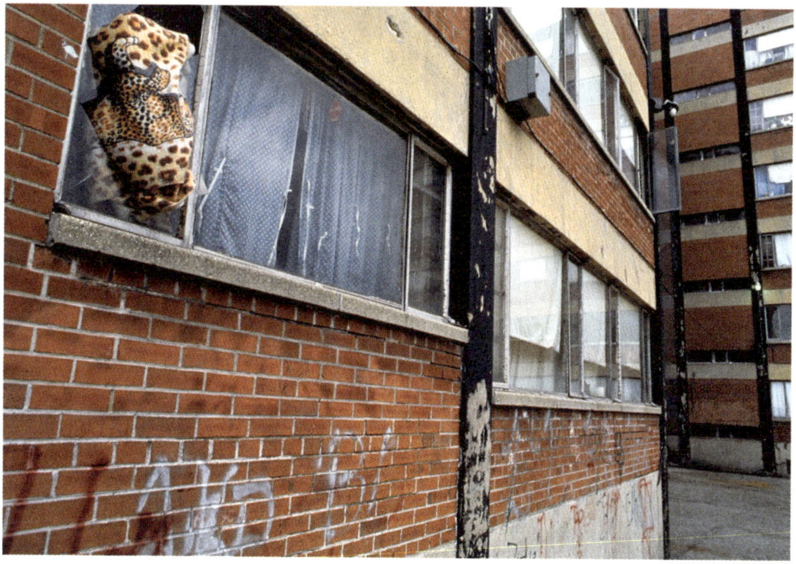

fig.14 and 15

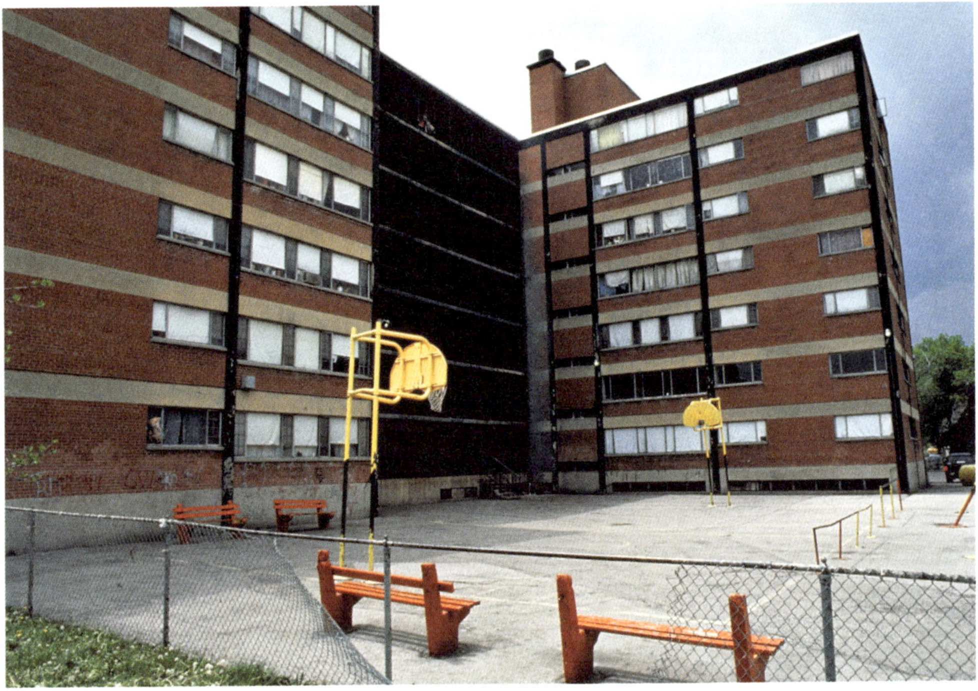

fig.16

educational and informed and not merely a charity project.' As proposed by the artists, the group was paid a design fee, which was subsequently used to set up educational programmes for children at Ogden Courts, and the artists participated in other fundraising efforts, such as shared dinners to support additional programmes for the resident community.

Core to the project were a series of discussion workshops focused on issues of economics, law, race, the construction of US homes, the history and philosophy of public housing, home decorating, colour theory, paint-chart design and the sociopolitical or demographic signification of colours. The resulting paint chart provided a US history of social housing and set local matters within this context. The naming of the selected hues was rooted in, for instance, individual colour choices within the resident community (e.g. 'Elois's Pink Lace'), national events ('FHA Gingerbread', referring to the National Housing Act of 1934 that created the Federal Housing Administration) or local events ('Cabrini Green', in memorial to an individual killed in another housing complex within Chicago). An interior view of the Blue Room of the White House adorned the front of the chart, which folded out to reveal a US map with images representing fifty government-subsidised housing projects, one for each state.

Plans to distribute the charts and associated paints through True Value Hardware stores across Chicago and in selected stores nationwide were not realised because the projected costs of production exceeded budgeted funds, which was the source of some dispute between the artists and Sculpture Chicago. The Ogden Courts complex was demolished in 2005.

We Got It! The Workforce Makes the Candy of Their Dreams (1992–93)

Simon Grennan, Christopher Sperandio and Local 552 of the Bakery, Confectionery and Tobacco Workers' International Union of America, involving the particular participation of Dorothy Barksdale, Richard Bowens, Leroy Brown, Barbara Fleming, Artemio Gil, Martina Herrara, Louis Mason, Minnie Mitchell, Willie Rias, Mary Ross, Thelma Smith and Regina Williamson – a dozen of the 800 production-line workers at the Nestlé factory in the Chicago suburb of Franklin Park – and more generally represented by Jethro Head, Union President.

—

As described in the 'Culture in Action' programme guide
'Twelve members of BC&T Local 552 and the artists have designed their own candy bar and its promotional campaign, which incorporate issues of individual to corporation, job to home, and the impact and meaning of products consumers confront daily.'

—

General point(s) of access
We Got It! chocolate bar produced in an edition of 30,000 and distributed to selected shops within Chicago. Eleven billboards promoting the bar were placed in Chicago, mostly on the South Side.

—

The artists initially wanted to work with the management and candy-makers at Fannie May, a local company with dedicated stores throughout the city that happened to share its name with the Federal National Mortgage Association (FNMA, commonly known as Fannie Mae). But when attempts at direct collaboration with Fannie May, as well as other companies, proved unsuccessful, the artists started to contact local unions instead. A fourteen-page plastic-bound booklet titled 'The Workers Make the Candy of Their Dreams: Project Outline for a New Artwork' was used to present the idea in meetings with union members.

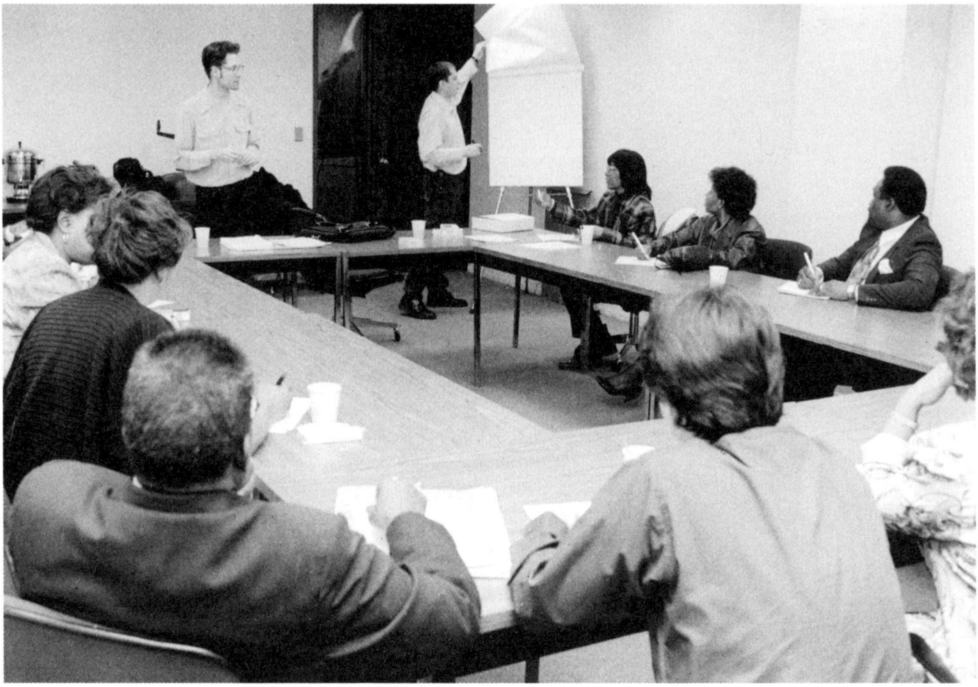

fig.17

Design-team workshop with union workers and Grennan and Sperandio in the board room of local law firm Sidley Austin LLP.

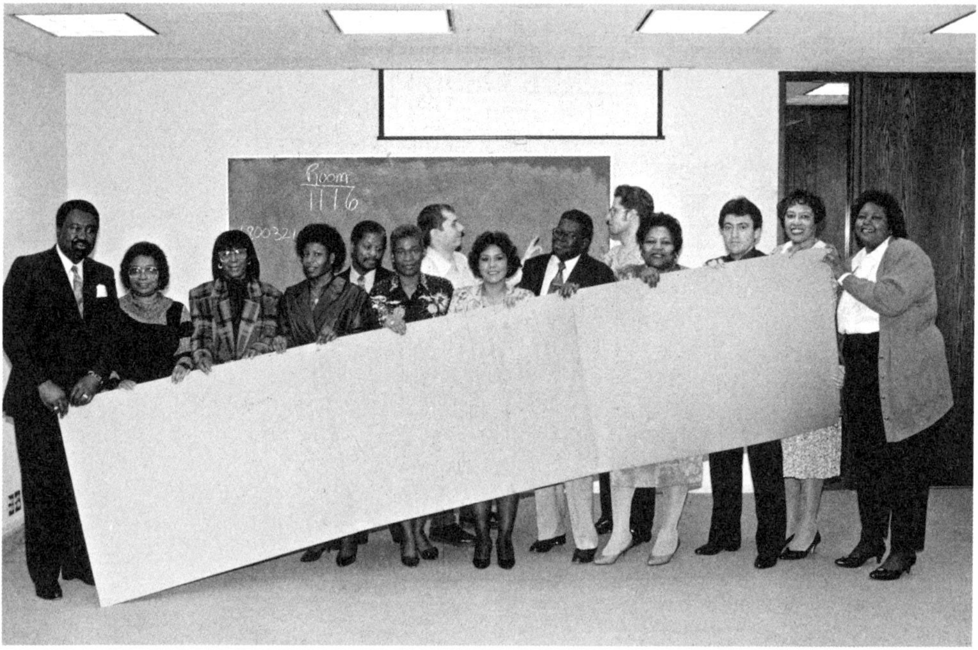

fig.18

Photograph that was used as the basis for the *We Got It!* box design and billboard campaign

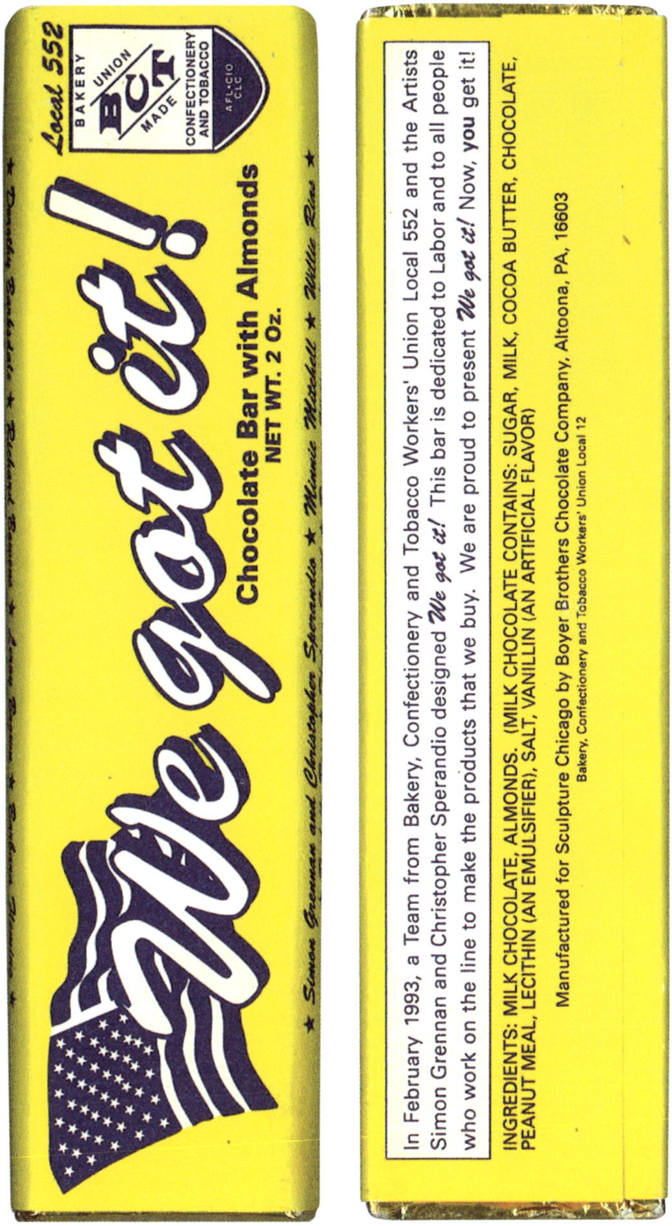

fig.19 and 20

The names of the artists and their collaborators were listed on the side of the chocolate bar.

In June 1992, the artists established relations with Jethro Head, the president of the union representing workers at the Nestlé factory in the Franklin Park district of the city. In September, the artists, representatives of Sculpture Chicago, Jethro Head and the factory's manager, Charles E. Brashears, gathered for a meeting. The company was not set up to make and distribute small product runs, but Head instigated a union election to generate a team of twelve members who would work closely with the artists on the design and promotion of a new candy bar. When Nestlé's international headquarters proved unsupportive, Head cited the project as a 'test of worker "empowerment"' in the local press (*Chicago Reader*, 14 January 1993). Brashears agreed to let the elected workers go on what he called 'art leave', on condition that they met off-site to contribute to the project and that no credit be given to the local factory division at Franklin Park.

In February 1993, the twelve elected workers took part in a forty-hour week of workshops in a law office in downtown Chicago – Sidley Austin LLP – made available as an alternative meeting site by Sculpture Chicago board member Jack Guthman. Facilitated by Grennan and Sperandio, these workshops generated the design of the chocolate bar, its wrapper and promotional campaign. The workers decided they would produce a chocolate bar with almonds, and that they would use an image of themselves holding the bar to promote it. Production of the bar and its packaging was arranged through union contacts and taken on by union members at a small factory in Altoona, Pennsylvania.

An offer to donate space on forty billboards originally made by Gannett Outdoor was withdrawn when the firm perceived the project to be a commercial venture. Sculpture Chicago subsequently agreed to a reduced commercial rate, and eleven billboards were put up in locations chosen by the project team – chiefly on the South Side, where many Nestlé factory workers lived. The 'Culture in Action' bus tour passed the billboard at 2235 North Western Avenue, at which point tour guide Rebecca Keller explained the project, typically while handing out chocolate bars to passengers.

Commercial distribution was difficult, particularly without Nestlé's support. Available soon after the exhibition opened, the candy bars were priced at 50 cents a piece, and sales were ultimately restricted to particular locations in central Chicago: at Eastern Lobby Shops within the Loop and from the high-end Market Place food store in Streeterville. Head staged an event at the Nestlé factory in Franklin Park, distributing the candy bar directly and for free, with accompanying information, to the workers on the site.

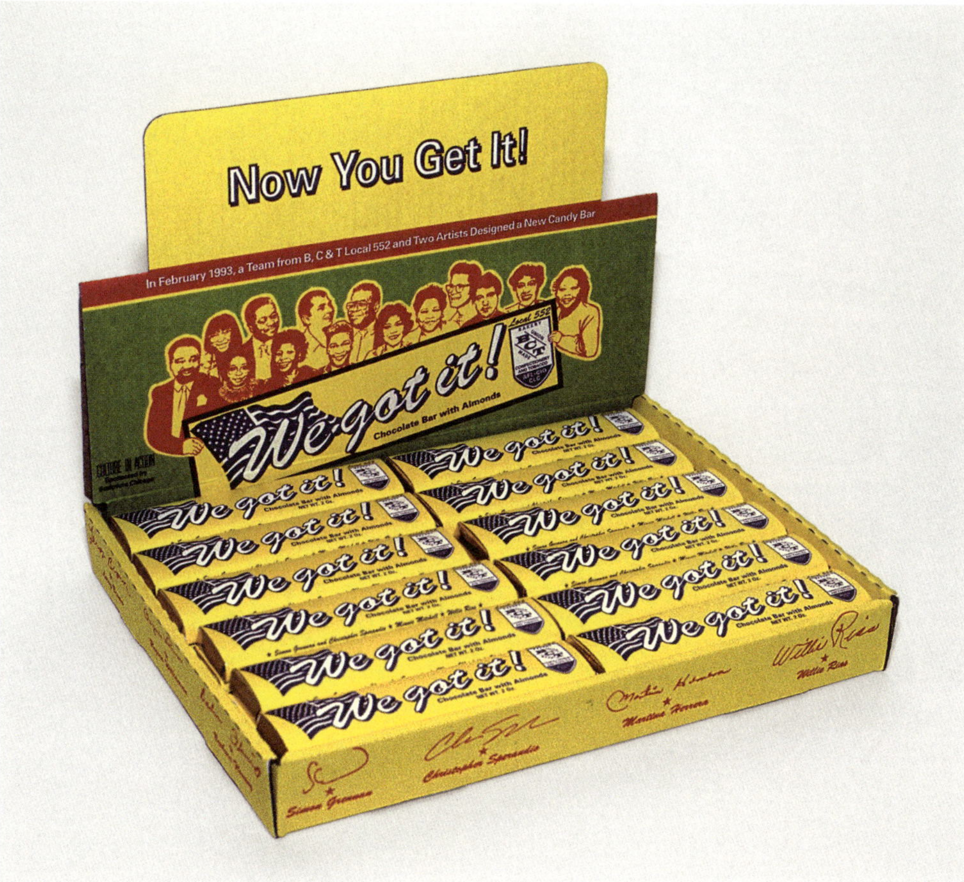
Now You Get It!
In February 1993, a Team from B, C & T Local 552 and Two Artists Designed a New Candy Bar
We got it!
Chocolate Bar with Almonds
Local 552
Simon Grennan
Christopher Sperandio
Martina Herrera
Willie Ries

fig.21

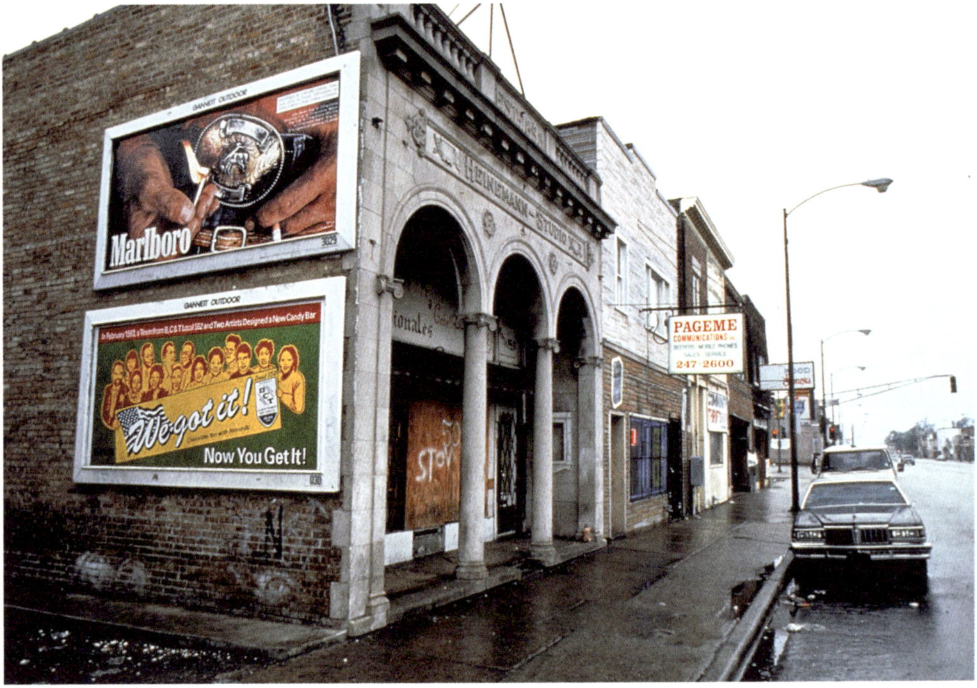

fig.22

The billboard explained the origin of the new chocolate bar, discreetly crediting 'Culture in Action, sponsored by Sculpture Chicago'.

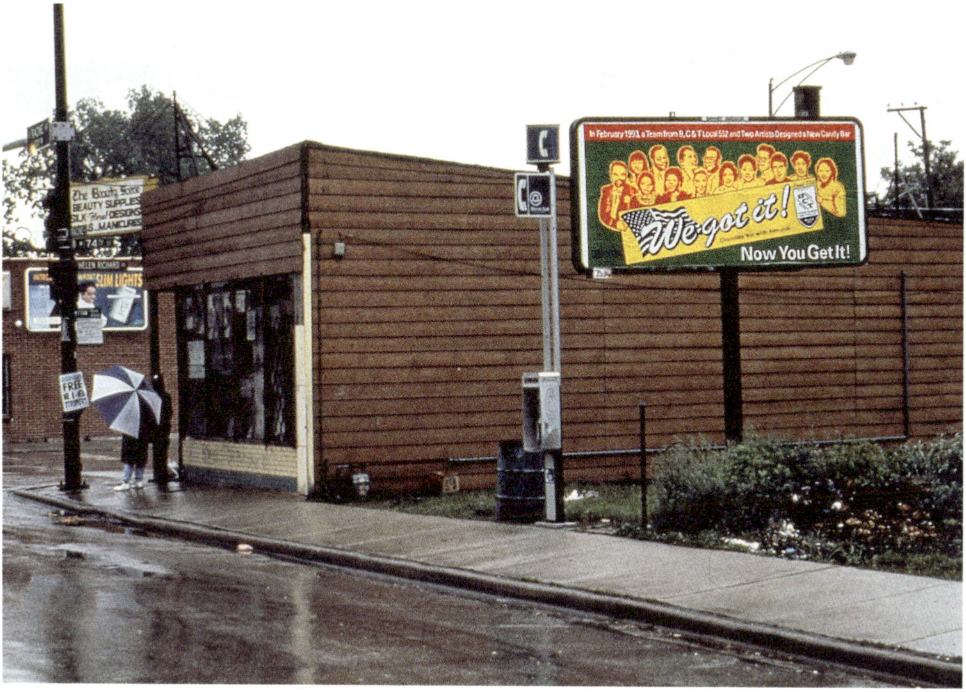
BEAUTY SUPPLIES
SLIM LIGHTS
In February 1993, a Team from B, C & T Local 552 and Two Artists Designed a New Candy Bar
We got it!
Now You Get It!

fig.23

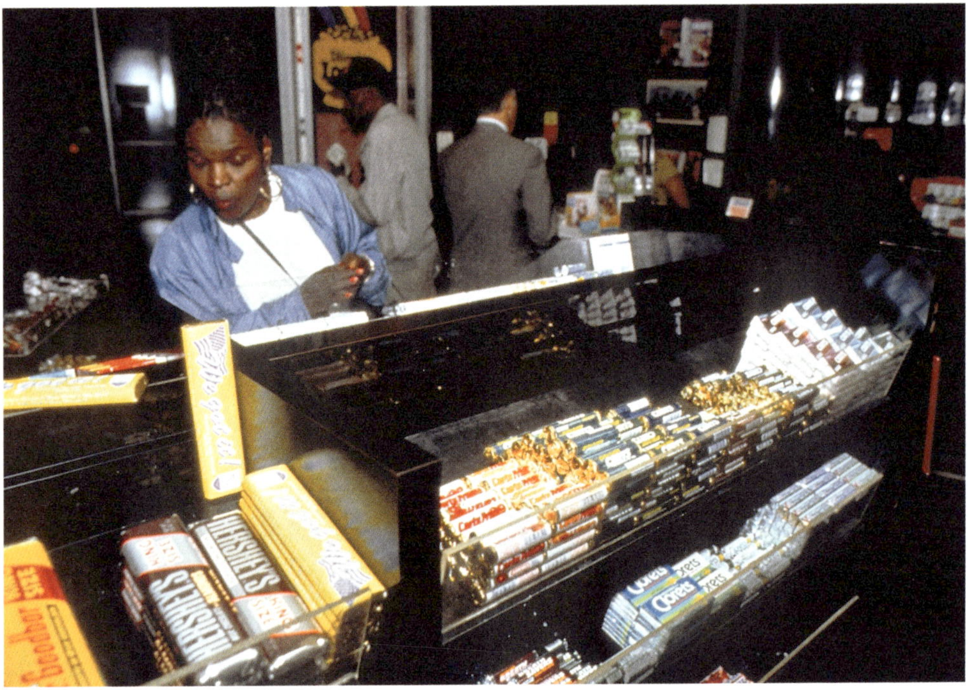

fig.24

The bar on display, at an Eastern Lobby store in the Loop (fig.24) and at The Market Place food store, Streeterville (fig.25).

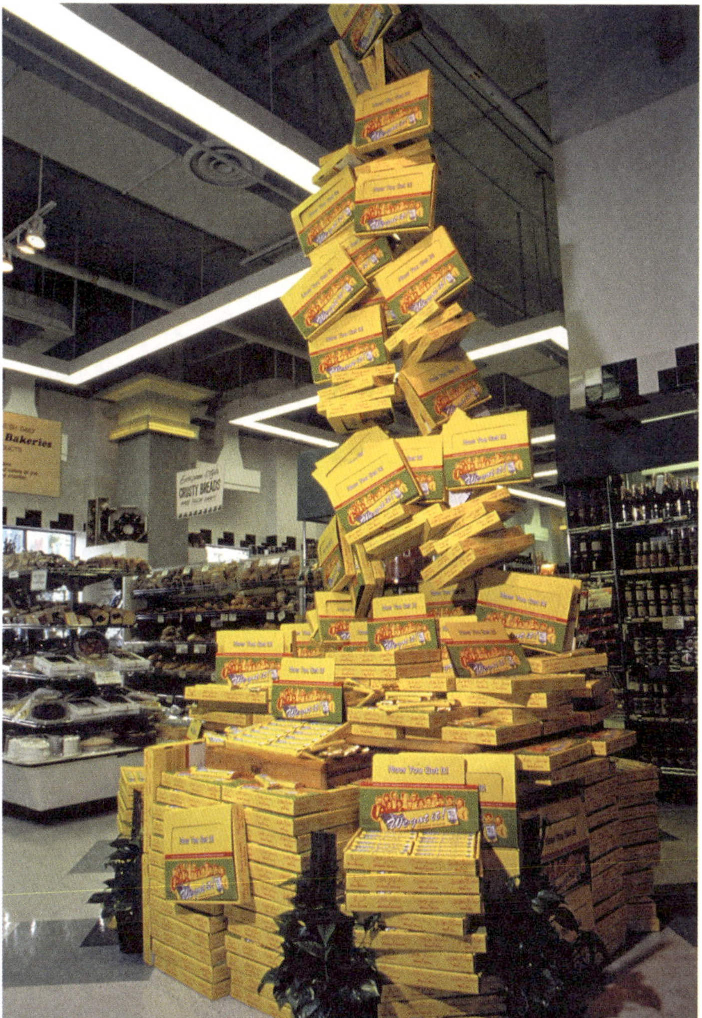

fig.25

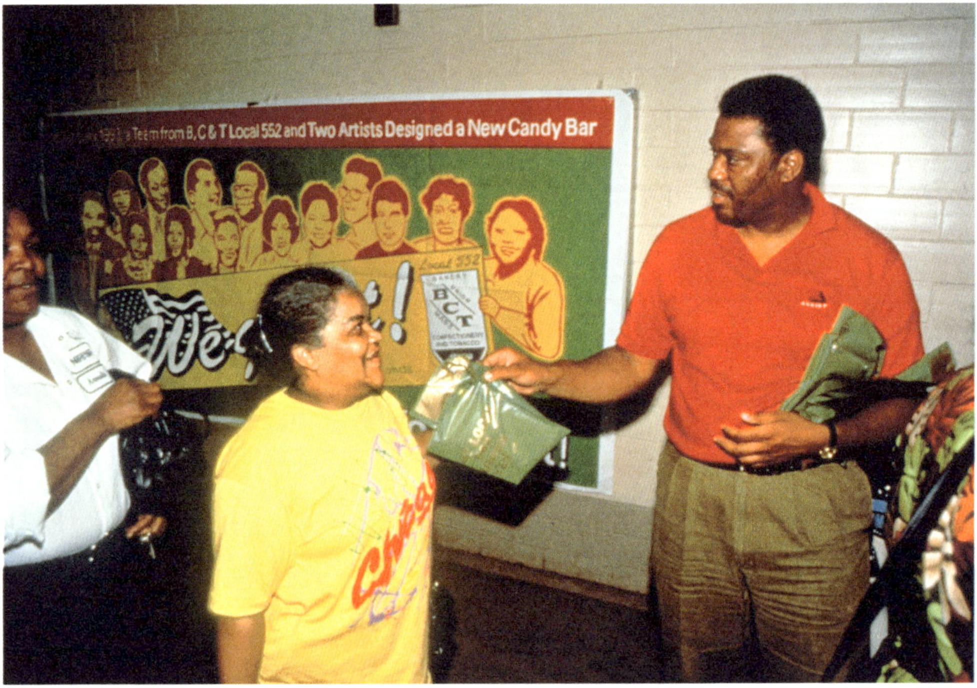

fig.26

Jethro Head distributing the chocolate bar and information about the project to Nestlé factory employees.

Map A

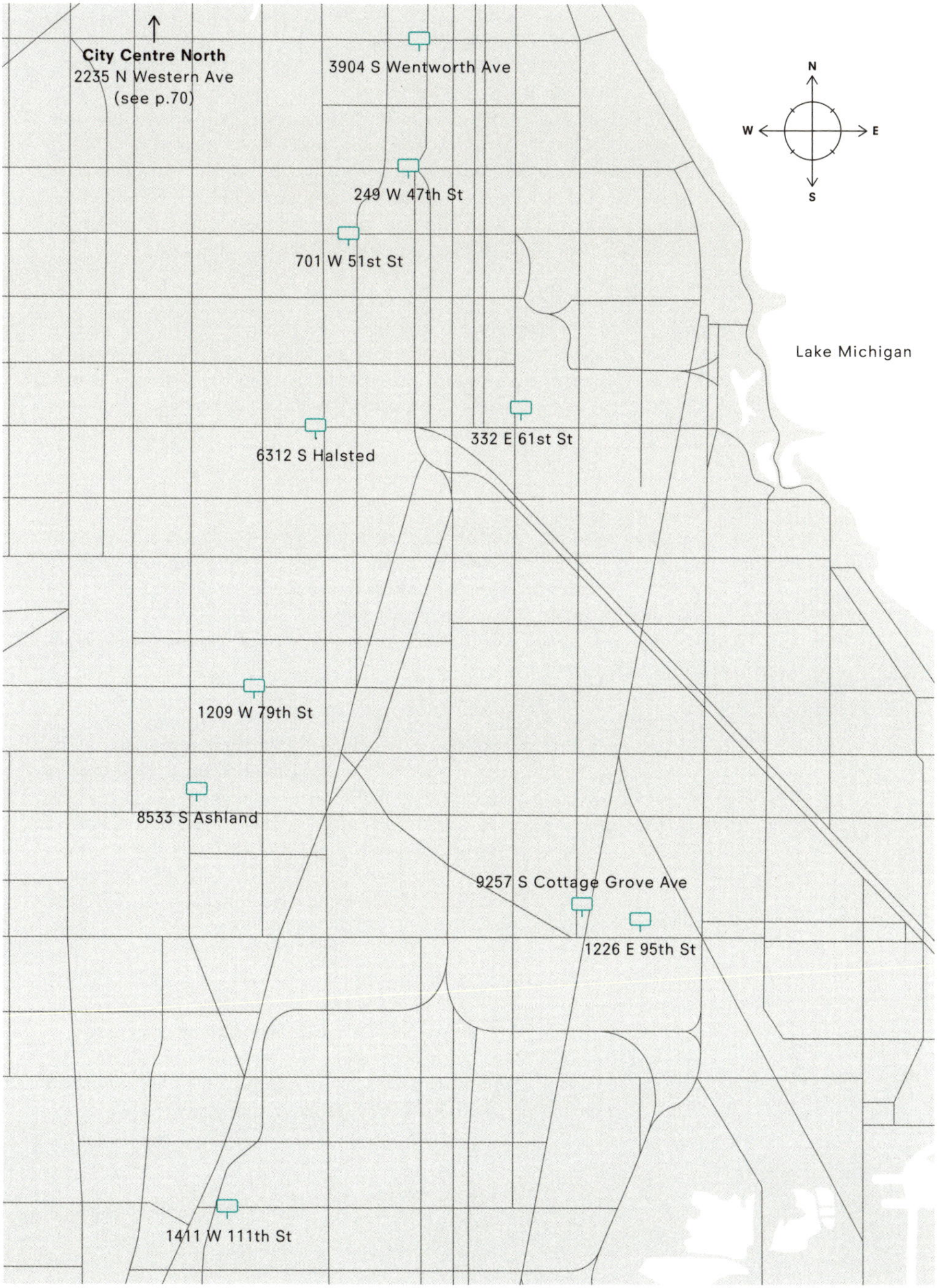
City Centre North
2235 N Western Ave
(see p.70)
3904 S Wentworth Ave
N
W
E
S
249 W 47th St
701 W 51st St
Lake Michigan
332 E 61st St
6312 S Halsted
1209 W 79th St
8533 S Ashland
9257 S Cottage Grove Ave
1226 E 95th St
1411 W 111th St

Flood: A Volunteer Network for Active Participation in Healthcare (1992–95)

Haha (Richard House, Wendy Jacob, Laurie Palmer and John Ploof) and Flood: A Volunteer Network for Active Participation in Healthcare, including Tony Alioto, Terry Amidei, Kristin Appelhof, Jennifer Bartlett, Jeff Black, Valerie Brodar, Kerryn Brunsting, Chris Campbell, Suzanne Flemens, Paul Garklavs, Bob Gonzales, Chris Hanson, Bob Hewitt, Jennifer Jankauskas, Zach Jennings, Diane Kelley, George Levin, Liang Lu, Carla Mayer, Kevin Nevills, Caroline O'Boyle, Jodi Osterreicher, Kelly Pierce, Amy Reichart, Bob Schultz, Rachel Selekman, Hendrika Sonnenberg, Derek Stroup, Beth Turk, Miwako Watanuki, Kurt Weston and neighbours and friends of the garden, located in the Rogers Park area, on Chicago's North Side.

—

As described in the 'Culture in Action' programme guide
'Artists and volunteers are cultivating a hydroponic garden to produce vegetables and therapeutic herbs for use by HIV/AIDS service organisations. The garden serves as a centre for community dialogue as well as a metaphor for caregiving.'

—

General point(s) of access
An indoor hydroponics vegetable garden in an empty Rogers Park storefront at 1769 West Greenleaf Avenue, open to the public from 21 May to 29 August 1993: Monday, Tuesday and Friday, 4 pm to 7 pm; Saturday, 1 pm to 4 pm; and Sunday, 1 pm to 5 pm. Weekly meetings took place on Tuesday evenings, and public lectures and special events took place throughout the summer.

—

The Chicago-based artists' collaborative Haha began their project with the idea of creating a community garden in the neighbourhood in which they lived, Rogers Park, at the time an ethnically mixed area with rising poverty and the fastest-growing rate of infection for HIV/AIDS in the city. When an outdoor site could not be found, the artists decided to move their project indoors. This developed into plans for a hydroponic garden intended as a source of food for people with HIV/AIDS, free from the risk of infection from soil-borne bacteria.

After attending a workshop on hydroponic gardening in October 1992, Haha started work in the empty storefront they had located. In the front of the space, plastic troughs were placed on tables a metre above the floor, and each had 24 holes filled with rock wool for growing the plants. The back of the space was arranged for meetings and educational activities, with reference information on horticulture, nutrition and HIV/AIDS along the walls.

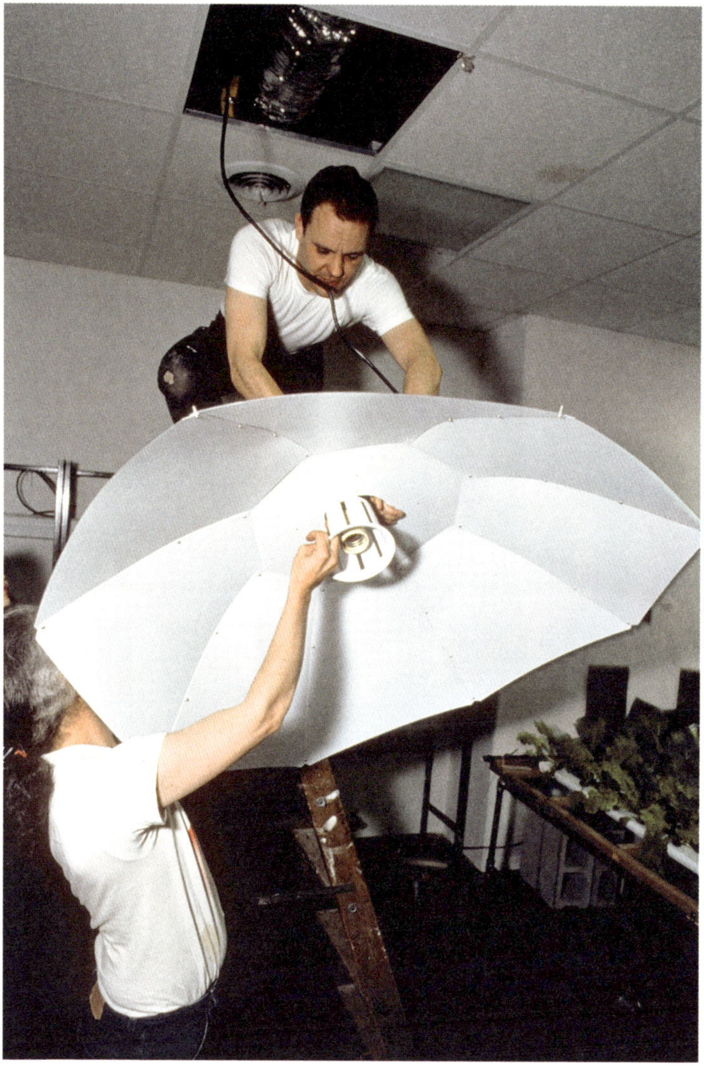

fig.27

John Ploof and Flood member Bob Hewitt installing one of the two 1000-watt metal-halide lamps that were on every day from 6 am to 10 pm.

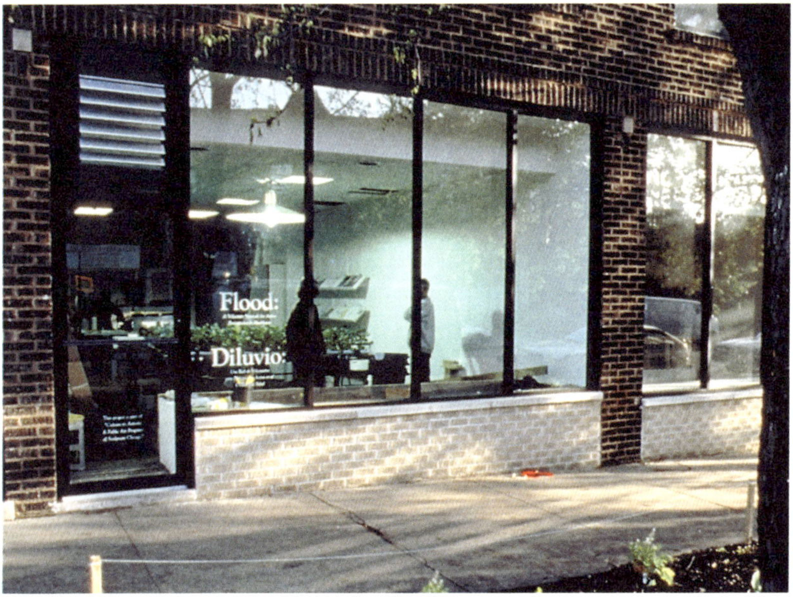

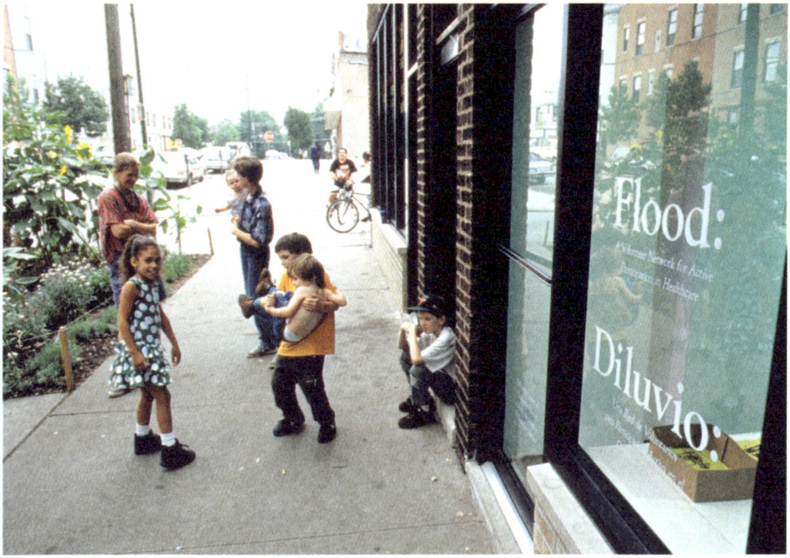

fig.28 and 29

Storefront with copies of the 'Culture in Action' programme guide visible in the window.

Flood members Zach Jennings and Caroline O'Boyle with visitors.

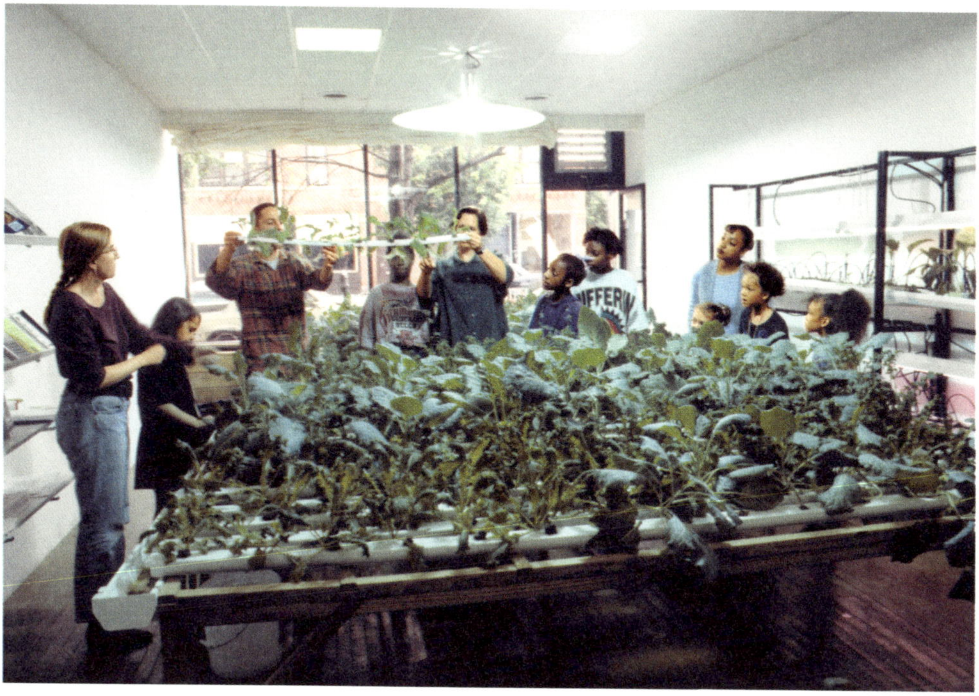

fig.30

By early 1993 the indoor garden was established, and weekly meetings with an open group of volunteers began in February. Initially participants were mainly students from local colleges and universities, but over time the constituency became more mixed – cumulatively including educators, writers, electricians, cooks, construction workers and more artists. Volunteers were involved in the maintenance (cleaning, watering, monitoring, harvesting) of the garden, and some also in the management and development of the place.

During the spring of 1993, Flood members met with HIV/AIDS support networks to discuss the distribution of herbs and vegetables from the garden. Flood volunteers began to assist with existing local services, such as the food-delivery service Open Hand Chicago. Meanwhile, the first batch of hydroponic greens – including kale, collards, mustard greens and Swiss chard – were sprouting and could be harvested. By May the garden was open to the public.

Up and running, the garden could feed about 75 people every six weeks. Produce was distributed through Better Existence with HIV (BEHIV), Chicago House hospice and Open Hand Chicago. School and summer-camp groups came to the space for discussion events. A logbook was used to record daily interactions with visitors, who could leave anonymous comments. They could also pick up free condoms. In the summer an outdoor garden was planted in a space adjacent to the building.

The 'Culture in Action' bus tour stopped at *Flood* over lunchtime. Typically introduced to the space by a member of Haha, passengers could browse the plants, information and comment cards, and were encouraged to enter into debate.

Flood's fundraising initiatives allowed the group to continue to function and to maintain the project when financial support from Sculpture Chicago ended in September 1993, after the public phase of 'Culture in Action'. The storefront remained open until 1995, and related gardening initiatives were developed with other locales and communities in DeKalb, Illinois, and Cedar Rapids, Iowa. Ongoing discussion and work by Flood members contributed to the consolidation of four organisations and services through the Howard Area Community Center, including a food pantry, an alternative high school, a community centre and counselling and medical referrals.

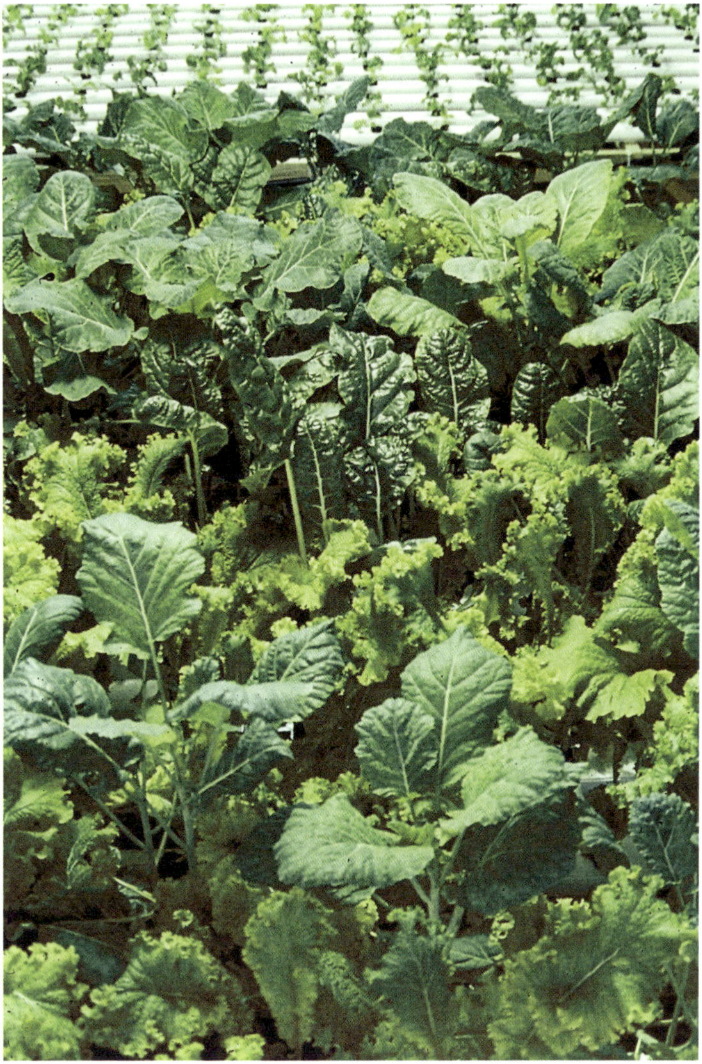

fig.31

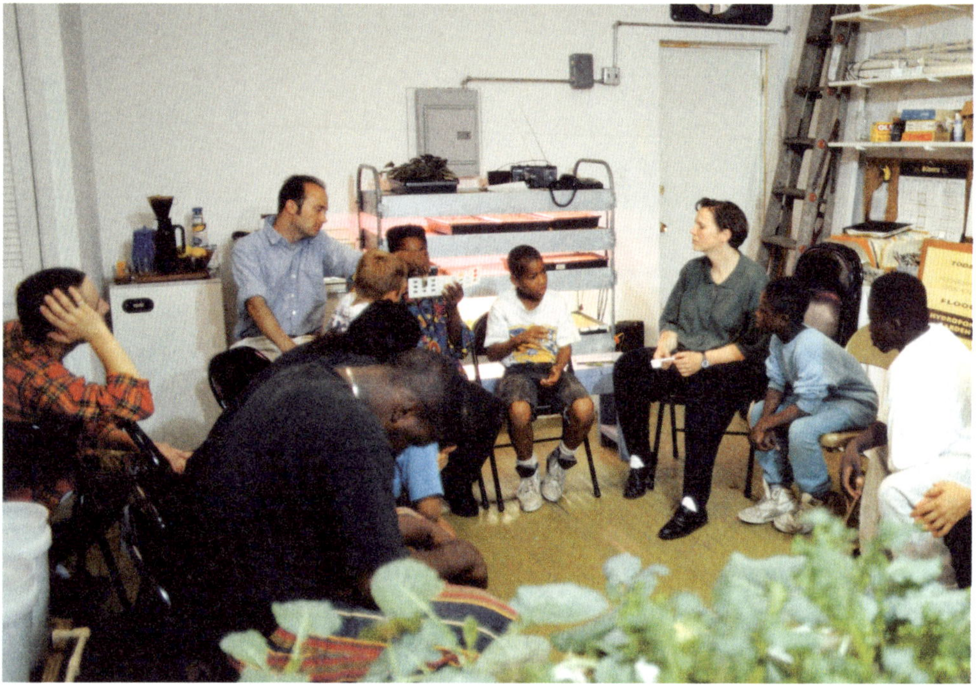

fig.32

Discussion led by Caroline O'Boyle and Richard House.

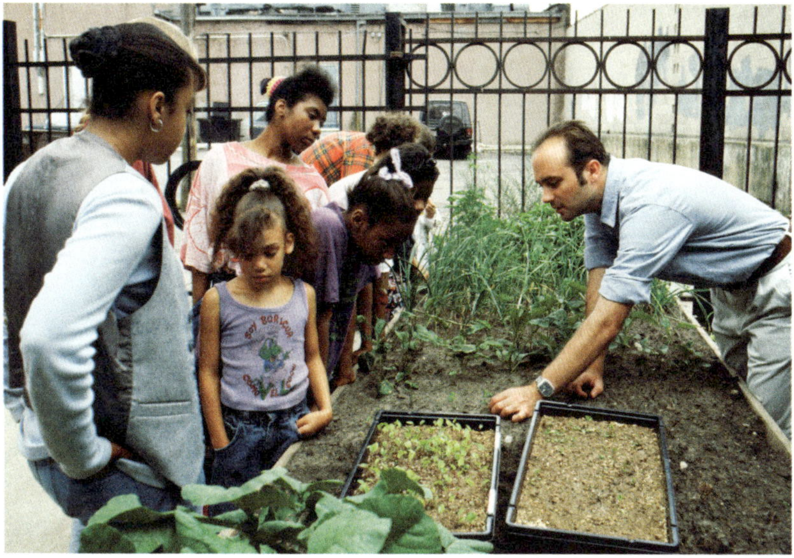

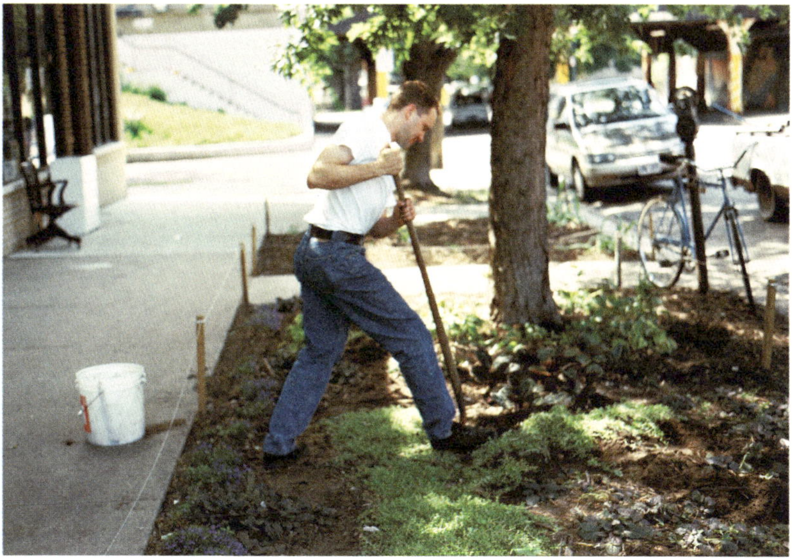

fig.33 and 34

Richard House and a group of participants tending to the outdoor garden at the rear of the building (fig.33) and John Ploof working on the garden at the front (fig.34).

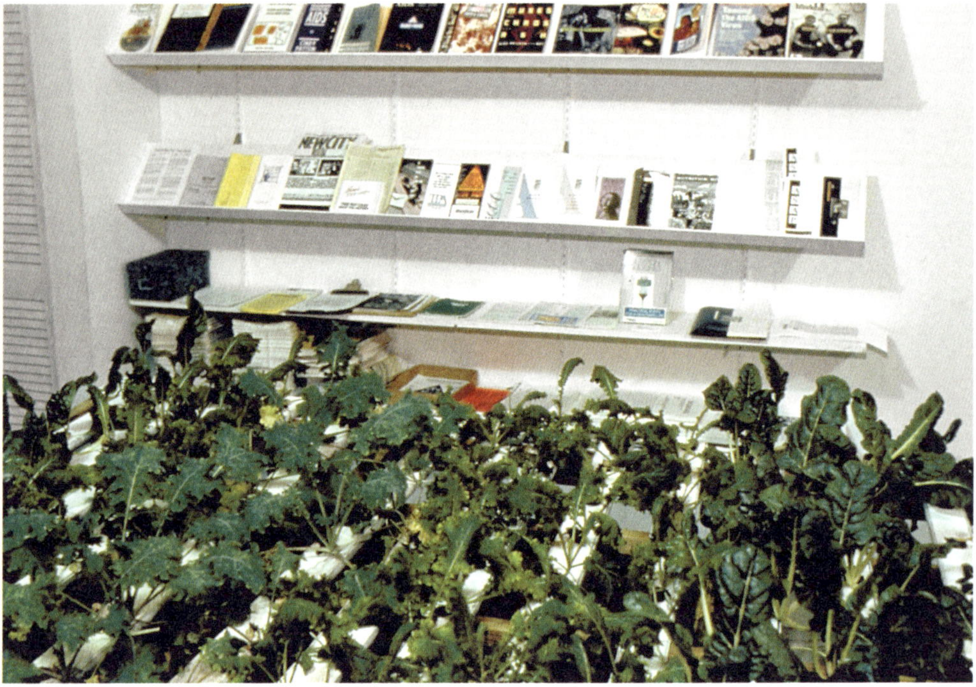

fig.35

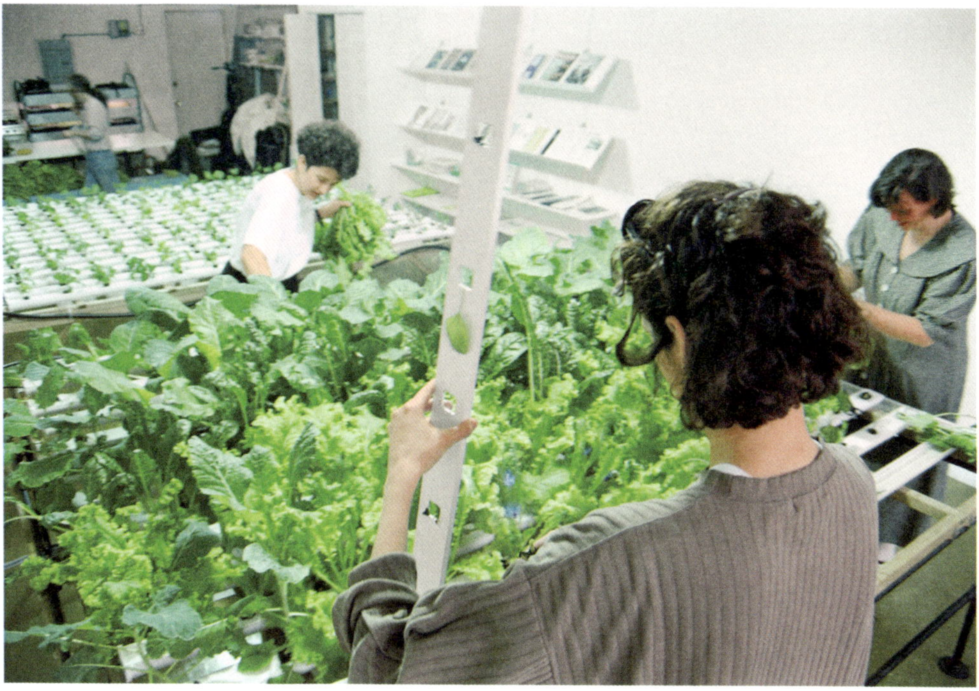

fig.36

Full Circle (1992–93) and *Dinner at Jane's* (1993)

Suzanne Lacy and a coalition of Chicago women: a steering committee and advisors, including Diane Chandler, Amina J. Dikerson, Joyce Fernandes, Nancy Flay, Stephanie Fogg, Sandra Furey, Michelle Gazzola, Camille Gerstel, Juana Guzman, Ronne Hartfield, Sharon Irish, Mary Ann Johnson, Barbara Kensey, Kanta Khipple, Grace Lai, Susan Larson, Juju Lien, Virginia Martinez, Esther Parada, Marianne Philbin, Kavita Ramdas, Eunita Rushing, Jane Saks, Ann E. Smith, JoAnne Stone-Geier, Janet Treuhaft, Thelma Tucker, Manny Tueter and Cheryl Yuen; a staff team of Mary McGall (*Full Circle* coordinator) and Tali Simon (administrative assistant); and a student team of Ericha Ahlschier, Shalona Byrd, Tracy Hudak and Mary Zerkel.

—

As described in the 'Culture in Action' programme guide
'Conceived in the spirit of Jane Addams, this [...] collaborative work looks at women's accomplishments in the past, their continuing commitment to community in the present and their ability to envision the future.'

—

General point(s) of access
A hundred limestone monuments, each honouring a woman from the Chicago region, installed on pavements within the Loop from May to September 1993. On 30 September 1993, a dinner for fourteen global women leaders was held at the Jane Addams Hull-House Museum, which was filmed and later edited into a 53-minute video co-produced with Michelle Baughan.

—

With the working title 'Ireland/Chicago', Lacy initially intended to focus on the political activism of working-class communities historically established through Irish immigration. Inspired by the social activist circle formed around pioneering Chicago reformer Jane Addams at Hull House at the turn of the twentieth century, the project then developed to acknowledge more broadly the current and past contributions of women to the city.

Noting the lack of major monuments to women in Chicago, and with reference to the spirit of public service and the legacy of Addams, Lacy decided her work would honour ten historical women and ninety living women for their contributions to public life in the city. Each woman would be represented by a limestone boulder with an accompanying bronze plaque placed in a prominent urban setting.

Lacy assembled a steering committee of fifteen women, with whom she solicited from the public – through field investigation and advertising – 350 nominations of women to honour. From this long list the committee selected ninety women and a historical committee drew up a list of ten historical figures.

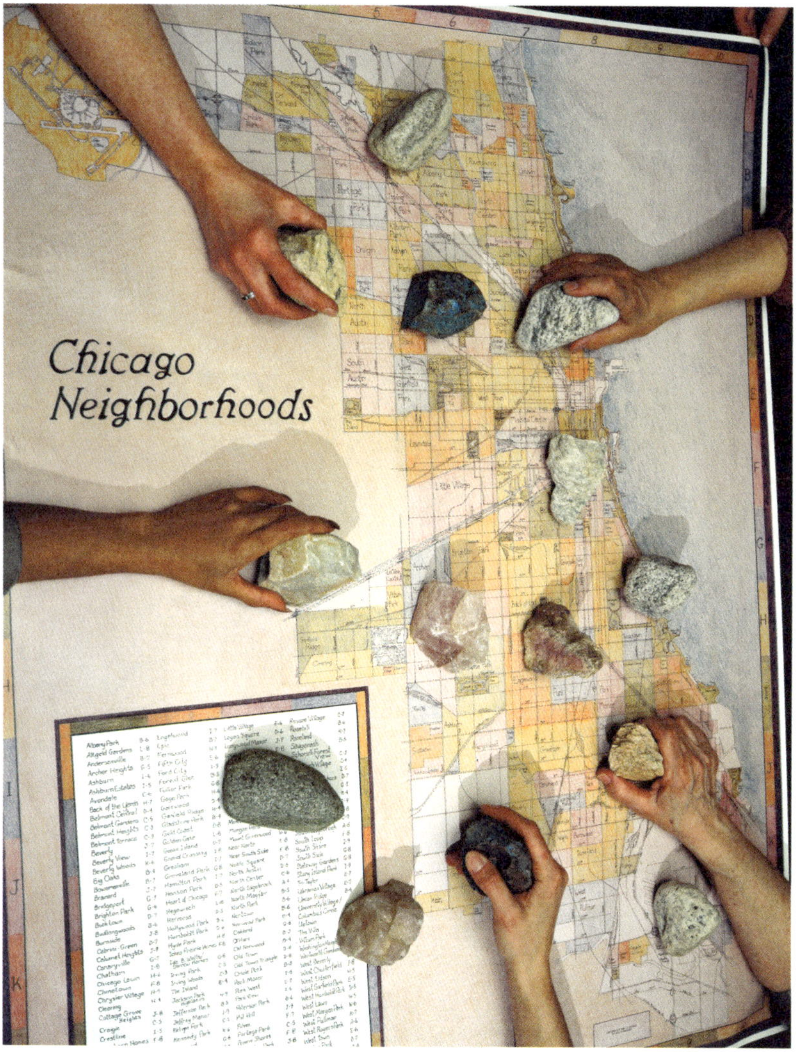

fig.37

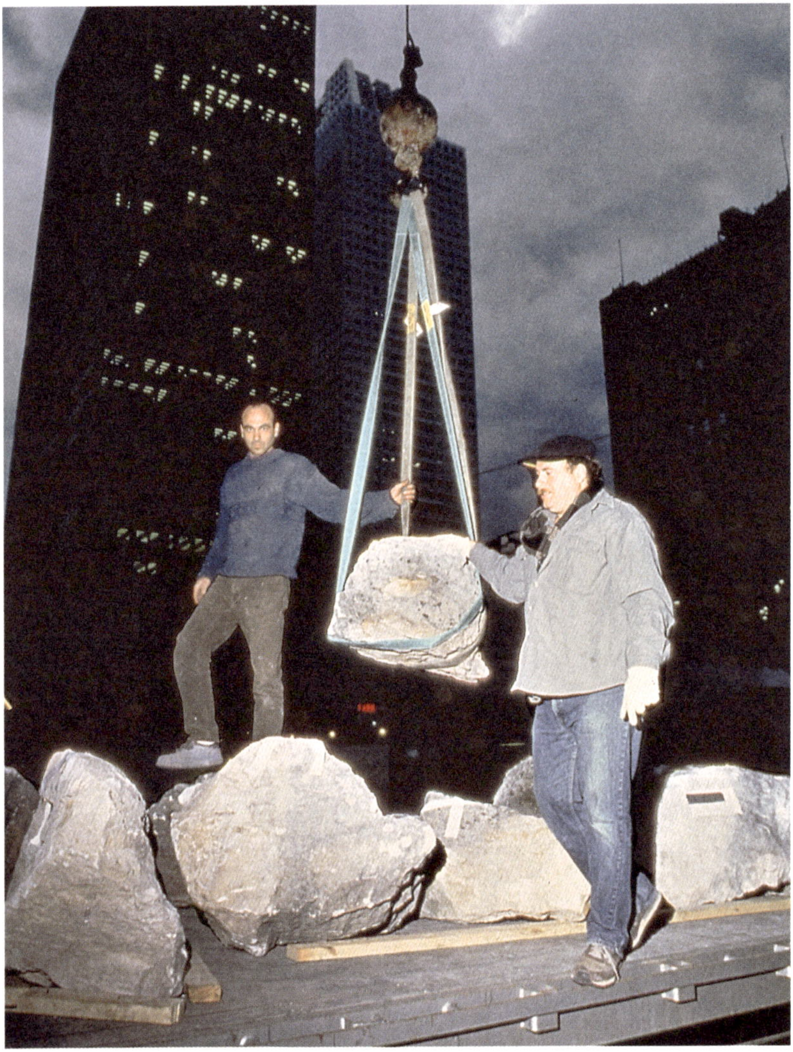

fig.38

Installing the boulders for *Full Circle*.

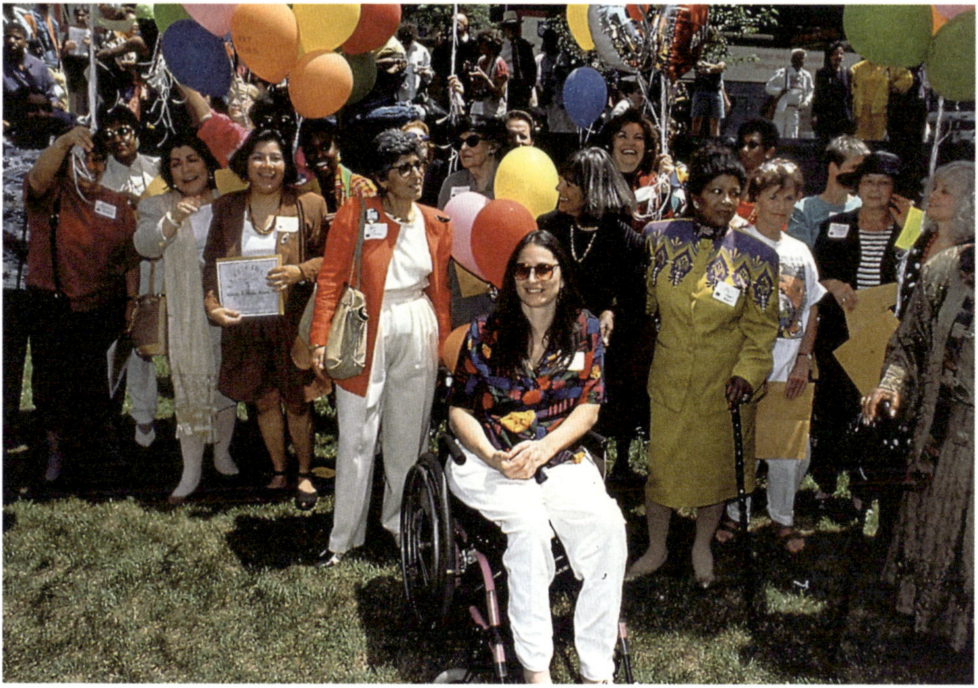

fig.39

Celebration for the *Full Circle* honourees, Pritzker Park, 22 May 1993.

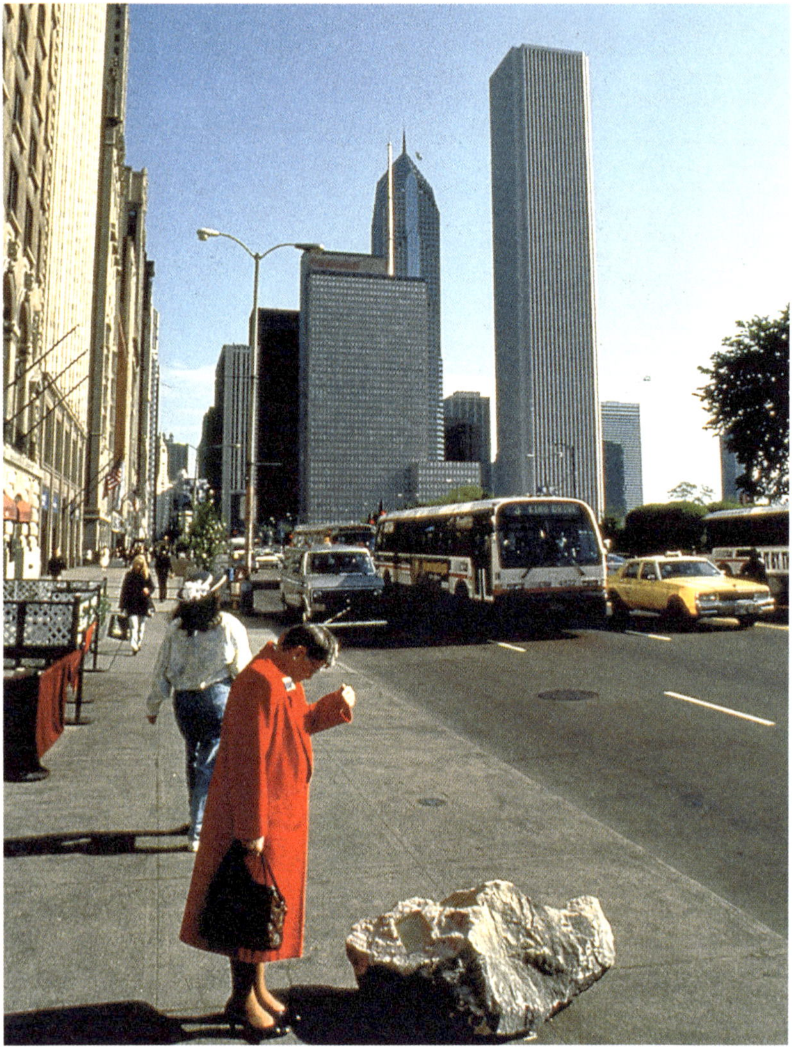

fig.40

The rocks were sourced from the Wapanucka Oolitic Limestone Quarry in Tulsa, Oklahoma, which was specifically selected as one of the few quarries in the United States under female ownership. Joanne and Ceci Gillespie, the owners, donated the limestone for the project, and each of the resulting boulders measured between 60 by 90 centimetres and 90 by 120 centimetres, weighing roughly half a tonne.

Each stone had a bronze plaque designed by graphic designer Leslie Becker attached, giving the name and a quotation or biographical note for the woman being honoured. The locations for the rocks were decided by Lacy and artist and Sculpture Chicago installation manager Ted Stanuga. After permission had been obtained from numerous private and public organisations, the rocks were installed throughout the night of 19 May 1993 by a crew of construction workers with cherry pickers and flatbed trucks.

On 22 May 1993, as part of the official opening of 'Culture in Action', a public ceremony celebrating the ninety living honourees was held in Pritzker Park, within the Loop, where each received a certificate produced by Chicago artist Esther Parada. Around 300 people attended the event in Pritzker Park, and each attending honouree then hosted a simultaneous celebration with friends and supporters at the site of her rock monument. An additional element of the project mentioned in the programme guide, involving the broadcast of 'public service announcements' on the radio by the living honourees between August and September 1993, was not ultimately realised.

Described variously in the local press as 'rocks of strength' (*Chicago Defender*, 26 May 1993) and 'insulting eyesores' (*Chicago Sun-Times*, 25 May 1993) public debate about the selection of women and the visual appeal of the boulders ensued. The monuments remained in place for four months, after which the Cultural Affairs Department of the City of Chicago contemplated finding a location for their permanent display, but neither this nor a subsequent plan to reduce them into gravel in order to create a permanent installation in Jane Addams Memorial Park near Navy Pier ever came to fruition. The 'rock women', as the nominees came to call themselves, held a reunion in 1994.

Lacy's was the first project to be discussed on the 'Culture in Action' bus tour, which started and ended at Pritzker Park, close to several of the monuments. The bus then drove westward past the Jane Addams Hull-House Museum, providing the opportunity to discuss Addams's legacy and the second part of Lacy's project, *Dinner at Jane's*.

Dinner at Jane's took place at the Hull-House site on 30 September 1993, with an international group of invitees, fourteen women from Egypt, India, Korea, Poland, South Africa and the US: Magdalena Abakanowicz (artist), Cheryl Carolus (Executive Committee member of the African National Congress), Chung Hyun Kyung (feminist theologian), Johnnetta B. Cole (President of Spelman College), Dr Mirna Cunningham (psychiatrist and writer), Dr Nawal El Saadawi (psychiatrist and writer), Susan Faludi

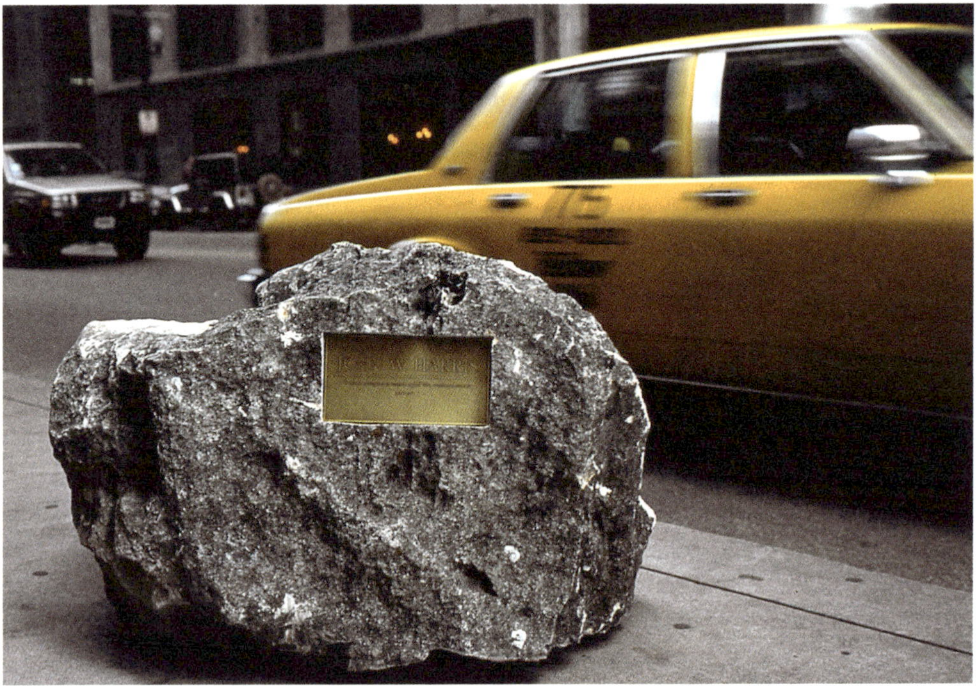

fig.41

A boulder honouring Joan W. Harris. The plaque included the statement: 'I can't imagine a meaningful life without music and art.'

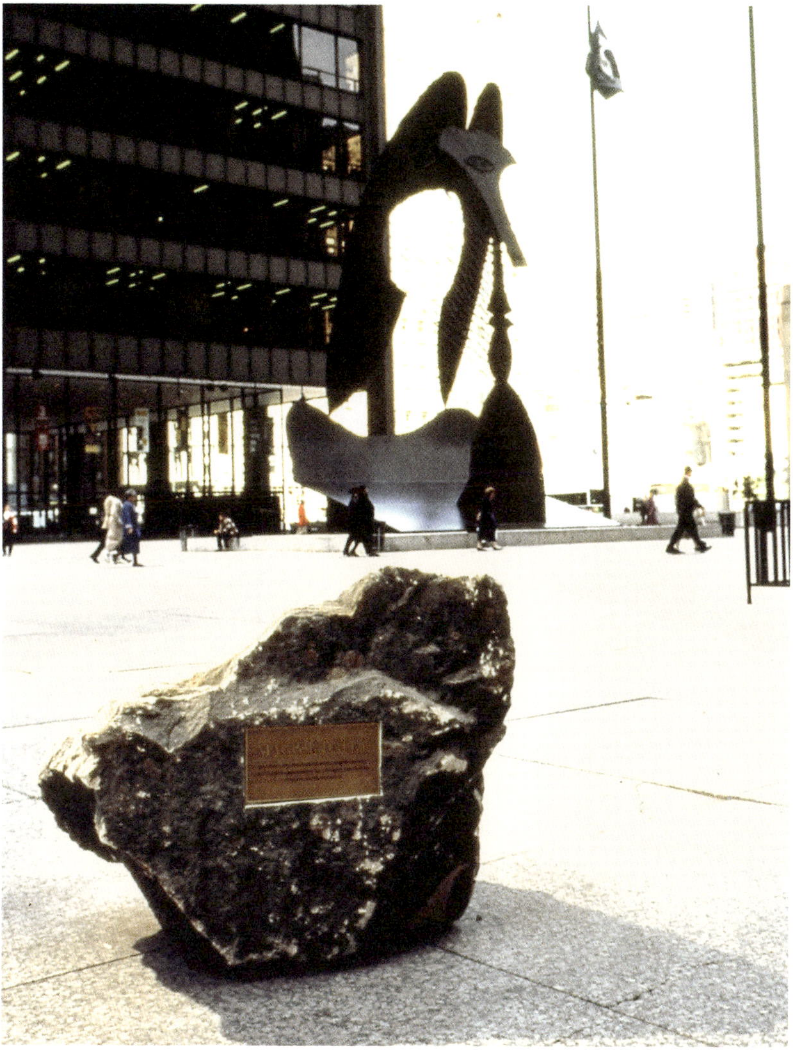

fig.42

Boulder honouring Maggie Daley, political figure and partner of then-Mayor Richard M. Daley, on Daley Plaza (named after her father-in-law, former Mayor Richard J. Daley), with permanent public art in the background.

(writer), Susan Grode (lawyer), Anita Hill (law professor), Dolores Huerta (organiser of the United Farm Workers), Devaki Jain (economist), Wilma P. Mankiller (Principal Chief, Cherokee Nation), Gloria Steinem (writer) and the Reverend Addie L. Wyatt (labour organiser). An unscripted discussion of the situation of women in their countries and globally was proposed by Lacy, to be captured by two three-camera film shoots directed by Phylis Geller of the Public Broadcasting Service (PBS) and Tom Weinberg.

Lacy conceived the private dinner as an intimate counterpoint to the highly public nature of the boulder monuments. It was held in the historic building where Jane Addams and Ellen Gates Starr founded the Hull-House settlement in 1889. Conceived as a performance referencing the gatherings of international reformers historically at the site, the private dinner is described in its audio-visual documentation as a 'symbolic and practical meeting of visionaries seeking change'.

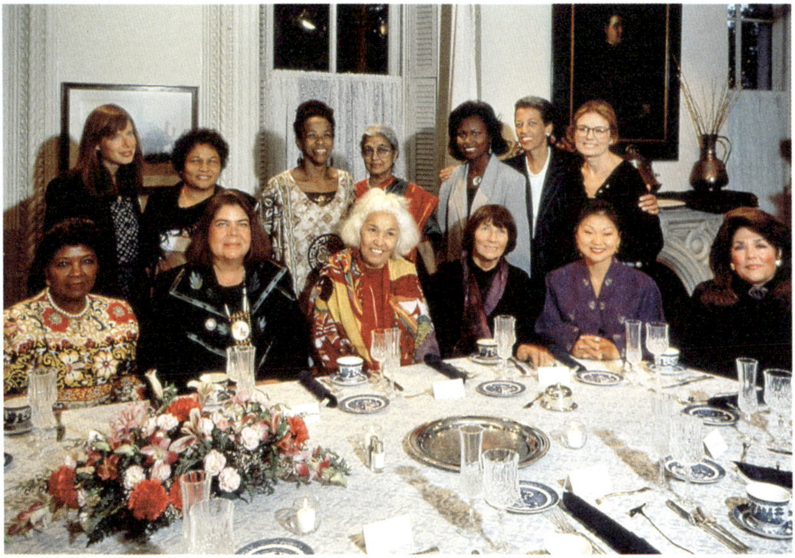

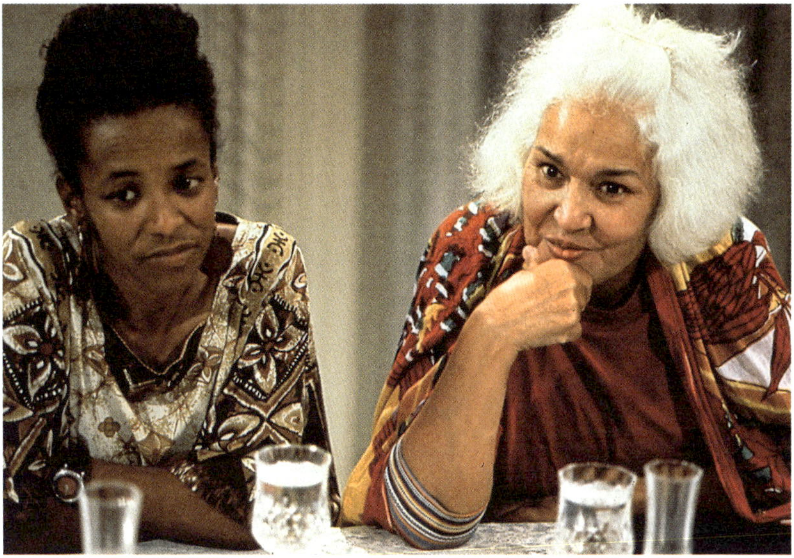

fig.43 and 44

Dinner at Jane's participants (clockwise from left) the Reverend Addie L. Wyatt, Susan Faludi, Mirna Cunningham, Cheryl Carolus, Devaki Jain, Anita Hill, Johnnetta B. Cole, Gloria Steinem, Susan Grode, Hyun-Kyung Chung, Magdalena Abakanowicz, Nawal El Saadawi and Wilma P. Mankiller (fig.43) and Cheryl Carolus and Nawal El Saadawi during the dinner (fig.44).

Map B

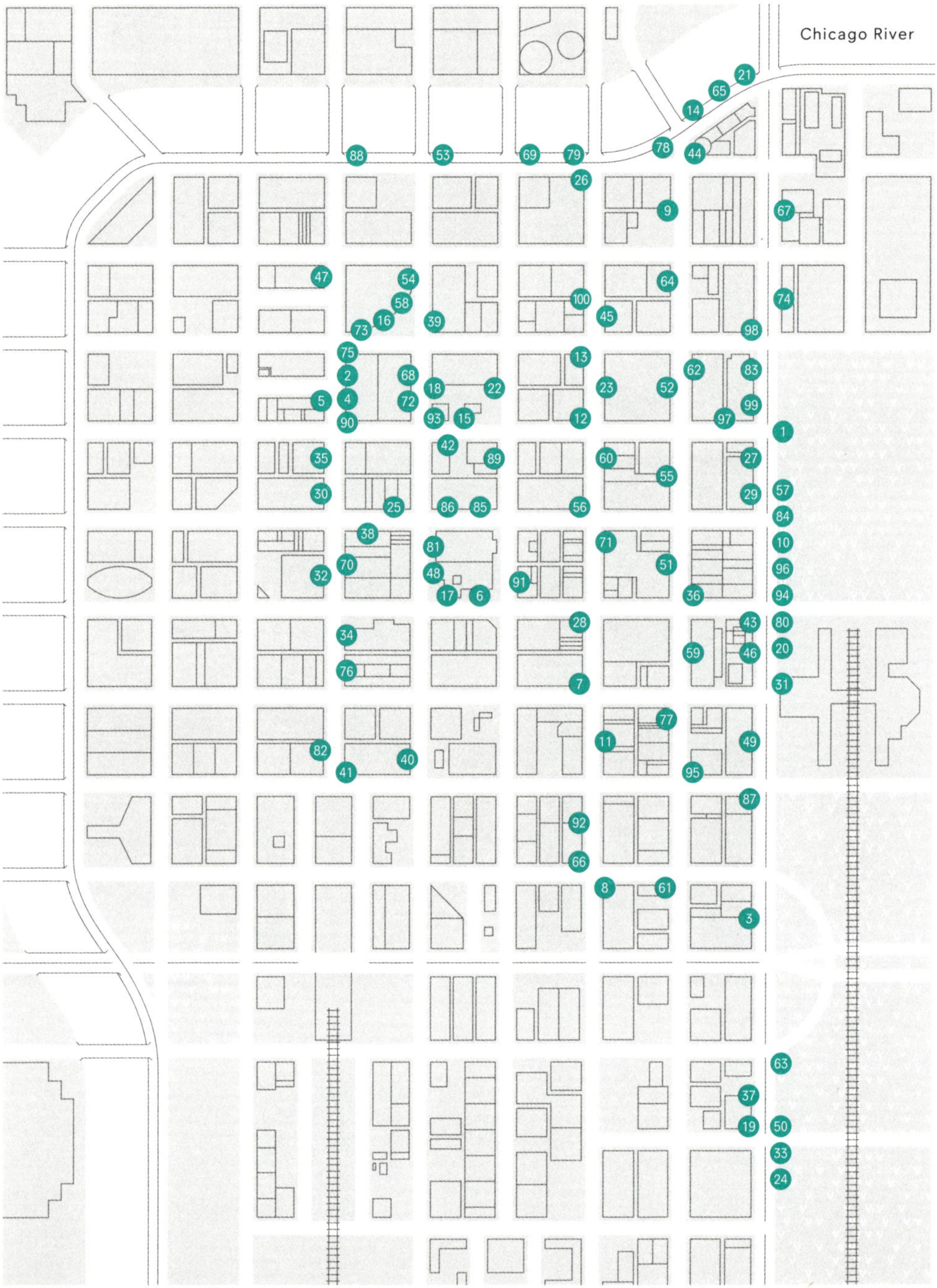
Chicago River
21
65
14
88
53
69
79
78
44
26
9
67
47
54
58
16
73
39
100
64
45
74
98
75
2
68
18
22
13
23
52
62
83
5
4
72
90
93
15
12
97
99
1
42
89
35
60
27
55
30
25
86
85
56
29
57
84
38
81
71
10
70
32
48
91
51
96
17
6
36
94
28
43
80
34
59
46
20
76
7
31
77
11
49
82
40
41
95
87
92
66
8
61
3
63
37
19
50
33
24

Boulders placed within the Loop for *Full Circle* honourees, May to September 1993. For the location of Jane Addams Hull-House Museum where *Dinner at Jane's* took place, and the wider central Chicago area, see map on p.70.

1 Jane Addams (1860–1935)
2 Blanca E. Almonte
3 Etta Moten Barnet
4 Rev Dr Willie T. Barrow
5 Marjorie Craig Benton
6 Dr Arnita Young Boswell
7 Marca Bristo
8 Gwendolyn Brooks
9 Abena Joan Brown
10 Dr Margaret Goss Burroughs
11 Jean Butzen
12 Judy Langford Carter
13 Ann Christophersen
14 Kay Clement
15 Rev Dr Johnnie Colemon
16 Ellen C. Craig
17 Dr Dolores E. Cross
18 Maggie Daley
19 Geraldine de Haas
20 Amina J. Dickerson
21 Catherine DuSable (c. 1700s)
22 Rose Farina
23 Sunny Fischer
24 Lupe Perez Marshall Gallardo (1911–1984)
25 Ann Ida Gannon, BVM
26 Susan Getzendanner
27 Helyn Goldenberg
28 Ines Bocanegra Gordon
29 Sandra P. Guthman
30 Joan W. Harris
31 Ronne Hartfield
32 Christie Hefner
33 Ellen Henrotin (1847–1922)
34 Rhona Hoffman
35 Nicole Hollander
36 Kate Horsfield
37 Ruth Horwich
38 Maha Jarad
39 Hazel M. Johnson
40 Marva Lee Pitchford Jolly
41 Tae Sue Kang
42 Kanta Khipple
43 Carol Kleiman
44 Ardis Krainik
45 Nancy Lanoue
46 Ngoan Le
47 Lucia Woods Lindley
48 Beatrice Cummings Mayer
49 Lucyna Migala
50 Harriet Monroe (1860–1936)
51 Peggy A. Montes
52 Jeannie Morris
53 Mary F. Morten
54 Senator Carol Moseley-Braun
55 Gladys R. Arana Nelson
56 Mary Nelson
57 Agnes Nestor (1880–1948)
58 Dawn Clark Netsch
59 Lisa Nigro
60 Camille Odeh
61 Sister Therese O'Sullivan
62 Sara Paretsky
63 Lucy Parsons (1853–1942)
64 Audrey R. Peeples
65 Betty Jeannie Pejko
66 Cindy Pritzker
67 Barbara Proctor
68 Aurelia Pucinski
69 Sue Purrington
70 Arlene Rakoncay
71 Guadalupe A. Reyes
72 Ruth M. Rothstein
73 Ilana Diamond Rovner
74 Bettylu K. Saltzman
75 Florence Scala
76 Adele Smith Simmons
77 Rita Simo
78 Andrea Smith
79 Faith Smith
80 Hannah Greenebaum Solomon (1858–1942)
81 Margaret Strobel
82 Tina Tchen
83 Indre Paliokas Tijunelis
84 Erma Tranter
85 Sister Margaret Traxler
86 Ngan-Hoa Chung Trinh
87 Helen Valdez
88 Jacqueline B. Vaughn
89 Mary-Frances Veeck
90 Carmen Velasquez
91 Val Ward
92 Anna Wasylowsky
93 Lois Weisberg
94 Ida B. Wells (1862–1931)
95 Thelma K. Wheaton
96 Francis Willard (1839–1898)
97 Jessie Anderson Woods
98 Reverend Addie L. Wyatt
99 Kiyo Yoshimura
100 Linda Yu

Tele-Vecindario: A Street-Level Video Project (1992–95 and evolving into Street-Level Youth Media, ongoing)

Iñigo Manglano-Ovalle and Street-Level Video (S-LV), the youth division of the Westtown Vecinos Video Channel (WVVC); including Miguel Boyas, Larissa Burgos, Jasmin Cardona, Veronica Cardona, Heriberto Carrion, Mike Cruz, Elbert De Luna, Jose Delcid, Wilfredo Gines, Natalie Miranda, Maria Ocasio, Anthony Oliver, Miguel Oliver, Edith Pauley, Ronnie Pauley, Alfonso Soto, Olga Soto, James Tavenner, Ken Turner, Luis Vega, Miriam Vega and others; and its staff members, Nilda Ruiz Pauley (field director), Maria Suarez (production coordinator), Paul Teruel (production director) and Troy Winston (field assistant).

—

As described in the 'Culture in Action' programme guide
'The artist and young adults are creating a series of video installations and video portraits in their neighbourhood. This video mapping aims to convey residents' sense of the street and to create a dialogue about social and cultural issues of place and community.'

—

General point(s) of access
This Is My Stuff: A Street-Level Video Installation on view at Emerson House Community Center, 645 North Wood Street, from 12 May to 28 August 1993. *Cul-de-Sac: A Street-Level Video Installation* by S-LV with Iñigo Manglano-Ovalle and Paul Teruel, at the Museum of Contemporary Art (MCA), Chicago, from 3 July to 8 August 1993. During June 1993, S-LV's videos were broadcast twice weekly on Chicago's Community TV Network (CTVN), and videos were shown at various venues throughout the spring and summer of 1993. *Tele-Vecindario: A Street-Level Video Block Party* took place on Chicago's West Erie Street, between Paulina Street and Wood Street, on 28 August 1993.

—

Manglano-Ovalle began his project in January 1992 under the title 'Sereno/ Tertulia': *tertulia* is the Latin American tradition of gathering outside in the evening to socialise and talk, and *sereno* is the figure who would – as remembered by the artist's grandfather – light the streetlamps and relay the time and local news to the community. Having recently moved to Chicago's West Town in 1991, Manglano-Ovalle initially proposed to introduce this ritual into the neighbourhood through the manual illumination of streetlights by young members of the community.

The project progressed throughout 1992 in dialogue with social-service agencies, from which it became clear that street gangs were a primary local concern. Seeking to address this, in September 1992 Manglano-Ovalle developed the idea that a fifteen-minute 'video map' might be produced by young people in the area describing their neighbourhood. By October video-training

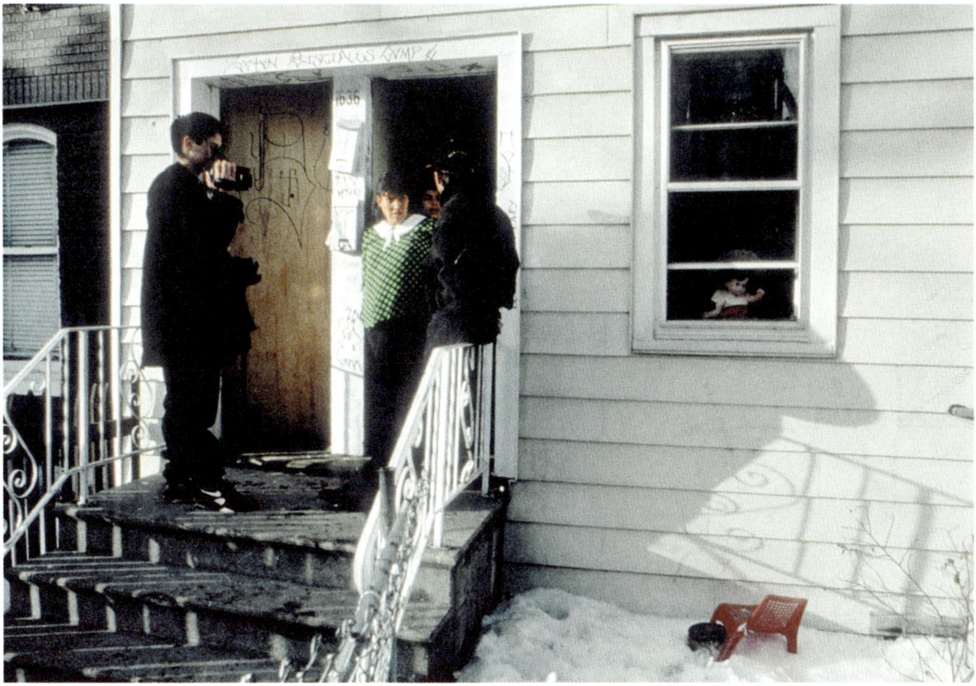

fig.45

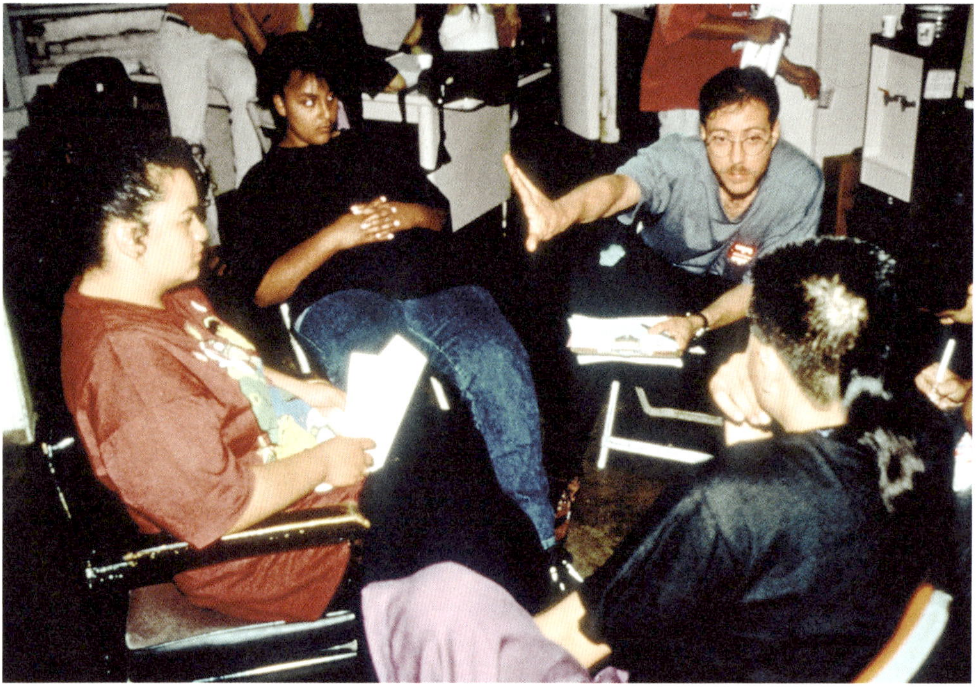

fig.46

Manglano-Ovalle with Natalie Miranda, Miguel Boyas and others during a production planning session at CTVN in 1993.

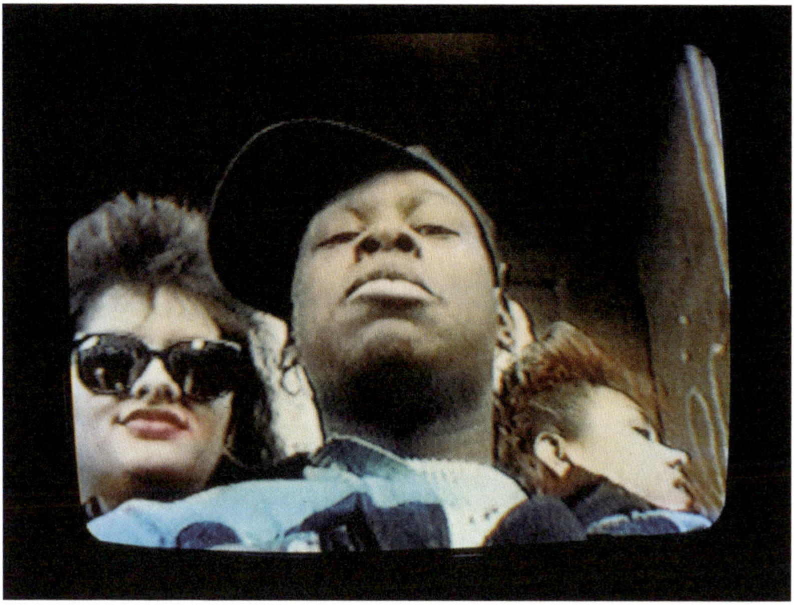

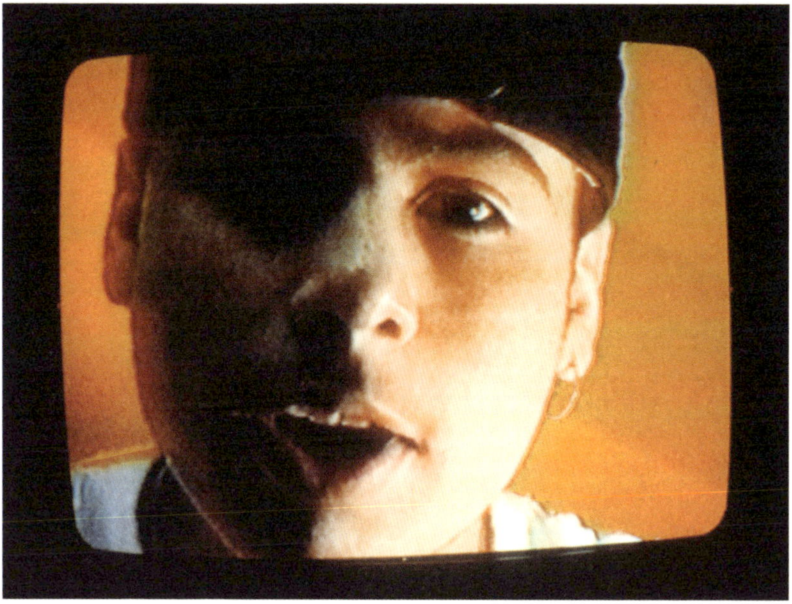

fig.47 and 48

Stills from *This Is My Stuff*.

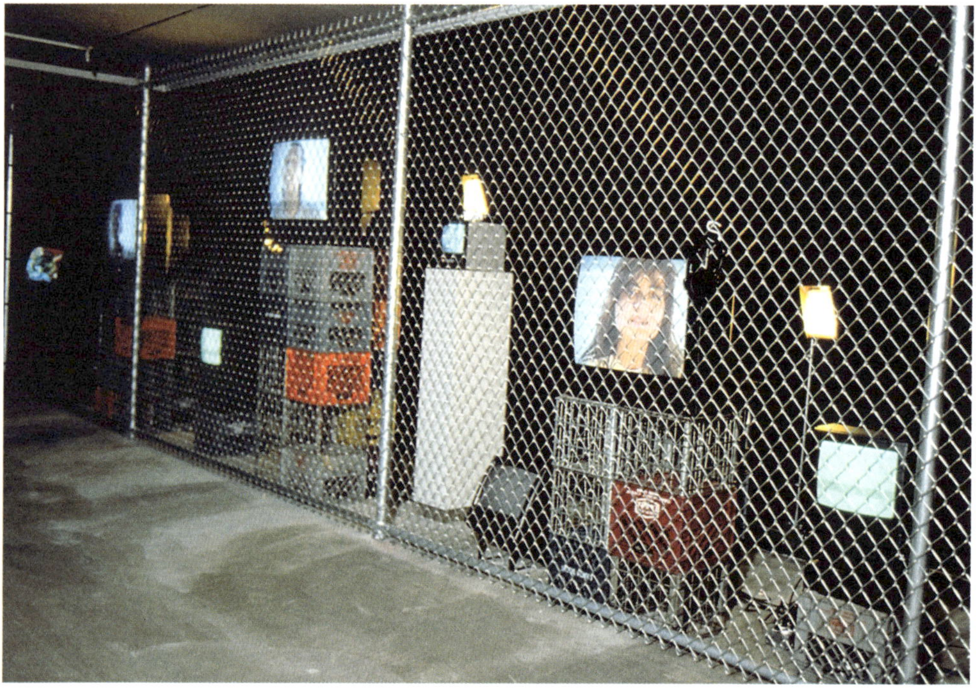

fig.49

Cul-de-Sac: A Street-Level Video Installation,
Museum of Contemporary Art, Chicago, 1993.

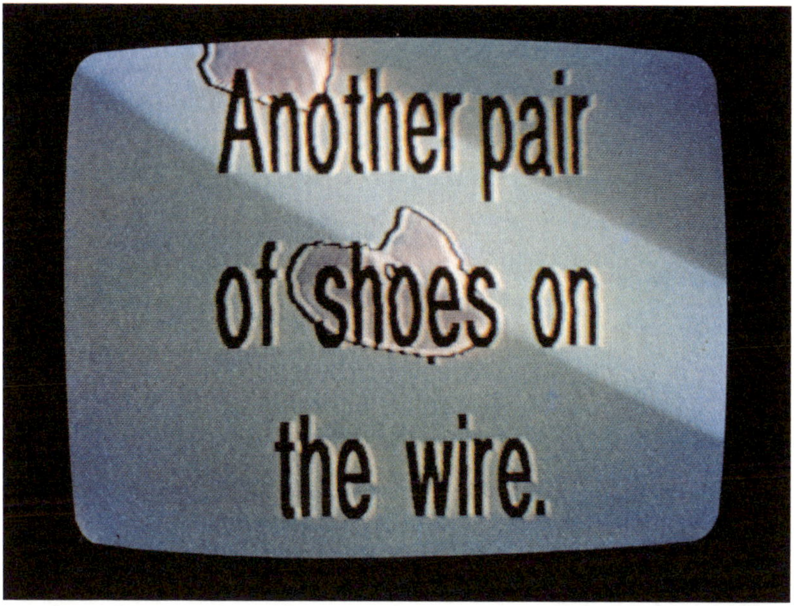

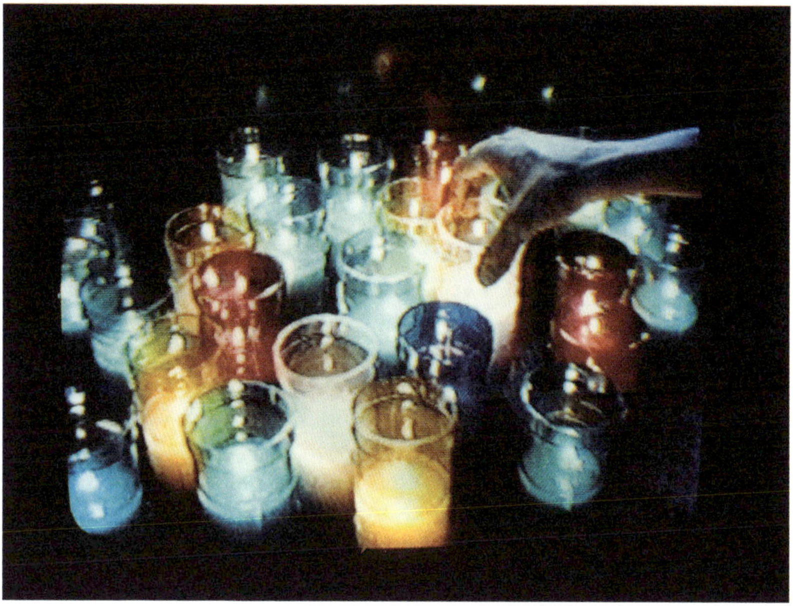

fig.50 and 51

Stills from *Rest in Peace*.

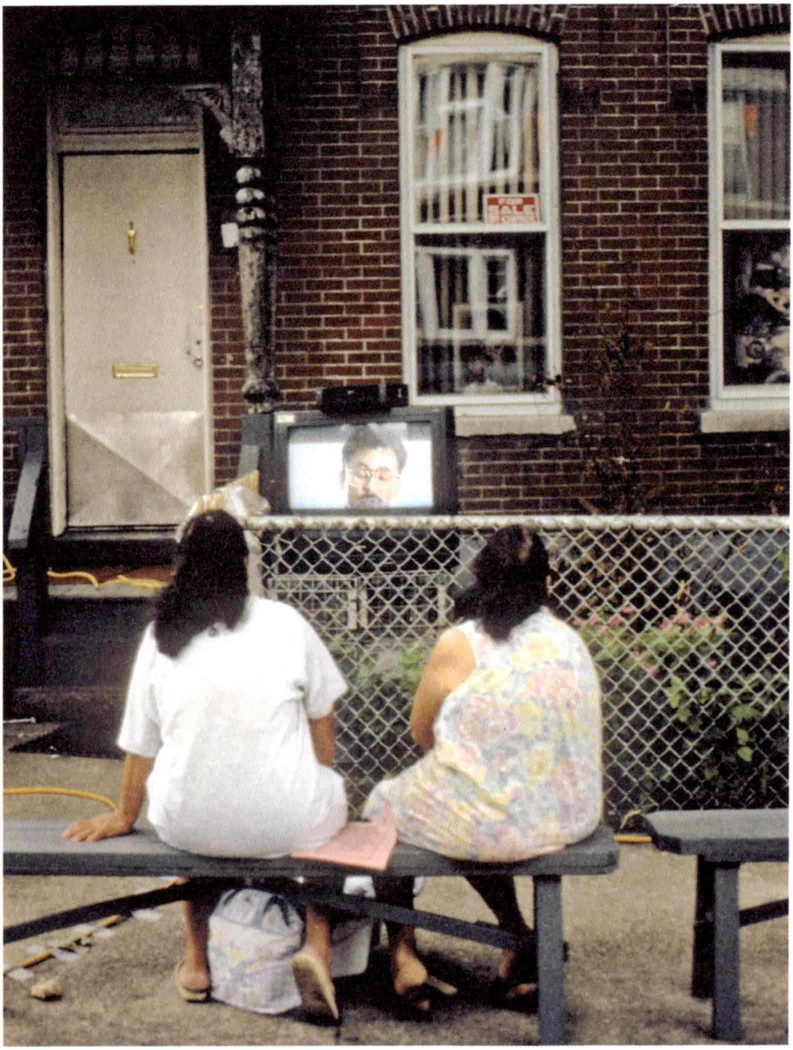

fig.52

Installation at *Tele-Vecindario: A Street-Level Block Party*, West Erie Street, 28 August 1993.

workshops had begun, and by the end of 1992 the project had transformed to focus solely on video dialogues between West Town residents.

The WVVC was formed from a coalition of individuals involved in youth-directed organisations such as CTVN, Emerson House Community Center, Erie Neighborhood House and the school-within-a-school programme at Wells High School. The S-LV division constituted an open group of around twenty young adults from West Town.

The S-LV group began to conduct video interviews with members of their community, including business owners, community organisers, families, friends and rivals. The first public outcome of this process was a display in the windows of Emerson House Community Center, *This Is My Stuff: A Street-Level Video Installation,* with the videos screening for most of the duration of the 'Culture in Action' exhibition and providing a focus for a stop on the bus tour. When broadcast twice weekly throughout June on Chicago's CTVN, S-LV's videos formed part of *Hard Cover*, a series produced by and for teenagers. The videos were also shown at various other venues in the spring and summer of 1993, including Wells High School, a local grocery shop, a video arcade and a hot dog stand.

Over five weeks that summer, the MCA displayed *Cul-de-Sac: A Street-Level Video Installation*, credited to S-LV with Iñigo Manglano-Ovalle and Paul Teruel. The work consisted of fourteen TV monitors, with eleven playing edited footage by S-LV that showed West Town streets, interviews with residents, video games and definitions of the word 'cul-de-sac'. The installation was lit by orange sodium lights and surrounded by an eight-foot-high chain-link fence. Outside the fence were three more monitors, detailing socioeconomic statistics – informally styled by S-LV – about West Town and offering aerial views and further footage of the neighbourhood. Manglano-Ovalle gave a talk at the MCA on the opening afternoon of the installation, 3 July.

The culmination of Manglano-Ovalle and S-LV's activities during 'Culture in Action' was the installation and block party *Tele-Vecindario: A Street-Level Video Block Party,* along Erie Street in West Town, on the last Saturday of August. Around seventy video screens were arranged in multiple installations – stacked on milk crates, placed in cars, on the street, in front gardens and on the steps of homes – all powered by plugging into the electricity supply of local residents. A new iteration of *Cul-de-Sac* was presented, and *Drive-By*, which shows clashing neighbourhood factions as filmed from a car; and an eleven-screen memorial in a vacant lot titled *Rest in Peace* was on view. A peace mural, *West Town Respect*, was also created as part of an installation titled *Graffiti*, a project that involved discussion between S-LV, local gang representatives and residents, before execution by graffiti artists Rafa, Zore and the Spray Brigade. A stage was set up for performers to use, and there was a street-fashion show. Security for the event overall was negotiated between four gangs with claims to the area and became another work, named *Truce* by Manglano-Ovalle.

Following 'Culture in Action', the monitors and video-editing equipment purchased for *Tele-Vecindario* remained with S-LV. They established their own base opposite Wells High School and continued producing videos in collaboration with Manglano-Ovalle, Paul Teruel and Nilda Ruiz Pauley. In 1995 the group established itself as the ongoing non-profit organisation Street-Level Youth Media.

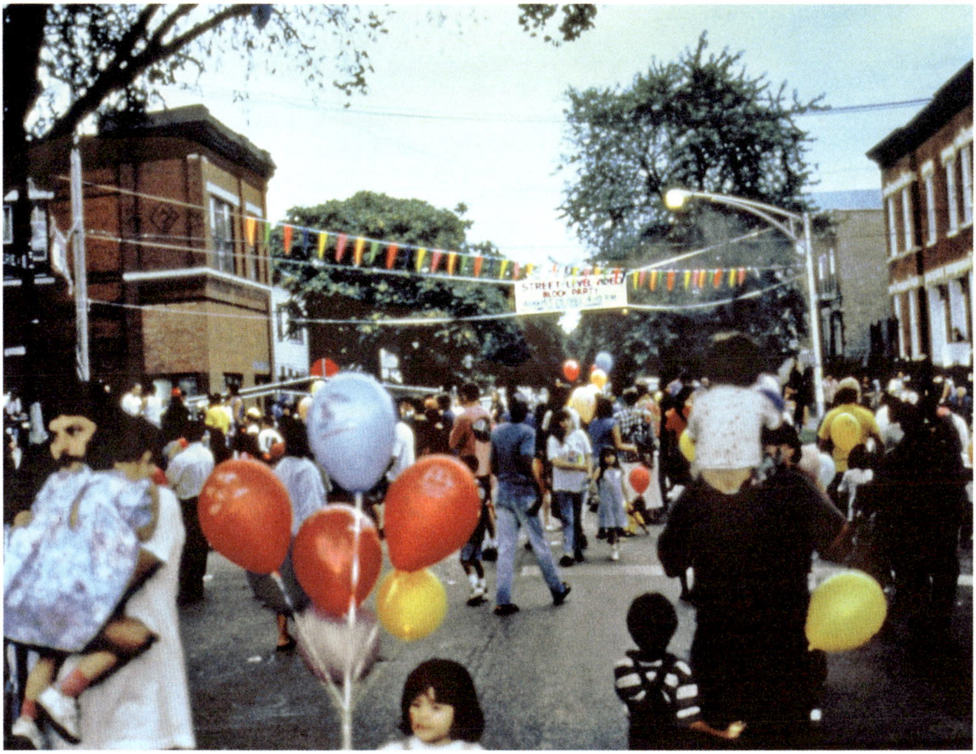

fig.53

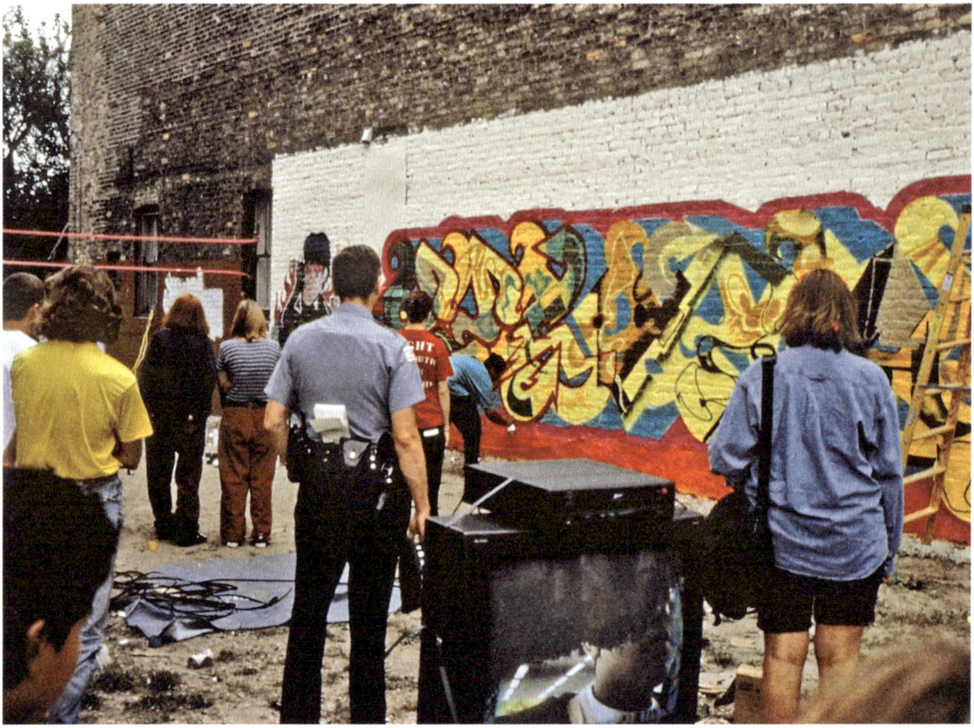

fig.54

West Town Respect mural and *Graffiti* installation.

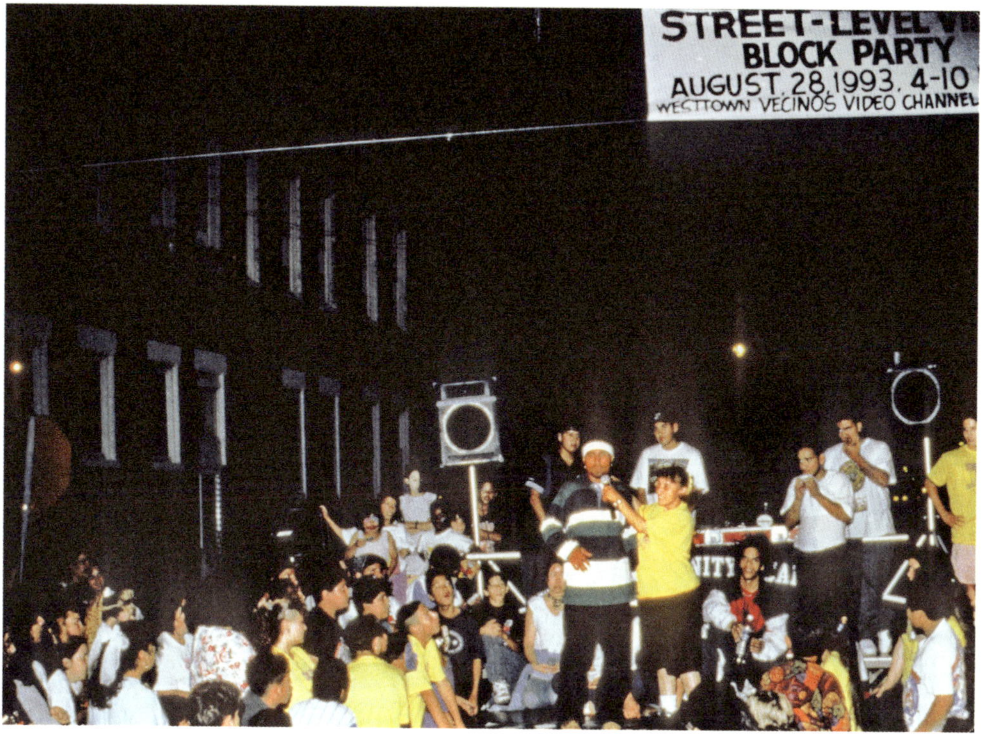

fig.55

Stage on the corner of North Wood St and Erie St.

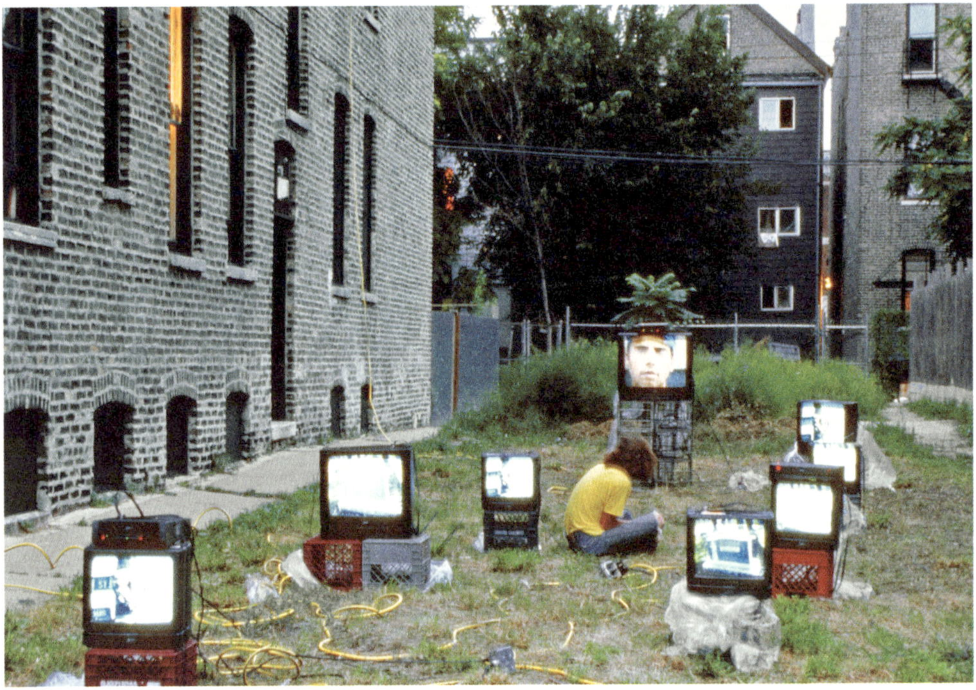

fig.56

Rest in Peace installation.

Map C

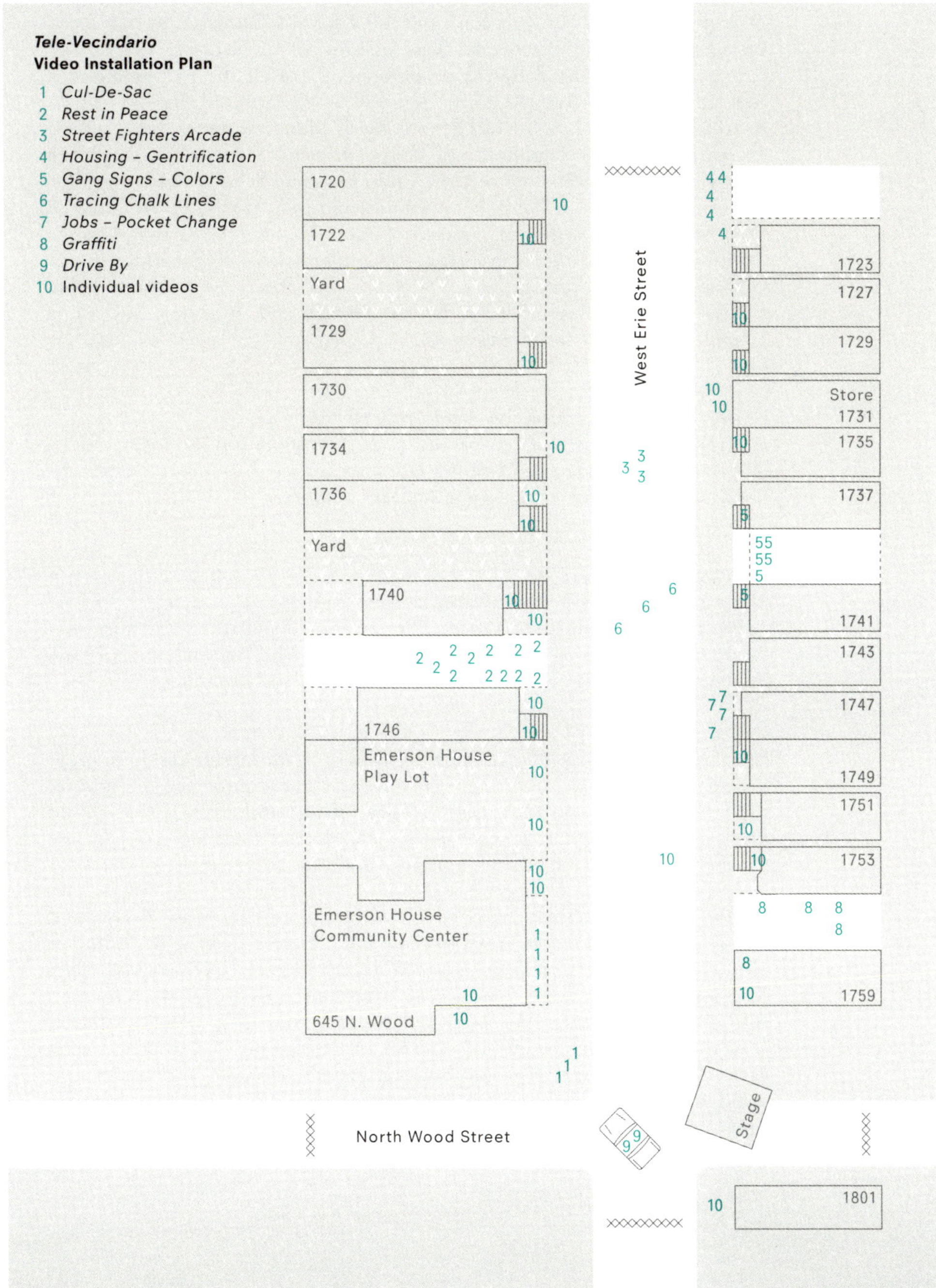

Tele-Vecindario
Video Installation Plan
1 Cul-De-Sac
2 Rest in Peace
3 Street Fighters Arcade
4 Housing – Gentrification
5 Gang Signs – Colors
6 Tracing Chalk Lines
7 Jobs – Pocket Change
8 Graffiti
9 Drive By
10 Individual videos
1720
1722
Yard
1729
1730
1734
1736
Yard
1740
1746
Emerson House
Play Lot
Emerson House
Community Center
645 N. Wood
West Erie Street
1723
1727
1729
Store
1731
1735
1737
1741
1743
1747
1749
1751
1753
1759
Stage
North Wood Street
1801

Consequences of a Gesture (1992–93) and *100 Victories / 10,000 Tears* (1993)

Daniel J. Martinez, VinZula Kara and the West Side Three-Point Marchers/ Los Desfiladores Tres Puntos del West Side for the *Consequences of a Gesture* parade, which, as listed by the programme, involved the participation of African American Arts Alliance, Aguijon II Theater, Alpha Phi Alpha, Austin High School, Cardenas School, Cash Money, Cooper School, de la Cruz School, Erie Neighborhood House, Farragut School, Henry Booth House, Henry Horner Boys & Girls Club, Jungman School, Make-up Boys, Marshall High School Band, New Sounds, Phi Beta Sigma, IOTA Chapter, Pros Arts Studio, Redmoon Theater, Salazar Elementary School, Shango Temple, the Spray Brigade graffiti group, Suder School, Taller Mexicano de Grabado (Mexican Printmakers Workshop), Temporary Juvenile Detention Center representatives, WGCI Dance Troupe and Whitney M. Young School; and project coordinators Angela Coleman and Elvia Rodriguez.

—

As described in the 'Culture in Action' programme guide
'A procession/carnival/ritual/parade and an installation exploring social movement and displacement within cities, specifically how urban neighbourhoods change as one ethnic group replaces another.'

—

General point(s) of access
The parade *Consequences of a Gesture*, at three consecutive locations on 19 June 1993, from 9.30 am to 1.30 pm. The outdoor installation *100 Victories / 10,000 Tears*, set up in a fenced-in area at West 14th Place and South Peoria Street, near the Maxwell Street Market's site, July to November 1993.

—

Martinez's project was propelled by his interest in the labour and immigrant histories of Chicago. In particular his idea was to refashion the tradition of public gatherings and May Day parades into a symbolic act that would bring distant communities together. He maintained a residence in Chicago for the duration of the project, a period of almost two years.

In 1991 Martinez began to identify and make contact with groups and individuals who played key roles in their communities, assisted by Sculpture Chicago staff and local project coordinators Angela Coleman and Elvia Rodriguez. Subsequently a series of community meetings were held to introduce and discuss the proposed parade. Martinez asked composer VinZula Kara to act as musical director of the parade, and invited a wide variety of participants – groups and individuals, children and adults – to decide how they wanted to represent themselves, but with an emphasis on surrealism and absurdity.

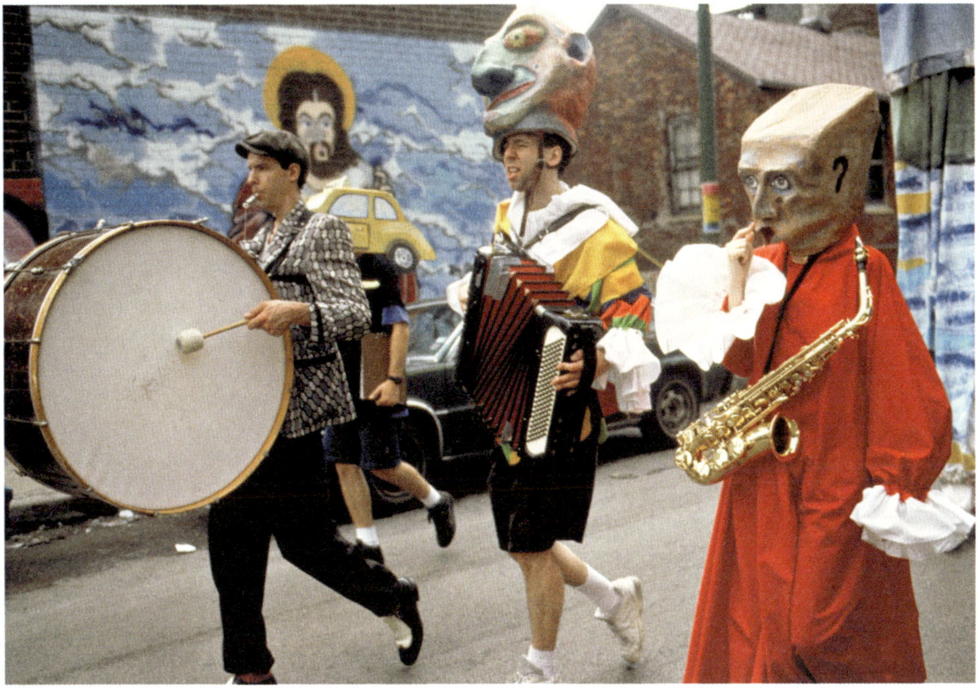

fig.57

The parade on its way through the Pilsen neighbourhood, on the way to Harrison Park.

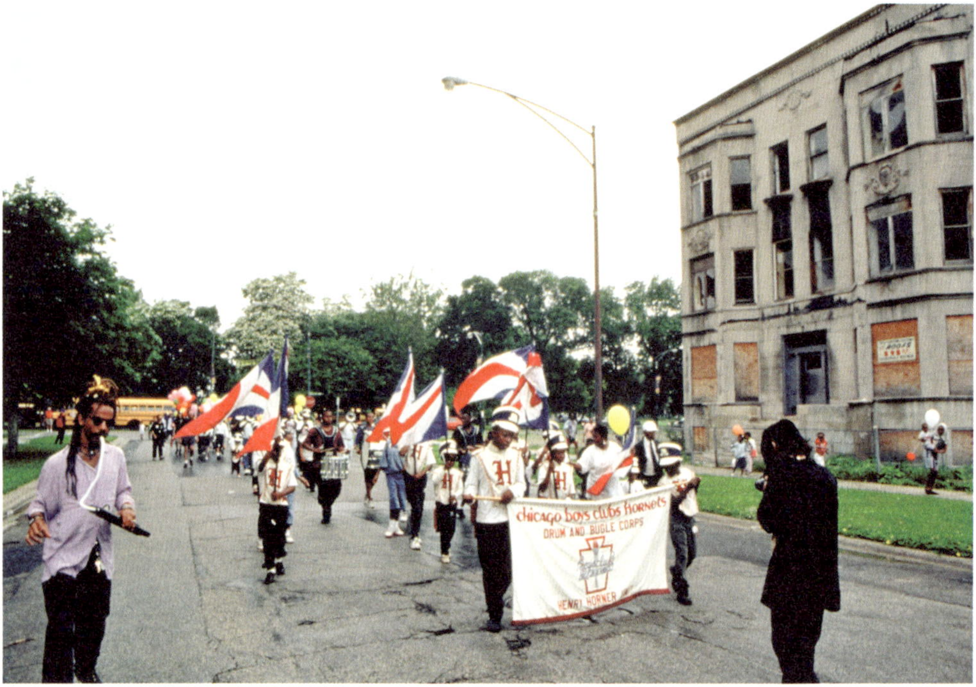

fig.58

The Chicago Boys Club Drum and Bugle Corps, Henry Horner Unit, with VinZula Kara (far left) and Daniel J. Martinez filming (front right) in Garfield Park.

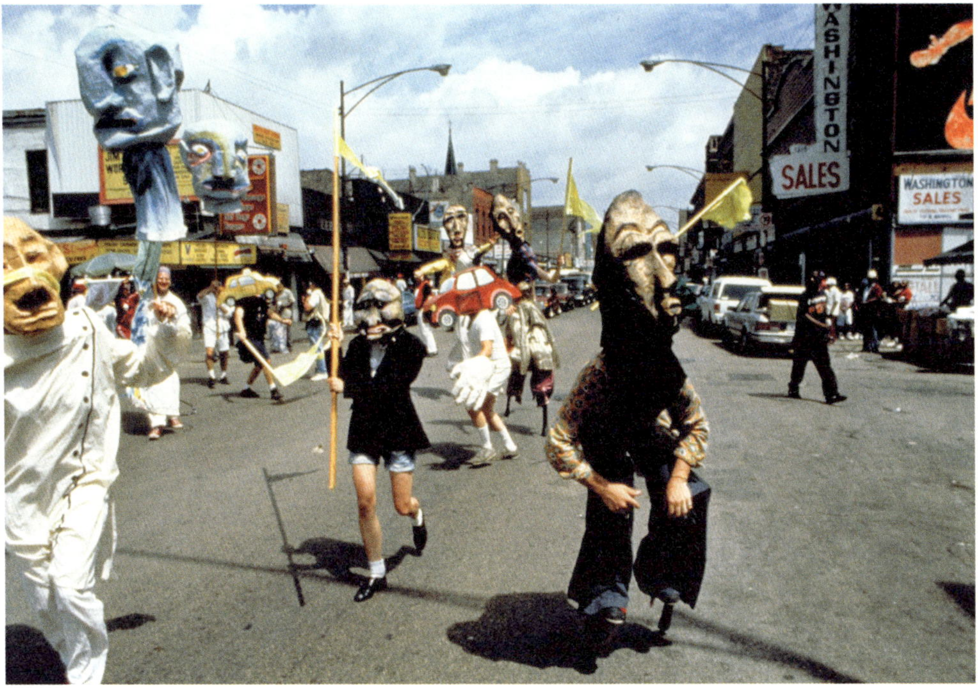

fig.59

Performers from the Redmoon Theater on Maxwell Street.

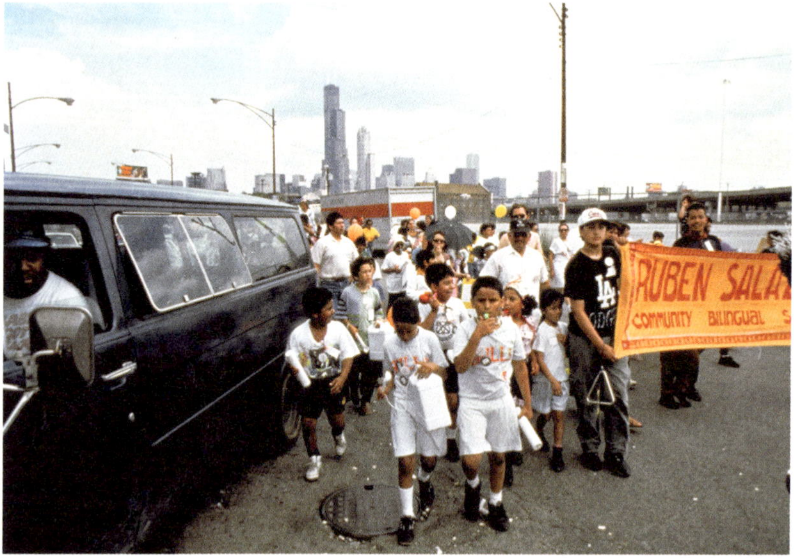

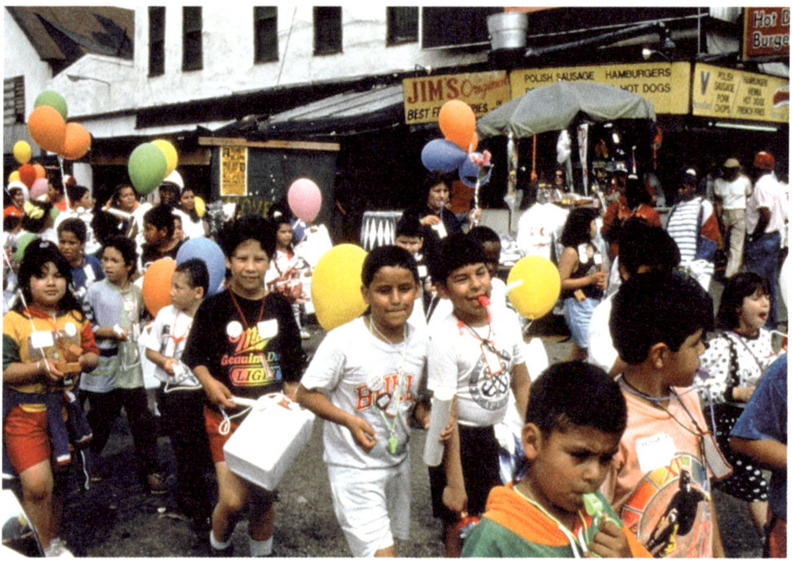

fig.60 and 61

Parade participants in the Maxwell Street area.

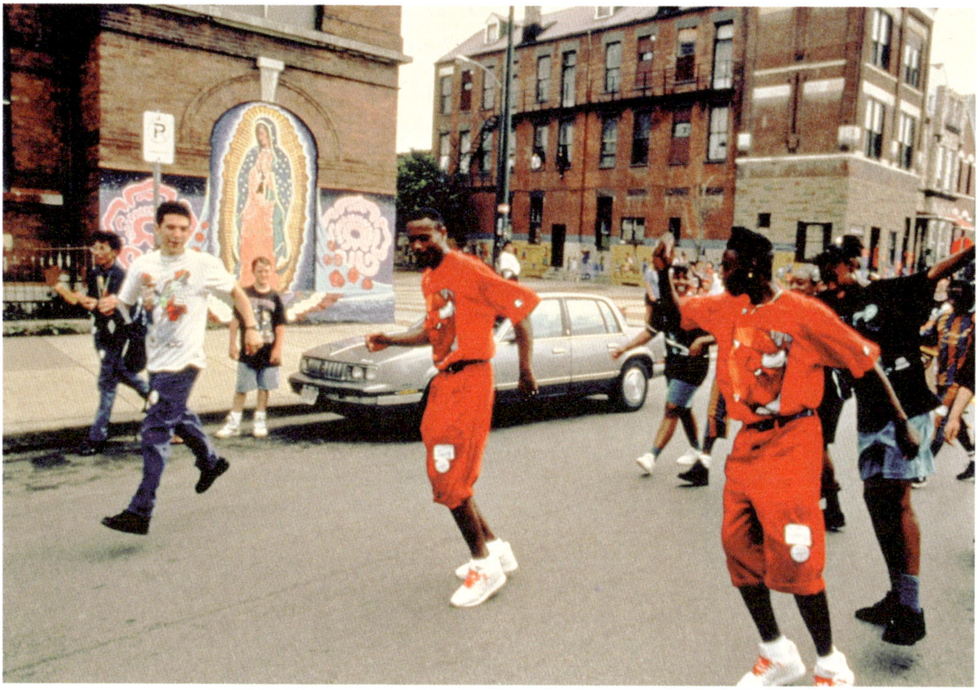

fig.62

Parade participants in the Pilsen neighbourhood, on the way to Harrison Park.

The parade was planned in three sections, following in part from Martinez's initial proposal to conduct 'an opera in four parts' at significant historical sites and public sculptures across Chicago. Locations were chosen to bring together culturally and geographically separate constituencies, in particular Mexican American and African American communities.

The parade began in Harrison Park, close to the predominantly Mexican American neighbourhood of Pilsen, and finished in Garfield Park, set within the predominantly African American neighbourhood known as East Garfield Park, after passing through a meeting ground for the two: the Maxwell Street Market area. The parade's path is significant within the history of Chicago's immigrants, as diverse communities – of Irish, Greek, German, Italian and Eastern European descent, for instance, as well as African Americans from the Southern United States – had settled in these West Side neighbourhoods during the late nineteenth and early twentieth centuries.

The parade comprised around 120 groups, organisations and schools, as well as food carts selling ice cream and tamales. Starting near Harrison Park at approximately 9.30 am, it moved on to Maxwell Street at around 11 am and finished at Garfield Park between 12.30 and 1.30 pm, with buses transporting participants between locations. The 500 or so people participating were joined en route by thousands of spectators, mainly people living in the neighbourhoods being celebrated. The parade also coincided with a United Farm Workers rally commemorating Cesar Chavez in Harrison Park, and also with Juneteenth, or Emancipation Day, commemorating the abolition of slavery and the emancipation of African American US citizens.

The Maxwell Street Market area is a historic site for labour struggles in Chicago, and less than two miles from the site of the 1886 Haymarket Riot, recognised as the origin of the international May Day parades. The market itself had been in operation since the late 1870s, and remained a popular site of commercial and social exchange for a diverse mix of low-income communities. At the time of 'Culture in Action', the University of Illinois at Chicago (UIC) had controversial plans to expand their campus into the market's site (trading eventually ceased there on 28 August 1994 and the UIC development was subsequently realised).

100 Victories/10,000 Tears (1993) was installed in July and remained for five months in a vacant lot owned by UIC, close to Maxwell Street Market. The idea developed through a chance meeting with Antonio Pedroso, owner of a local granite and marble business. At the time, elements of the UIC campus designed by Walter Netsch were being dismantled, and Martinez learned that Pedroso's company would be transporting the valuable granite slabs to a salvage yard. Martinez proposed that a selection of the slabs and other features of the university's former plaza be covertly appropriated to create a monumental sculpture – in the artist's words, 'a people's plaza'. While permission had been secured to use a lot owned by the City of Chicago – one which the City had already forced the Maxwell Street Market to stop utilising – the Sculpture Chicago board withdrew support at the last minute;

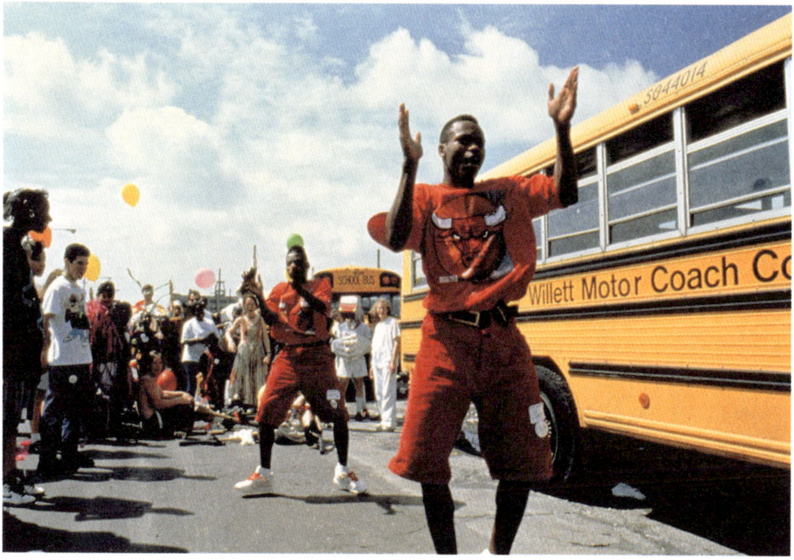

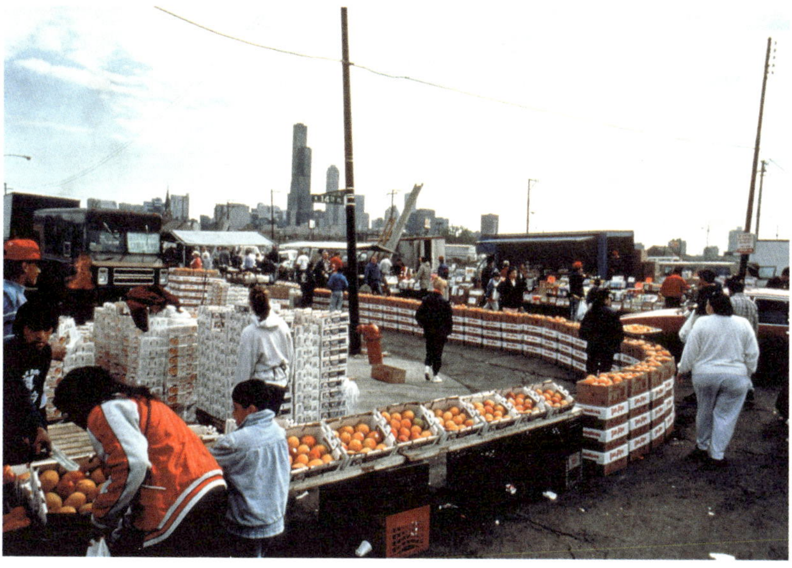

fig.63 and 64

Buses transporting participants from one location to another during the parade, here seen on Maxwell Street (fig.63) and the Sunday Maxwell Street Market, 1992 (fig.64).

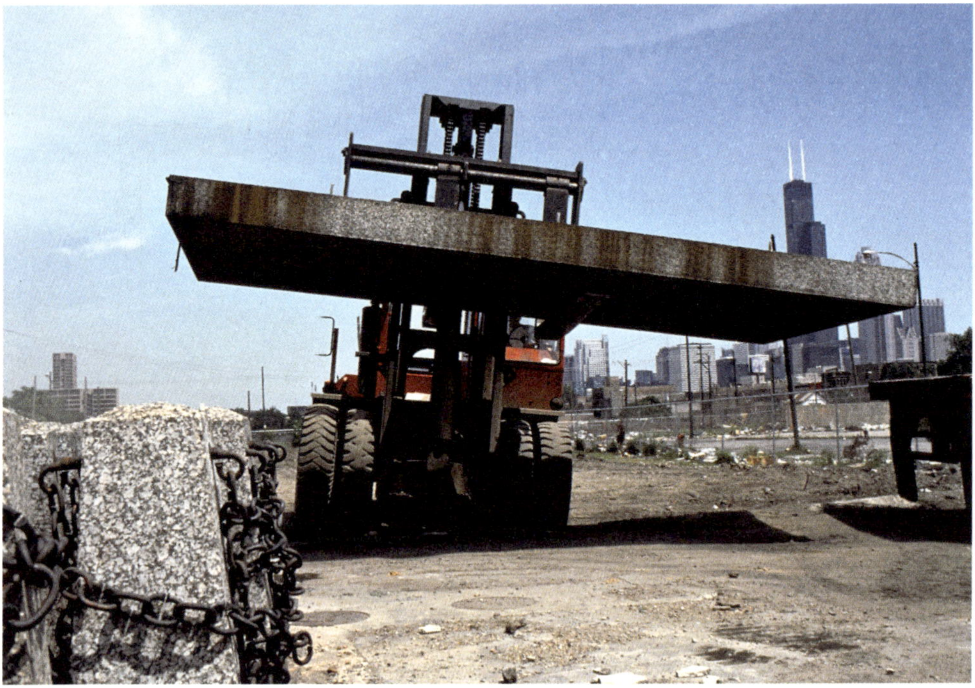

fig.65

Installation of *100 Victories / 10,000 Tears*.

without their or the university's knowledge, the work was installed illegally in a vacant UIC-owned lot.

Each slab measured approximately 2.5 by 7.5 by 0.3 metres and weighed around forty tonnes – so heavy that only one at a time could be moved. On the fence around the site Martinez produced 24 signs in the style of existing 'No trespassing / UIC property' signage, which the 'Culture in Action' bus tour took in on its route. Half of the signs referred to decisive moments in the labour history of Chicago and the other half featured unattributed philosophical and poetic remarks supporting revolutionary causes, such as the Surrealist slogan adopted by the Situationist International: 'Take your desires for reality'. The standing slabs were removed five months later, but the granite base remained in place for another two years.

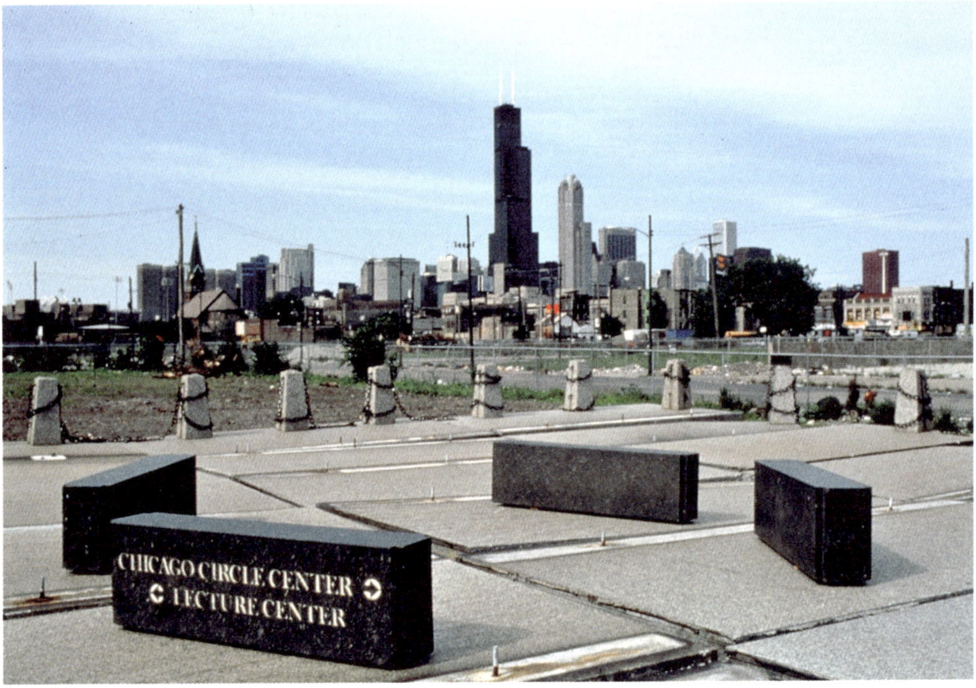

fig.66

View of *100 Victories/10,000 Tears* with the Chicago skyline in the background.

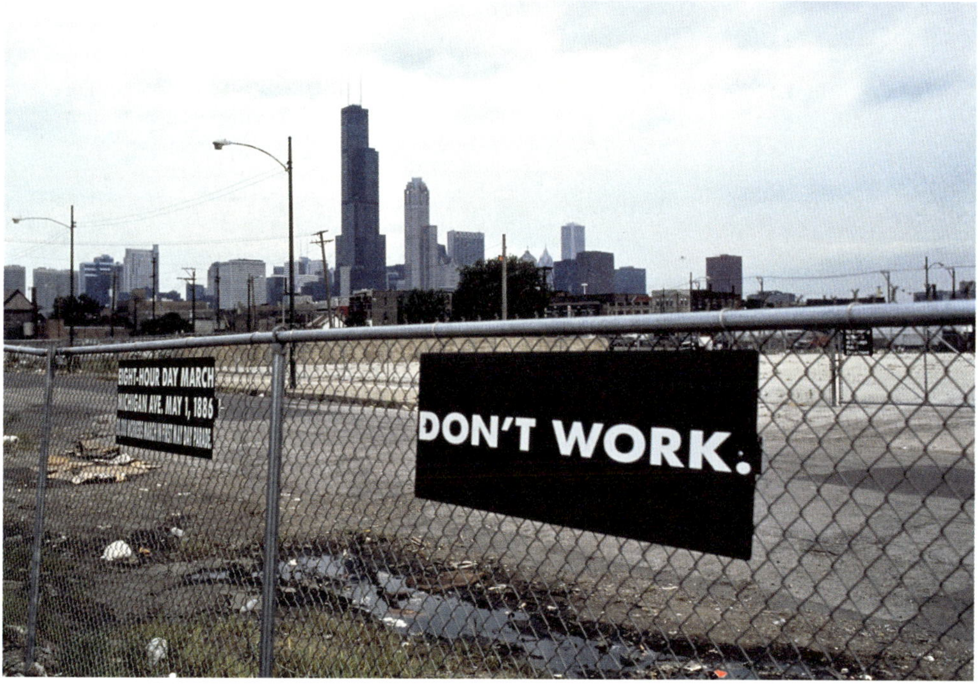

fig.67

View of the installation fence. The sign on the left reads: 'EIGHT-HOUR DAY MARCH / MICHIGAN AVE. MAY 1, 1886 / 80,000 WORKERS MARCH IN FIRST MAY DAY PARADE.'

Naming Others: Manufacturing Yourself (1992–93)

Robert Peters with Mushroom Pickers, Ghosts, Frogs and other Others. Participants included individuals at the Urban Life Center (now Chicago Center for Urban Life and Culture) and the Resource Center, a non-profit recycling and reuse organisation, and other respondents to Peters's public solicitation.

—

As described in the 'Culture in Action' programme guide
'As a way to understand how all Chicagoans and Others form and respond to social classifications, the artist and collaborating organisations and individuals engage in a process of "name-calling" – everyday acts of naming – from the playful and careful to the abusive.'

—

General point(s) of access
An interactive telephone line, 1-800-808-THEM, made publically available between 12 July and 30 September 1993, based on an earlier written questionnaire and public solicitation. Cards placed on Chicago Transit Authority (CTA) bus routes between July and August 1993 advertising this number. 'Meeting Grounds', a two-day symposium, took place at the Chicago Cultural Center on 12 and 13 November 1993.

—

Following a preliminary research project in Indonesia, Peters planned to develop his work on 'the liminal spaces experienced when working and moving between cultures'. He began his 'Culture in Action' project as an exploration of tourism and cultural identity, initially proposing an installation at Chicago's O'Hare International Airport. But inspired by a compilation of names he found in a pioneering linguistic study from the mid-1960s charting terms of abuse in the Chicago area, and engaged by the issue of how a given culture is recognised from within and from outside, Peters decided to develop an 'alternative lexicon' based on the specific practice of name-calling.

Peters began by designing a questionnaire structured by various social categories – such as occupation, religion and race – to collect language heard or used to name individuals and groups. Public participation was solicited through adverts in local newspapers, newsletters and a market research agency, and through 1-800-246-4ART, the official 'Culture in Action' information line. Peters also conducted interviews with individuals at the Resource Center and with students based at the Urban Life Center, some of whom also interviewed additional participants.

Altogether 224 people, aged 16 to 72, filled in the questionnaire. The collected information then informed the design of a computer-controlled telephone survey whereby callers could choose their route through various

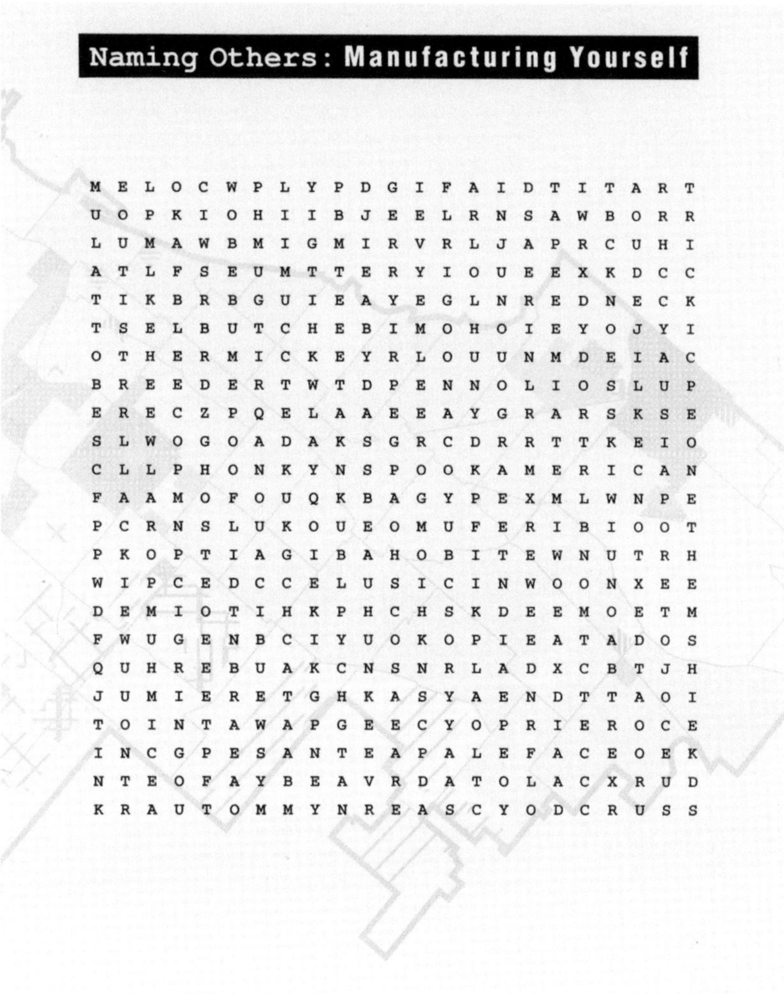

fig.68

Cover of the questionnaire booklet.

A number of years ago I came across a compilation of "Terms of Abuse for Some Chicago Social Groups" by linguist Lee A. Pederson (*American Dialect Society*, 1964, no. 42, University of Alabama Press). I have a persistent and unsettling reaction to Pederson's list which is lodged in the recognition that I know unspeakable terms for others; this shift into socially unacceptable space makes me acutely aware of how I acknowledge and produce difference. It also brings to mind the elaborate naming acts and euphemisms with which we bury difference in politeness; that is, in some cases the more conscious we become of difference the more fearful we are of precisely naming it. In *Naming Others: Manufacturing Yourself* I look at the ways we form and respond to social classifications by engaging participants in everyday acts of "naming" that range from playful and careful to abusive. I expect this probing to provoke participants, particularly when they confront cultural stereotypes that intimately affect them. But my intent is to encourage us to look beyond our immediate emotional reactions to an appreciation of the fact that we all name and are named by others. — Robert Peters

The project has been integrated into the progams of organizations that are engaged in sensitizing individuals to difference and alternative world views, such as the Urban Life Center, or agencies whose constituents represent specific economic, social, religious, or ethnic groupings, such as the Resource Center. Other participants include you and individuals solicited through local newspapers, newsletters, and by a market research organization. The collected materials of *Naming Others: Manufacturing Yourself* form a set of templates with which each of us shapes others and with which each of us is shaped. These templates will be made available to the general public from July 4 to September 30, 1993 through an 800 telephone number. *Naming Others: Manufacturing Yourself* is part of "Culture in Action: A Public Art Program of Sculpture Chicago" and is co-sponsored by Randolph Street Gallery.

fig.69

Introduction and a completed first page (fig.70) of the nine-page questionnaire.

3 X

Naming Others: **Manufacturing Yourself**

This survey collects any language you know, have heard, or have used that names individuals and groups with respect to Geographic Residence, Occupation, Social and Economic Status, Religion, Body, Age, Sexual Orientation, Gender, Race, and Nationality. This language will range from the playful and careful to the unspeakable. At the end of this form you are asked to describe your subjective responses to the act of recalling these terms and to speculate on the origin of one term (see "Recapitulation ").

Your responses to this survey will be kept confidential. Your name is not required in order to participate in this project.

Geographic Residence

Did you grow up in an urban, suburban, or rural setting? SUBURBAN

Where did you grow up? Outside Philadelphia and New York city. In what city, neighborhood, and/or suburb do you live? Chicago. Lakeview.

Do you feel a part of your community ? Not particularly.

Would you please list below terms or short descriptive phrases you have heard, used, or know that name geographic places or individuals in relation to their geographic residence?

Urban (individuals): *e.g.*, city slicker

uptown girl, yuppie, matron, man about town, career girl, downwardly mobile, savvy, street smart, cool, provincial, pre-Copernican,

Urban (places): *e.g.*, Gotham, tinsel town (LA), second city (Chicago)

the big apple, Philly,

Rural (individuals): *e.g.*, yahoo, hick, stubble-jumper

provincial, cheese head, hick, salt of the earth, down to earth, boy/girl next door

Rural (places): *e.g.*, boondocks, nowheresville

provinces, the country,

→ I don't like where you're leading me with these questions - they bring out basest prejudices which aren't necessarily a fair view of ~~my assumptions~~ or how I see these people/places.

Regional (places): *e.g.*, Bible belt (Midwest), land of fruits and nuts (California)

1

fig.70

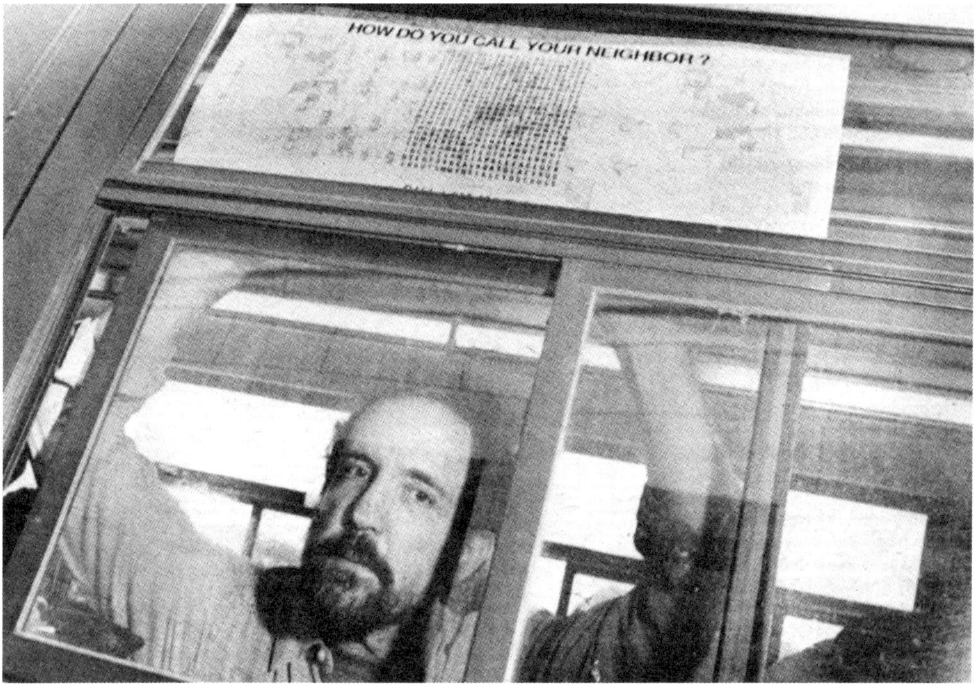

fig.71

Robert Peters holding one of the advertising cards against the window of a CTA bus.

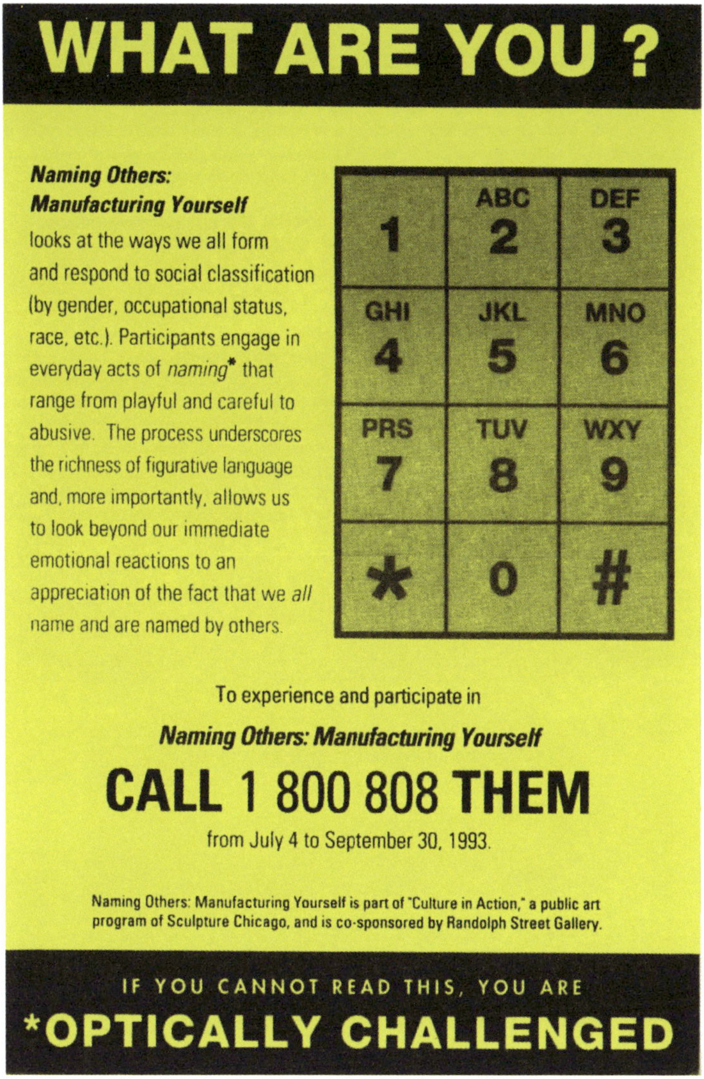

fig.72

Tear-off slips with details of the project were attached to the cards placed in CTA buses.

RACE-COLOR (6A, 6B)

S For those who value individuality of something it is disturbing to have that individuality diminished by classifications and generalizations.. *(Muzak comes under)*

G You mean labels like bird, bee, person or penguin ?

S Yes. In some circumstances it is enough to know that birds chirp, bees buzz, persons talk and penguins live in the cold looking as though they wear tuxedos. In other circumstances such as when a female person is a bird or a person of gender much more must be known...

S What is your color? If you are a person of non-color press zero, zero. If you are a person of color press P, C If you are a person of both color and non color press X, X

OO, PC, XX (7)

(alternating voices male and female over dubbed so very dense)

chink, whitey, feather heads, flange heads, nigger, yellow horde, peckerwood, chief, coon, honkey, moulagnani, redneck, darkie, half-caste, oreo, apple, coconut, banana, Uncle Tom, Geronimo, spic, jap, gringo, jigaboo, half breed, spade, WASP, gook, Cafe au Lait, Stepin Fetchit, all look alike, Tonto, Kim, Sambo, mulatto, white trash, Injun, Negro, Buddha's, Redskin, black, colored, chalker, gray, fade, pinkey, ghost, Zulu, Ethiopian, rice eater, mongrel, zebra, spookerican, slant, tight eyes, mestiszo, ofay, shade, no balls, blue eyed devil, short leg, can't dance, no rhythm, dipped, lunch meat, chop suey, white folk, paleface, nip, boy, spear chucker, troglodyte, bright skin, spic, jungle bunny, greaser, Afro American, buckra, chicken lips, boot lips, Klu Kluxer, long knife, the man, roundeye, ball face, monkey, white palmed, missing link, Kemo Saby, Mister Charles, sickle cell, colonizer, white meat, smoked Irishman, blanco, unbleached American, melanin impoverished,Velcro head, hayeater, some of my best friends

fig.73

Extract from the recorded survey script, which was read by George Kase and Sarah Peters.

categories of terms, before being asked to name themselves accordingly; they were then invited to add to the presented lexicon. The system for navigating the survey addressed listeners in relation to their own social position and identity, with automated questions such as 'What is your sex? If male press M; if female press F, if uncertain press X.' Short dialogues and philosophical musings on the power of words were spliced between the listings of terms, and it could take up to twenty minutes to go through the entire sequence.

Shortly after the telephone-survey line was open, Ameritech (now AT&T), the company donating the 1-800 toll-free number for the public to call, withdrew their service due to internal complaints. Instead they referred callers to a number with a 708 area code – a pay service not operated by Ameritech – and added a lengthy disclaimer which advised that the service contained 'explicit and vulgar' material and that teenagers should seek parental permission (despite Peters's inclusion of a disclaimer within the existing script).

This unanticipated censorship led Peters to engage in a long and largely unreciprocated correspondence with Ameritech, questioning their decision to act as gatekeepers of the public space of telecommunications; asking, for instance, why the service was altered and which parts of the script were offensive to them. Peters persisted for a year but the corporation resisted. At the time, he noted his additional dismay at the 'hands-off' response of Sculpture Chicago (*Art Papers*, November – December 1993).

Although this project could not be visited on the 'Culture in Action' bus tour, tour guide Rebecca Keller offered information and reflection on it during the long drive from Iñigo Manglano-Ovalle and Street-Level Video's *Tele-Vecindario* at Emerson House to Haha and Flood's storefront in Rogers Park.

In November 1993, after the official public programme of Sculpture Chicago had ended, Peters presented a two-day symposium 'Meeting Grounds' at the Chicago Cultural Center, organised in collaboration with Randolph Street Gallery, which had co-sponsored the *Naming Others* survey. The symposium, initially titled 'How a culture presents itself to itself and to Others' in reference to Peters's original proposal, set out to question how cultural representations take shape in an increasingly globalised world where social, economic and cultural factors continually intersect and have an impact on each other. With the subtitle 'a public gathering across cultural divides', the symposium drew together a wide range of practitioners, including artists, anthropologists, sociologists, traders and historians, chosen for their transcultural experiences. Those taking part included anthropologist Terence S. Turner and Kinhiabiéiti, a Kayapo videographer, on uses of electronic media and self-representation; historian Lisa Brock on differing notions of race across the African diaspora; and James Luna, a Pooyukitchum and Mexican American artist performing in conjunction with his simultaneous installation at Randolph Street Gallery.

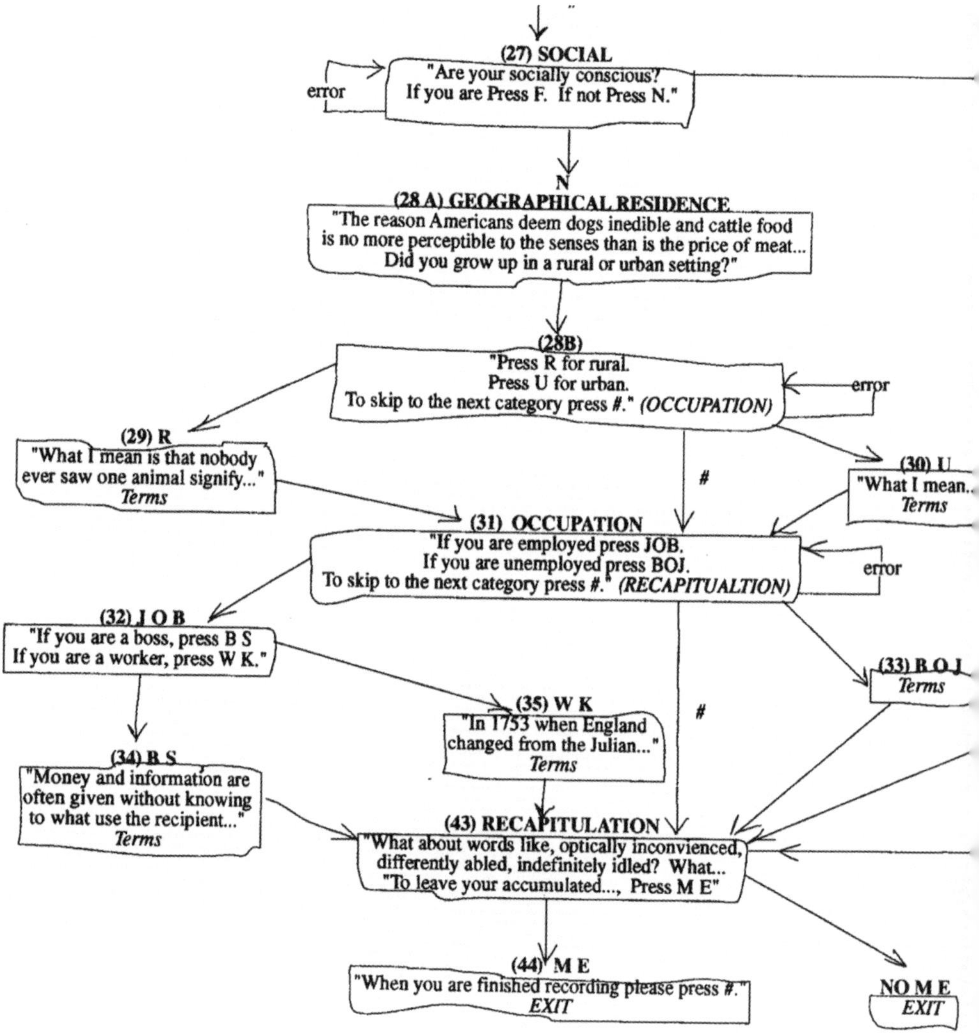

fig.74

Detail of Peters's flow chart mapping the survey sequence.

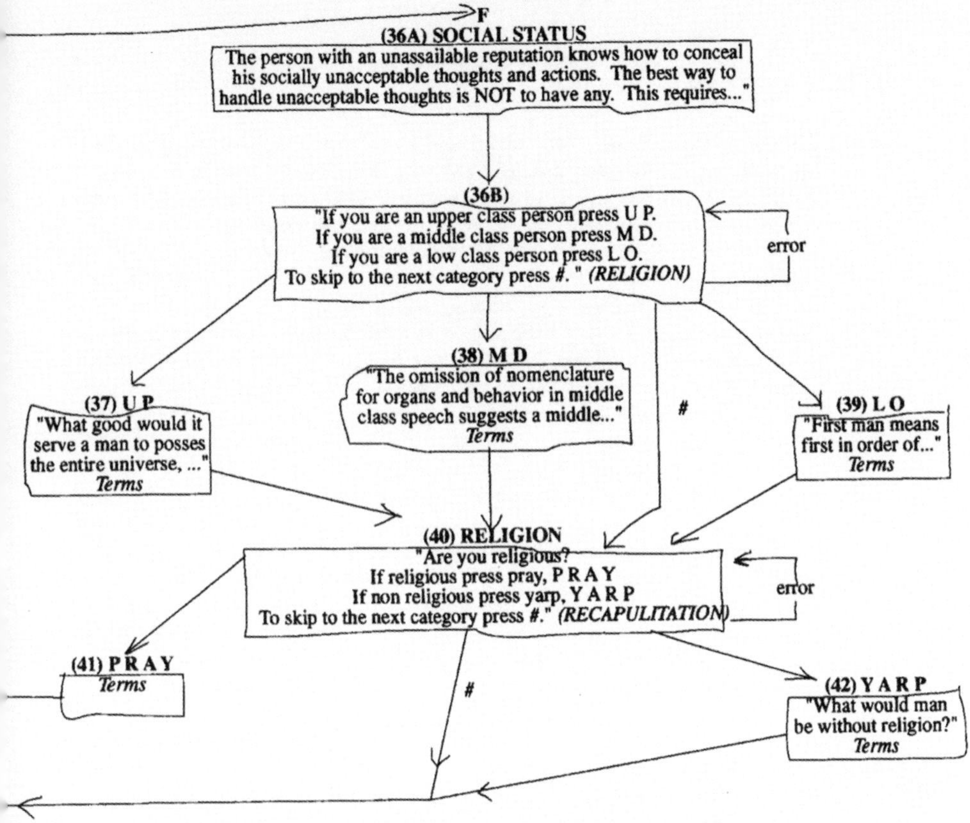
F
(36A) SOCIAL STATUS
The person with an unassailable reputation knows how to conceal his socially unacceptable thoughts and actions. The best way to handle unacceptable thoughts is NOT to have any. This requires..."
(36B)
"If you are an upper class person press U P.
If you are a middle class person press M D.
If you are a low class person press L O.
To skip to the next category press #. " (RELIGION)
error
(37) U P
"What good would it serve a man to posses the entire universe, ..."
Terms
(38) M D
"The omission of nomenclature for organs and behavior in middle class speech suggests a middle..."
Terms
#
(39) L O
"First man means first in order of..."
Terms
(40) RELIGION
"Are you religious?
If religious press pray, P R A Y
If non religious press yarp, Y A R P
To skip to the next category press #." (RECAPULITATION)
error
(41) P R A Y
Terms
#
(42) Y A R P
"What would man be without religion?"
Terms

The New Public Art: As Opposed to What?[1]
— Hafþór Yngvason

Part I: Contemplation prompted by the 14th International Sculpture Conference in Philadelphia, June 1992

Conservation and pollution, racial and social divisions, ethnic prejudices, housing, crime, health, unemployment... the list is incomplete, but it indicates the variety of issues addressed by public art. It is a list of public concerns – common, ordinary and close. In a presentation by Mary Jane Jacob at the International Sculpture Conference in Philadelphia last spring, this list summed up a rather unusual emphasis in public art programming.

'Culture in Action', a new programme curated by Jacob for an independent public art agency in Chicago (Sculpture Chicago), involves eight artists and collaborators who have been commissioned to work over several months with local groups and institutions. Rather than emphasising solely the creation of art objects or installations as an artist-in-residence programme might, the programme's main goal is social interaction. Working with high school juniors, residential councils, community activists, factory workers and city officials, the artists will engage in informal dialogues with the groups. Already, a series of lectures, panel discussions and symposia have been organised. This summer (1993), after two years of planning and public exchange, the projects are expected to culminate in such unorthodox art productions as a public education brochure, a hydroponic garden, a new line of candy, an alternative city tour, an ecological field station and collaborative installations involving temporary markers and monuments to subjects outside official history.

If 'Culture in Action' poses a radical move beyond established approaches in public art, there is more at stake in its departure than an Oedipal reaction to earlier movements. It must be remembered that the wish to provide more intimate relationships between art and its publics has been the driving force behind public art from the beginning. As a means to achieve that goal (by providing public amenity, for instance), the art object has served a different purpose in public art than it has in more museum-oriented forms. Rather than seeing 'Culture in Action' as mere experimentalism, it is better understood as an attempt to re-evaluate and overcome the terms, or limits, that public art has had to contend with and has too often accepted and internalised.

The ground for this re-evaluation became particularly clear at the conference in a panel called 'Can Sculpture Survive the Public Art Process?'. If the panelists – Athena Tacha, Jody Pinto and Albert Paley, all well-known pioneers of the public art movement – dutifully recounted the burden of bureaucracy on the creative process in numerous humorous and not-so-funny

—

[1] Editors' Note: This text was first published in *Public Art Review,* vol.4, no.2, Spring–Summer 1993, pp.4–5. It is reprinted by kind permission of the author and publisher.

anecdotes, the framing of the question seemed to distort what their struggle as public artists is about.

In a passionate plea for the creation of 'meaningful' public spaces that would unify their communities on the model of the public plazas and forums of historic Europe, panelist Athena Tacha's concern was not with the resilience of solitary creation at all. Significantly, her concern was whether a true 'gathering place' can be created in a society where there are no common beliefs and where parking lots and streets seem to have priority in city planning.

If Tacha's concern put the social goal of public art into perspective, it also offered a vantage point on its social limits. Based on an over-simple conception of 'community' as well as of the artist's role in society, the model of the medieval plaza – with its ideal of 'harmonious community' centred on common function – calls for the recreating of the 'common life' so conspicuously missing from modern cities by simply updating the spatial symbols of civic unity. It is a model, as panelist Jody Pinto insisted, that at best is irrelevant to the diversity of American society and has proven unresponsive to changes in lifestyle and population in European cities as well.

It is in response to this re-evaluation of older models that the 'Culture in Action' programme takes its departure. It is not a re-evaluation of the artistic achievements of public art but of the assumptions of urban development that public art has customarily worked within – assumptions about 'community' and 'neighbourhood'; 'participation', 'representation' and 'cultural identity'; 'public design', 'art' and 'architecture'. This can be seen by looking at a few of the project descriptions.[2]

- To consider and counter the prevailing perception of a now predominantly Mexican American neighbourhood, Daniel Martinez intends to 'interconnect … an overlay of issues relating to housing, labour and migration that have impacted' the development of the neighbourhood, a former Jewish ghetto and a major place of settlement for many European immigrant groups. fig.57–67

- Kate Ericson and Mel Ziegler intend to 'reveal … the utopian beginnings, architectural history and conceptions/misconceptions we hold about [federally funded city housing projects] and their residents'. fig.14–16

- Suzanne Lacy 'will explore issues of women, immigrants and the working class'. Drawing inspiration from the struggle for fair labour practices, education, health and other social and political reform by the social activist circle formed around Jane Addams's Hull-House at the turn of the century, the project will focus mostly on present-day service activities of immigrant women. fig.37–44

—

[2] EN: These reflect the artists' in-progress projections and proposals.

fig.17–26

- Simon Grennan and Christopher Sperandio 'will explore the relation of employees to employer and individual to corporation through the real-life collaboration among artists and management and workers of a candy company'.

fig.45–56

- Iñigo Manglano-Ovalle's project will focus on processes of bridging social, generational and cultural isolation of individuals and groups within localised communities. Through evening gatherings, a set of interrelated issues affecting the neighbourhood (family, immigration, employment, class, city service priorities, etc.) will be explored and an attempt made to 'reach an understanding of the complexity and the views of the community'.

If these short excerpts suggest a social-scientific research programme, that impression may be partially true. Several of the artists will work with sociologists, urban planners and other specialists to research and analyse social issues. However, the programme is a response to social conditions rather than to a scientific goal, and the approach is a public exchange rather than a scientific method. The research is better seen, then, as acknowledgment of the fact that the complexity of public issues cannot be avoided – not only are there no simple solutions available to public art: there are no simple problems. If loss of community characterises city life, it is not clear what is to be unified or what will count as community in a pluralist society. And if a sense of irrelevance to public concern has become the predicament of public design, hence of public art, the problem is not simply that the power of design has been overestimated but that its social significance has not been fully acknowledged.

It is in the face of this recognition that 'the new public art' has to proclaim its public-ness. It has, as Mary Jane Jacob stated most convincingly in her presentation at the Sculpture conference, 'To test out new methods of involving and collaborating with community members that go beyond the traditional mural-painting model, to engage others in the conception, execution and ownership of public art. To do so, new strategies for art must be developed that involve the artist with community over time and may even create a sense of community where there was none; new modes of exchange between artist and audience need to be identified where public art can also be a vehicle for popular education; and new sites – where art in the form of objects, dialogues and events can take place – need to be created to bridge the gap between art and everyday life.'

—

Part II: Contemplation on 'The Artist In The Community' forum, Providence St Mel High School and Erie Neighborhood House, Chicago, 5 December 1992[3]

If the question of the artist's role in the community has been raised on occasion over the past twenty years of public art, it is now being asked in a more urgent, certainly more self-conscious manner. There was nothing arbitrary or casual, for instance, about the way it was asked during a public forum on the 'Culture in Action' programme held in Chicago last December. Rather than community involvement being relegated to administrative workshops on 'outreach', as it has been so often in the past, it was the focus of the forum. This is not surprising, of course, because cultural identity, diversity, representation and audience have become increasingly central to art criticism and cultural studies. However, it was striking how directly relevant to the art itself – as opposed to some external conditions of its siting – the question appeared to be. The very posing of the question seems to have become integral to the way public art addresses itself to its own cultural conditions – which is to say that 'public' art has finally come to openly acknowledge how problematic its own claim to public relevance is.

This self-criticism, far from being self-absorbed, is a necessary element in public artists' attempts to come to terms with the social shortcomings of what can be called the 'integrationist' model of public art. As public art has developed over the last two decades, its emphasis has been on techniques of integration – not just to incorporate art physically into buildings and parks but also to foster social assimilation. While 'site specificity' – privileged in public art circles as the public form of art – has provided a means to introduce art into neighbourhoods without the glaring irrelevance of what has been called 'plop art', it has rarely gone beyond the idea of responding to established ideas or 'facts' about communities to participating in a public sphere where such facts can be examined and contested. The more an artist seeks to adapt his or her art to pre-established notions about a community, the less the art may speak to community members' understanding of their relation to their community and other levels of modern society.

It is in response to this dilemma that 'the new public art' has emphasised 'participation' over 'integration'. The difference between the two emphases is not simply a matter of degree of community involvement, for community members (usually children) are often included in some aspects of integrationist art to facilitate its acceptance. The difference is rather a matter of conflicting notions about the role of art in public life. This, I would like to suggest, is a matter of conflicting views of what constitute the problems of modernity.

—

[3] EN: The 'Culture in Action' round-table forum, 'The Artist In The Community', took place on 4 and 5 December 1992. The afternoon session on the first day was held in the ballroom of the Blackstone Hotel, Chicago; it began with introductions to the programme by representatives of Sculpture Chicago, followed by participating artists and community representatives from their projects responding to questions by Carol Becker. The second day was held at Providence St Mel School, the site of Mark Dion's project, and Erie Neighborhood House, an important site for Iñigo Manglano-Ovalle's project. It began with introductory presentations by site representatives and artists working there, followed by round-table discussion sessions involving participating artists, some of their collaborators and local and international professionals in fields related to public art. The concluding plenary session was chaired by Mary Jane Jacob and featured contributions from Yves Aupetitallot, Ian Hunter, Joseph Mannino, Lynne Sowder and Noreen Tomassi.

While the integrationist model presupposes that modern societies are, in the words of the social theorist Seyla Benhabib, 'communities integrated around a single conception of the human good' – i.e. a conception that can be responded to in an unproblematic fashion and revitalised through simple design, such as a public plaza – the participatory model is based on the notion that '[modern] societies are marked by a "plurality" of visions of the good, and of the good of association itself'.[4]

Without such a pluralist conception, it would be hard to appreciate the complexities of at least some of the projects commissioned for the 'Culture in Action' programme. Simon Grennan and Christopher Sperandio's project, fig.17–26 'The Workforce Makes the Candy of Their Dreams', may seem like just another expansion of public art into new contexts – a candy factory this time – but it fits no established categories of public art. It's neither a patronising act of putting good art in the factory for the benefit of the workers' cultural education (plop art), nor an integrationist attempt to respond to the workers' 'proletarian culture' ('site specific art'), nor for that matter an attempt of misplaced constructivism involving artists in capitalist production ('design collaboration'). What distinguishes Grennan and Sperandio's project from such approaches is the awareness they have incorporated into their work of how problematic their claim to public relevance is. Thus, if they do make attempts to engage the workers in 'participation', it is not to promote the established order at the plant but to examine the uses and abuses of participatory rhetoric. That at least was the impression given at the forum by one of the participants in the project, the president of the Bakers, Confectioners and Tobacco Workers' Union, Local 522. The employer claims to already have a workers/management participation programme in place at the plant, developed at the plant's expense for the workers' benefit, but the workers see it as a structure of empty words and view Grennan and Sperandio's project as providing a way to examine or test its foundation.

fig.14–16 Nor can Kate Ericson and Mel Ziegler's 'Housing Project' be reduced to an integrationist response to 'facts' or values indigenous to tenants of public housing. As part of their project, they will develop a paint chart of official colours used for public housing, not in an attempt to make their art specific to its site, but to chart the powers at play in everyday life through participatory examination of how facts and values are constituted in people's lives and of how they are related to other value systems.

What these two examples show is not only the complexity of the pluralist vision but also a development away from the integration of art into presumably undifferentiated value schemes to involvement in the complex reality of power relations. While the integrationist vision sees the problems of modernity in 'the loss of a sense of belonging, oneness and solidarity', as

—

[4] Seyla Benhabib, *Situating the Self: Gender, Community and Postmodernism in Contemporary Ethics,* New York: Routledge, 1992, p.79.

Benhabib has put it, the participationist sees the problems 'more in the sense of a loss of political agency and efficacy'.[5]

The participatory vision of public art grew, as Suzanne Lacy stressed at the forum, out of the grass-root efforts of the 1970s, influenced significantly by the great community activist Saul Alinsky. Public artists have been part of the so-called 'new social movements',[6] fighting along with environmental, peace and feminist activists for qualitative social and cultural change. In urban politics, they have aligned themselves with tenants and squatters, consumer advocates and welfare-rights militants, and against the faceless bureaucracy of 50s- and 60s-style social programmes and urban planning. It has been a fight not just against unwanted highway plans and gentrification but for active involvement of ordinary people in the decisions affecting their own lives.

As with these new social movements, 'the new public art' has often concentrated on the positive side of the equation. The Ericson/Ziegler project is a good example of this; Suzanne Lacy's large-scale art project with aging women is the classic prototype of an attempt to empower through participatory examination of values, prejudices and alternative visions. The success of such projects does not depend on whether the communities engaged will come to accept them – for without their active involvement from the beginning, the projects will not even get off the ground. Rather, the test is whether the art plays a real role in the participants' lives and leaves them with a fuller sense of their political and cultural power.

—

[5] *Ibid.*, p.77.

[6] For a more thorough examination and description of these movements, see Carl Boggs, *Social Movements and Political Powers: Emerging Forms of Radicalism in the West,* Philadelphia: Temple University Press, 1986.

'Culture in Action'[1]
— Joe Scanlan

> *In 1986* The Wall Street Journal *cited that 'the number of corporations collecting art has risen fifty percent in the past five years, to about a thousand'. By and large, these are contemporary collections since this art is more affordable and more plentiful: this demand alone has had an impact on sustaining a large number of artists and galleries. New branches of the art field have also sprung up to service these needs and interests: corporate curators, registrars and art advisors...*
> Mary Jane Jacob[2]

p.15

When Mary Jane Jacob took over as guest curator of Sculpture Chicago after the success of her public sculpture project 'Places with a Past', Sculpture Chicago had an erratic ten-year history at best. From its inception, the non-profit organisation's affiliation with River City Condominiums, the Printer's Row and Dearborn Street Station developments and the Chicago Dock and Canal Trust had overshadowed all but a few of the artworks it generated, making its brand of ragged and insensitive public art an even sorrier pawn than usual in the urban real estate development process. Jacob's arrival promised not only to improve the sensitivity of Sculpture Chicago's projects but also to greatly sophisticate its interaction with the city of Chicago, real estate developers and major corporate and foundation underwriters. It should be noted that Jacob's knowledge of the Chicago community dates back to her tenure as Chief Curator of Chicago's Museum of Contemporary Art (1980–86), particularly her facilitation of four magnificent satellite installations by Jannis Kounellis in conjunction with his 1986 retrospective.

'Culture in Action' set out to provide forums for culture in otherwise underserved communities by generating art from within the communities themselves, as opposed to simply serving up a local statue or mural. Each of its eight component projects was executed by an artist/community-group team and was developed over an extended period of time, necessitating long-term relationships with each artist's volunteer group, a host community centre and community residents in general. The success of creating such labour-intensive and open-ended art experiences was underscored by the fact that the prevailing aesthetic trait of 'Culture in Action' was its invisibility: not only in the sense of many of its operations not being evident, but also of their not being easily consumed. By fundamentally contradicting high art's aesthetic principles, its privileging of vision and the commensurate disengagement of passive viewers from static objects – i.e. the physically

—

[1] Editors' Note: This text is a lightly revised version of an article originally published in *frieze,* no.13, November–December 1993, pp.22–27.
[2] Mary Jane Jacob, 'Art in the Age of Reagan: 1908–1988', in M.J. Jacob and Ann Goldstein (ed.), *A Forest of Signs: Art in the Crisis of Representation* (exh. cat.), Cambridge, MA: The MIT Press, 1989, pp.18–19.

alienating experience of most cultural institutions – 'Culture in Action' framed its artists, its communities and its audience as the structure and content of its art.

Ironically, this decentralisation of 'Culture in Action' was most often characterised as *inconvenience* by the art-viewing public, a criticism often levelled against Chicago's Museum of Contemporary Art due to its location in the upscale retail atmosphere of North Michigan Avenue, a condition 'Culture in Action' explicitly set out to circumvent. In this respect 'Culture in Action' was no less exclusive than Chicago's esteemed cultural institutions, in that it assumed community-based art to be de jure more accessible than art located in museums. This is a dangerously naïve assumption in such a territorial city as Chicago, one that two of the projects (by Iñigo Manglano-Ovalle and the team of Daniel J. Martinez and VinZula Kara) directly addressed. What happens when communities and their residents become the subjects of art? Prospects to be mined by underwriters on a social mission in the form of culture? The former question is an old one and the latter response indicates a looming dilemma, in that it appears that upper-level funding for public art and community projects currently exceeds the expressed need or desire for it, creating a situation where art (culture) is being dictated – even invented – by the agencies who sponsor it more than the artists and communities they serve.[3] Sadly, the most telling aspect of 'Culture in Action' was the disparity between what Sculpture Chicago and its sponsors claimed to accomplish through these projects, what most of the artists knew was really possible, and the concomitant scepticism about whom the culture was really for.

fig.45–56; fig.57–67

For the exhibition's artists, it was whoever showed up on a given day, but certainly not everybody, not even rhetorically. The success and lasting impact of such projects is the depth and quality of their participants' engagement: it doesn't matter how many people are involved so long as those people who do come are sufficiently enriched. Nor can such projects hope to solve any of their respective community's problems; at best they can act as a first step towards increasing the general awareness of a community's issues, which might then lead to changes in attitude – or someday, even results. However sympathetic Mary Jane Jacob might be to such subtleties as a curator, as a representative of a public service agency she seemed far more concerned with emphasising the concrete accomplishments of 'Culture in

—

[3] Joe Scanlan, September 2013: In the early 1990s social betterment had become a stated goal in the funding guidelines of such cultural-funding agencies as the National Endowment for the Arts and the Rockefeller Foundation (both of which supported 'Culture in Action') – in equal if not greater measure than aesthetic excellence or artistic achievement. This was in large part due to the backlash created when the Corcoran Gallery in Washington DC cancelled its planned Robert Mapplethorpe retrospective in 1989, and NEA Chairman John Frohnmayer vetoed individual artist grants for Karen Finley, John Fleck, Holly Hughes and Tim Miller – the NEA Four – in 1990. Both controversies had a profound chilling effect on any artist eligible for corporate or governmental funding.

Action', thereby trivialising its more ephemeral, long-term effects. To borrow an observation by Witte de With Director Chris Dercon on the hoopla surrounding documenta 9: 'I am reminded of [French film critic Serge] Daney's cautionary words whenever works of art come into the realm of publicity … and the visual effects and jargon of publicity take over the space that actually belongs to works of art. "Publicity", wrote Daney, "is only interested in the exemplary, in the empirical, in evidence."'[4]

fig.1–13 Take Mark Dion and the Chicago Urban Ecology Action Group. Dion began by conceiving of a backwards and interesting way of teaching a group of high school students about ecology and the interdependency of local ecosystems. Rather than choose a simple model where flora and fauna are fig.2–5 few (and thus their ecological roles obvious), Dion began by taking his group on a field trip to two tropical rainforest preserves in Belize.[5] To paraphrase Dion: appreciating and maintaining an ecosystem has as much to do with a sense of scale as it does with hard science. Even the middling complexity of Chicago's environment obliterates whatever knowledge might be gained from mapping a simple textbook or laboratory ecosystem, so Dion intuited that first studying the extraordinarily complex ecosystem of a rainforest would make a temperate, urban ecosystem seem manageable by comparison, and render its traits more pronounced and site specific.

fig.6–13 Once back in Chicago, the sculptural manifestation of Dion's project involved procuring a site (the dormant headquarters of the former Lincoln Park Casting Club) and engaging the immediate 'natural' surroundings. Dion and his crew cleaned out all of the Club's lockers, rearranged them in perpendicular stacks to create a series of stall-like spaces and generally painted and cleaned up the place. A long room in the rear of the building reserved for fly-tying – replete with workstations of vices and flexible jeweller-style magnifying lamps – had the eerie charm of a 1950s high school chemistry lab and remained intact. From here Dion and his group conducted micro-expeditions to the Lincoln Park Zoo, the lagoon and the surrounding park; collected samples, conducted discussions and experiments; and kept a running tally of all garbage collected during their outings (leading one CUEAG member to remark that the average park visitor must be a promiscuous, chain-smoking alcoholic). They also made very little art to speak of – although the accumulated materials and charts in just about any section of the Casting Club could have been recontextualised and framed as such. The beauty of Dion's project was its indefiniteness, its constant activity and non-productiveness a parallel for his fascination with and scepticism of scientific method. The same might be said of Dion's approach to art as a form of social betterment.

—

[4] Chris Dercon, 'Am I Now Getting Sentimental?', *Parkett*, no.33, September 1992, p.155.

[5] EN: Dion started by teaching weekly classes on Saturdays, initially to prepare for the trip and afterwards to reflect on, among other issues, the local situation by comparison. The narrative sequence of events is given in the project description on pp.72–83 of this book.

An equally subtle but more mischievous project was *Naming Others: Manufacturing Yourself* by Robert Peters and 'Mushroom Pickers, Ghosts, Frogs and other Others'. It was completely invisible and yet, absurdly, the most vision-based of the projects in that it was inspired by a thirty-year-old list of 'Terms of Abuse' that Peters had discovered, an encyclopaedic account of derogatory names and slang compiled from the Chicago area. Peters became interested in the notion that, however inflammatory they might be, such terms were an integral part and product of Chicago culture. As a way of challenging Chicagoans to confront their prejudices, Peters first asked participants to fill out survey forms with as many contemporary terms of abuse as they could think of, all of which were then made available via a widely advertised toll-free telephone number. Callers could surf through the phone line's network by choosing options from a series of generic menus (sex, occupation, religion, race), each of which served up a cacophony of relevant slurs (cracker, dune-coon, sperm bank, pointy head, dick-for-brains) in addition to philosophical insights on the nature of language and naming.

fig.68–74

fig.68–70

fig.73, 74

When the detailed content of Peters's project became apparent to them, the Ameritech company backed out of providing toll-free service for the survey, despite Peters's entreaty that they try to appreciate the context in which it was being presented. Eventually they compromised by providing the toll-free number, but outfitted with a recorded disclaimer and a regular number that people interested in the survey could then call. Regardless of these corporate wranglings, Peters's project was successful: he was wise enough to incorporate Ameritech's reservations into the structure of his project as perverse proof of its complexity. As sociology, the survey results were highly informative and entertaining; and yet, since callers could categorically represent themselves however they wanted, the empirical veracity of the entire enterprise was undermined by its own perniciousness.

Writing on his public sculpture project for Münster, Michael Asher discussed the artist's relationship to the power inherent in public art commissions.[6] In such partnerships, power struggles of access and privilege develop between the artist's desire to realise an otherwise unfeasible project and the interests of the project's sponsors. In believing that they can manage their budgets, the details of their sites, and therefore successfully shape the public's experience of their work, artists often begin to believe that they can also control (if not blot out) the motives of their organisers and funders, their perceptions of the public and the public's perception of *them*. Thus, in public projects like 'Culture in Action', who's in control not only determines the scale of a given project but the subsequent quality or quantity of its public role. 'Culture in Action' was most provocative and successful in precisely those areas that Sculpture Chicago couldn't control; not because of any incompetence in the organisation or its facilitators, but

p.*20*

—

[6] Michael Asher and Benjamin H.D. Buchloh, *Writings 1973–1983 on Works 1969–79*, Halifax and Los Angeles: The Press of the Nova Scotia College of Art and Design and the Museum of Contemporary Art, 1983, pp.164–73. See also J. Decter, 'Culture in Action: Exhibition as Social Redistribution', in this volume, pp.14–43.

because control in general breeds didacticism and allows few accidents or ambiguities to occur.

Of all of the artists in 'Culture in Action', the Chicago-based collaborative Haha (Richard House, Wendy Jacob, Laurie Palmer, John Ploof) and their volunteer group Flood were perhaps the most familiar with the social and political terrains to be negotiated. They thus seemed most able to frame their proposal and realise their project without being deluded into thinking they were in control of things they weren't, or worrying about accomplishments beyond the function and maintenance of their project. Haha began by making installations about beauty, community engagement and personal contact that operated outside the art world's established structures. This was in 1987, the same year that Mary Jane Jacob left the Chicago MCA to become chief curator at the Museum of Contemporary Art (MoCA) in Los Angeles, where she co-organised the wholly inbred 'Forest of Signs' exhibition in 1989. Thus it was perhaps Haha's field experience that allowed them to take Sculpture Chicago's social mission with a grain of salt and carry

fig.27–36

on in a practical and faithful way. The lasting impression of *Flood: A Volunteer Network for Active Participation in Health Care* was the group's insistence that it remain modest and realistic in terms of what it might accomplish.

Flood began with Haha's desire to create a community garden, where local residents might interact in the course of self-sustenance. Their research into urban-gardening methods and their first-hand experience of the AIDS crisis led them to wonder how gardening might act as a sort of nurturing therapy for people with HIV and AIDS, and how hydroponic gardening – vegetables grown with nutrient-enriched water only, without soil – might be an alternative source of nutrition for people with HIV and AIDS, as well as a rich metaphor for people who need to monitor their systems very carefully in order to live. The fact that leafy vegetables like Swiss chard, mustard, kale and collard greens are fast growing, less readily available and rich in beta-carotene (which has been linked to cancer prevention and tumour reduction) further focused the details of their project.

Flood, then, first entailed the construction of a hydroponic garden in a vacant storefront of their North Side neighbourhood, the materials and rent for which was provided by Sculpture Chicago. At the same time, members of Flood were enlisted and trained. Once the garden was up and running, networks for distributing the vegetables to local clinics were organised, along with regular discussions on safe sex, caring for people with AIDS, hydroponic gardening and how to get the word out. By the end of the summer, the group had also designed several in-home hydroponic gardening units that could be made from readily available hardware-store materials.

Flood was also remarkably beautiful. The functional necessity of the garden gave its formal appearance an exhilarating ruthlessness and bluntness, a sense that in lieu of aesthetics every material decision and construction

fig.30, 31, 35, 36

technique was dictated by the project's technical demands. The plant stands were made of screwed metal and wooden pipe, metal strap hangers held clear plastic hoses in place and PVC plastic plant troughs (with nylon-stocking filters) were illuminated by ultraviolet lights. The installation was visually reminiscent of Kounellis's untitled room (1967) at Galleria L'Attico, Rome, or Helen and Newton Harrison's *Lagoon* (1973). Above the pipe structures and water pumps and beneath the cold glare of the lights, the plants wrinkled and stretched their leafy greenness, exalting their privileged status in the colourless room. The greens were at once vibrant and delicate, hearty and thread-like, patients themselves in a spick-and-span plant ward. The more one looked, the more the metaphor of the plants on their nutrient-enriched group IV became evident. And yet this metaphor of illness and maintenance was deferred by Flood's extroverted objective as the project moved freely from beauty to service and back again: if its medical practicality were to be challenged, *Flood* asserted its symbolism as art; and if beauty was to be seen as an aesthetic cipher irrelevant to social concerns, there was still food and therapy for the sick. This dialectic was superseded however, by the notion that beauty and symbolism *are* relevant to assuaging pain, anxiety and self-esteem. Matisse lives.

The remaining projects were executed by Kate Ericson and Mel Ziegler and a resident group of Odgen Courts Apartments (*Eminent Domain*, a 'Tru-Test EZ Paint' colour chart to be displayed in local hardware stores, with the colours named by the group as commentary on the drabness of government housing); Simon Grennan, Christopher Sperandio and twelve members of the Bakery, Confectionery and Tobacco Workers' Union (*We Got It! The Workforce Makes the Candy of Their Dreams*, which turned out to be a chocolate bar with almonds); Suzanne Lacy and a coalition of Chicago women (*Full Circle*, a hundred limestone boulders fastened to sidewalks throughout Chicago, with a bronze plaque commemorating a significant Chicago woman attached to each); Iñigo Manglano-Ovalle and Street-Level Video (*Tele-Vecindario: A Street-Level Video Project*); and Daniel J. Martinez, VinZula Kara and the West Side Three-Point Marchers (*Consequences of a Gesture*).[7]

fig.14–16
fig.17–26
fig.37–44
fig.45–56
fig.57–67

Of these, Manglano-Ovalle's and Martinez and Kara's were the least painfully obvious, particularly when each took to the streets in their host communities for a respective block party and an inter-neighbourhood parade. Throughout the summer, Manglano-Ovalle had been working with a teenage video crew, filming his predominantly Latino West Town neighbourhood, conducting street interviews with residents on the concepts of territory, identity, ownership and gentrification.[8] These interviews became the context through which the youths learned technical video training and the subtler means of formulating questions, steering interviews and editing material – mediating information. These interviews and finished videotapes were the focal point of a culminating block party in late August, when some sixty televisions were installed up and down the street on front stoops, in resident houses and

fig.52–56

—

[7] EN: See the project descriptions in this book, pp.67–157, for more details.
[8] EN: Manglano-Ovalle began work with this group early in 1992. The narrative sequence of events is given in the project description on pp.122–35 of this book.

gardens and in vacant lots. There was a stage for live-music performances and step demonstrations. As the sun set, the streets filled with people, including members of rival Latino gangs who had participated to varying degrees in the video project and who had called a (temporary) truce for the occasion.

fig.57–63 In July, Martinez, Kara and the Three-Point Marchers organised an 'Absurdist Parade' which began in Harrison Park (a.k.a. Zapata Park), a predominantly Mexican neighbourhood, and finished to the north and west in Garfield Park, a predominantly black West Side neighbourhood. Residents from each of the two neighbourhoods – who do not usually mix – participated in the free, come-one-come-all parade. However effective or meretricious as gestures, the street components of both Manglano-Ovalle's and Martinez and Kara's projects were successful in that their content was fundamentally uncontrollable. They bristled with the nervous energy of a social event that knows neither its magnitude nor its consequences until those present take personal responsibility for the event and shape it into whatever they might.

Since the contemporary version of public art did not arise in order to meet the expressed desires of neglected communities but as a proactive response to the suspicion held by a handful of perceptive artists and institutions that traditional art was having little if any effect on most of the population (particularly minority and lower-class communities), its difficulty has been finding methods to serve communities in ways that are relevant to them. How can the enthusiastic resources of foundations and corporate America be applied to meet the needs of beneficiaries without distorting culture beyond recognition in the process? It's not surprising that the most sensitive and successful of recent public art has occurred at intimate levels, on the model of John Ahearn, John Malpede or Rigoberto Torres. In these cases it is personal interest and motivation that precludes however much funding is available for a project. Thus, if anything can be learned from 'Culture in Action', it is that culture – at least culture in the anthropologically profound, socially embedded sense of the term – cannot be produced with the same expediency as art objects.

It is to Mary Jane Jacob's credit that all of the artists in 'Culture in Action' were already personally involved in alternative art forms, politics and community activism. But did Sculpture Chicago's more sophisticated relationships with cultural funding institutions necessarily translate into more intelligent and effective public artworks? Or would these projects have happened anyway – on smaller scales definitely, perhaps in different places and over longer periods of time – just minus all the hoopla and hype? I think so. If that's the case, Sculpture Chicago was only responsible for making them happen on a massive scale, together, adding little to the projects themselves but certainly following recent (government) guidelines that art be useful and have immediately measurable effects. It would be absurd to cite the dichotomy of 'official' and 'unofficial' art in the post-War Soviet Union as relevant to this discussion if it were not for Ilya Kabakov's installation being on view at the Museum of Contemporary Art during most of July and August. The poetic justice of his Russian pavilion at this year's Venice Biennale; the poignancy of *Incident at the Museum or Water Music* (1992) at the MCA; and the various ways he and his artist colleagues persevered throughout the 1950s, 60s, 70s and 80s would suggest that culture 'in action' is usually not that which is sanctioned.

'Chicago Is Culture in Action' — Mary Jane Jacob[1]

> *'Culture in Action' was unique to Chicago, the only place it could happen, intellectually ... It was counter to the mainstream and Chicago was not mainstream – not New York or Los Angeles. Chicago has always been a crossroads. So those from different geographic positions could converge there.*
> Daniel J. Martinez[2]

Art in Public Places and in Museums

There are always a number of institutions operating at once in the art world. One that determines how contemporary art is delivered is the museum, and in that Chicago is no exception. Another is public art, and there Chicago had won some distinction beginning in 1967 with the an outdoor sculpture by Pablo Picasso in Daley Plaza. The 'modern art monument' movement it launched continued as sculptures came to populate public land to the distaste or disinterest of the populace, or so the press would have had us think.[3]

As a result, those in what we might call the 'art-know' feared letting in the public; in order to preserve quality, it was believed the selection process needed to be guarded by experts. But to my mind, as a curator and a private citizen, there was a lot of public art, too much, that failed for one reason or another. Did it have to be this way? I asked myself, what if the art was located where people live and work, on the street rather than in parks, where they, at best, go for recreation? What if it dealt with the things that concern them in their everyday lives? Most of all, what if we let them in on the process? These became motivating questions in shaping 'Culture in Action'.

As a curator you also always have to ask yourself: where is contemporary art going now, and how can I show it? To me the interesting art was happening outside of galleries, but *not* in the form of public art commissions. My last big museum exhibition had been in 1989, at the Los Angeles Museum of Contemporary Art (MoCA), and titled 'A Forest of Signs'.[4] Its list of artists

—

[1] Editors' Note: This reflection by the curator of 'Culture in Action' is based on the transcript of a conversation with Charles Esche and Pablo Lafuente on 19 February 2013.

[2] Daniel J. Martinez in conversation with Michael Brenson during the symposium '"Culture in Action": Public Art in Chicago 20 Years Later', organised by Threewalls and held at the University of Chicago, 5 October 2013.

[3] Early in the current century this museum-without-walls model was employed to wide acclaim at Millennium Park in Chicago, with Anish Kapoor's *Cloud Gate* ('The Bean') becoming a new city symbol. But in 1990 Millennium Park was nowhere on the horizon; it was literally a below-street-level convergence of trains – a hole in the ground.

[4] 'A Forest of Signs: Art in the Crisis of Representation' was on view at the Museum of Contemporary Art, Los Angeles, from 7 May to 13 August 1989. See Mary Jane Jacob and Ann Goldstein (ed.), *A Forest of Signs: Art in the Crisis of Representation* (exh. cat.), Cambridge, MA: The MIT Press, 1989.

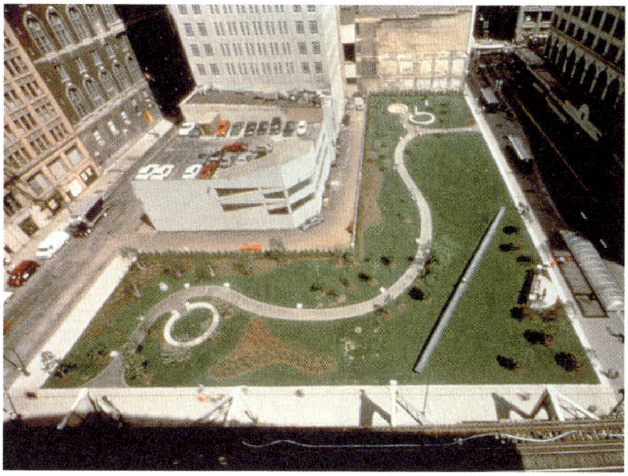

Ronald Jones, *Pritzker Park*, 1990–2008, commissioned by Mary Jane Jacob for Sculpture Chicago, in collaboration with the Department of Planning, City of Chicago. Courtesy the artist

comprises a kind of who's who of the period. These artists offered sharp social criticism, deconstructing power relationships at play in the world. Taking up such topical issues within the gallery setting, though, didn't seem enough to me. Placed inside the museum, the works didn't have an effect outside of it. The frame of the museum added a kind of irony rather than gravity to the subject matter – the museum was never going to be the place to facilitate the social change to which the works pointed. They needed a context that could magnify their message.

'A Forest of Signs' was the final point in my growing dissatisfaction with the rarefication of the museum and the controls that fearful administrators exercised, perhaps unconsciously or in the name of professionalism. If artists wanted to contribute to political change, the museum was not the place – the real world was. But some artists, even some in that show, were already out there, engaging difficult subjects such as AIDS in public places, bringing their messages to an undifferentiated, general public. Their means of delivery became modes like billboards or buses. Appropriating the look and mechanisms of mainstream media advertising seemed right.

—

Public Art Commissioning and its Problems

In the US in the 1980s, public art was commissioned through public systems at different levels of government. There was funding for new government buildings through the National Endowment for the Arts (NEA), the Government Services Administration (GSA) and the Department of Veterans Affairs. Some cities, like Chicago, also had ordinances that legislated a percent-for-art. The other route for commissioning was corporations. Overall it was an art-in-architecture model, and in all these cases, the resulting work was to be permanent – whether a sculpture, a mural, a painting – because this was an investment of money. Doing something temporary was out of the question, and pretty much still is (the City of Chicago's Cultural

Affairs Department is just now considering a change, but the discussion is still in the early stages). 'Social art practice' wasn't even a term, and undertaking anything like that within these commissioning systems was impossible.

As a museum curator, I sat on tens of selection panels around the country, each time charged with naming a shortlist of artists by sitting for a day in a conference room; looking at slides we each brought to the table; and, in most cases, never seeing the city or the site. Typically there were three national experts who were there to ensure quality, and three local panelists with some interest in the arts who were to represent the voice of the community. From all the selection panels on which I served, only a fraction of the projects were ever completed, and those that were hardly ever lived up to expectations. Compromises had to be made, not just for the lack of money, but also for the shortage of imagination and lack of creative, cooperative problem-solving. And since these programmes were tied to buildings or adjacent outdoor spaces, it was often a case of the architect battling for power with the artist. There is a different relationship between architects and artists today, but at that time it was hostile.

Another problem was the lack of real 'public-ness'. 'Public' was defined by location – who owned the building or land – but, as I said, the process was guarded. There was a fearfulness about the potential loss of artistic quality, maybe emanating from the guidance of museum directors at the inception of these government programmes. Because there was an unwillingness to let the public in, there was no community involvement. As a panel participant, I was witness to a desire to contain community in the name of upholding standards. On the part of government agencies – understaffed and without the means to implement other creative processes – there was a demand to keep things going. It seemed to me that things could be done another way, and that practices of curating, rather than administering, could be applied to the commissioning of public art.

When the members of the public did play a role, it was done independently, often leading to murals, or through not-for-profits like the Chicago Public Art Group that since 1971 has carried out a formula for community mosaics; they are all over the place – on schools façades, playgrounds, highway underpasses. I thought there has got to be a better way – a better process that can lead to serious contemporary art, on the order of those modern art monuments but in the idioms of today, and still have room for the public. Instead, why not invite members of the public to come into the thinking, to inspire and provoke it, give it purposefulness and be in continuous dialogue with the artists throughout the process? So I was excited when the artists in 'Culture in Action' proposed ways for others to participate that did not mean executing a part according to plan.

—

Sculpture Chicago

Sculpture Chicago was started in the 1980s by a group of arts-and-business supporters who were also active in the city's art museums, but who wanted to do something outdoors for the city and for artists. It was a period when the downtown district was in need of coming back, and the practice of turning former retail and manufacturing corridors into mixed-use living spaces was being initiated. The board of Sculpture Chicago had a deep reach into commerce and culture. So they helped make available to artists some underdeveloped areas of the Loop, in the city's downtown, for what became a summer programme of outdoor sculpture, with the advantage of bringing wider attention to these districts. Yet the process of undertaking this project seemed to me conventional and overdetermined: artists submitted maquettes to be juried, and those selected would scale up their work on site, utilising a tent as a temporary studio. Board connections maximised resources, bringing materials and services to artists that they could otherwise not muster, but these, too, spoke to what kind of art could be supported.

Yet the passionately emotional experiences of individual board members impressed me. They realised how seeing artists at work had a transformative power on the citizens who came to watch and on themselves. It was revelatory: the audience came to know through experience who artists are, why what they make matters, and how others contribute and play a part in the art process. So while Sculpture Chicago started with the double goal of helping artists make 'big work' and of making more visible locations seeking further development, the founders had discovered deeper meaning along the way.

When I returned to Chicago from Los Angeles in 1990, I listened to board members talk about what mattered to them – it was the process, it was the public's reactions. One example given was of a crane operator who had worked with an artist during the week. He came back on Sunday, his day off, to visit with his family, showing with pride what he had been a part of. Bingo! Why not do that? Keep the process and the public, and scrap the maquettes. This is what inspired and, at the same time, allowed 'Culture in Action' to happen.

—

'Culture' 'in Action'

In our initial grant applications I used the very mundane title 'New Urban Monuments' because I was confronting the practices of making public art in cities, asking what else could art be if it was about the public as well as about art. For me, getting to the answer always begins with sharing questions with artists, and 'Culture in Action' started with a morass of questions about art in public space.

During Daniel J. Martinez's first visit, a lecture was spontaneously organised by the Mexican Fine Arts Center Museum (now the National Museum of Mexican Art) to take advantage of his presence in the city. It took place one evening in the backroom of a turn-of-the-century bar in Pilsen, the neighbourhood where the museum is located – itself a start-up organisation of activist teachers who wanted to change their community. I was there, and Daniel got his steam up talking about what was at stake in America at that time, about why making art mattered and why society needs artists. He said 'this is culture in action', and in an instant I knew that was our title because Daniel was talking about art as a living thing.

This was the period of the so-called 'culture wars' around NEA's funding of artists. As the right was closing down on the freedom of artistic expression, people were demanding cultural change under the banner of 'multiculturalism', the word of the moment. This dichotomy was not coincidental: the former was motivated by fear and control, the latter by civil rights and democracy. The dynamism of the time was provoked by a need to change systems within society, and contemporary artists had a lot to say about their freedom and that of others.

So 'culture' was very much a word in practice at that time. It referred to people, and where they came from and their heritage, and art was an aspect of that. 'In action' meant being alive and having the right to participate in what affects your own life. When I was at MoCA in Los Angeles – a vast, multicultural metropolis – the museum wouldn't address that subject. I could have never shown Martinez, who lives there. But here in the backroom of this bar, as he has said, 'we believed we were winning the culture wars'.

—

Naming Artists' Practices with Audiences

Respecting the audience in the early 1990s meant valuing civil rights. I think that is probably always the case, but it felt urgent then. But respecting also meant not seeing those without art degrees as deficient, not deeming those without high art refinement as lacking culture. But it felt to me like the art field was all about who is in and who is out of art. It was not just an issue of representation (whose story is told), of location (outdoors instead of inside the museum) and more. I wanted to change the way we looked at who experiences art and to shift the demographic that equates the quality or depth of experience with an individual's educational, class or financial status.[5] So it was not just about the public being the subject or getting to do something in public. It was sharing concerns and people getting to know each other, deeply. The artists had face-to-face encounters with people who would otherwise have been invisible to the art world. This shared process I often cited as shared authorship, but over the years that became bogged down in art theory debates about who determined what in a project, who was in control and who made what. Sharing isn't about equal parts of the pie. Maybe 'being together' says it better. It was about coming to an understanding, but I do not think the art field understands that process very well. These works were not about doing social work but about co-generating ideas, having a genuine exchange, having insights together and, yes, coming to

—

[5] See M.J. Jacob, 'An Unfashionable Audience', in Suzanne Lacy (ed.), *Mapping the Terrain: New Genre Public Art,* Seattle: Bay Press, 1995, pp.50–59.

common understandings. So I would say it was about putting the audience – an uncommon audience – into the equation. That was crucial.

Back then I felt that in order to rethink audience we needed to take a leap in practice that might at some point have an effect on the public art system. This meant taking the institution out of the equation. Sculpture Chicago was in many ways a non-institutional frame: it was not a major player in the city, it was not a museum. Because 'Culture in Action' was something different from what that organisation had ever done, it meant creating new systems of working, bending the institution for the programme and for artists' needs. And because I raised nearly all the cash, the artists and I had a good deal of autonomy to use this as a laboratory.

'Culture in Action' was a declaration that there could be an alternative to big sculpture in finding a way to realise public investment in contemporary art. So it also offered other institutions a way to think about what they were doing and how they were delivering art to people. This was the reason we received a Challenge Grant from the NEA that provided nearly a third of our funding. NEA programme officers were also questioning whether there could be another way. In making art that involved temporary, ephemeral actions or built works that were only there for a time, we gained a good deal of freedom that public art commissioning couldn't garner – and this was at a time when the culture wars were seeking to shut down all federal arts spending.

Not having a name for this practice also allowed for experimentation. For years after, in conversation, I'd refer to 'culture-in-action-type projects'. Michael Brenson has said that he felt at that time an openness among people who wanted to engage, though they were exposed to something for which there was no language. He recalls that you had to *be* with the work, not because it didn't exist but because you had to let it reveal itself. It was raw, not institutional language. The term 'socially engaged art' came later. As we have seen, many other names were posited, too. While the term 'community art' brought with it associations far from the world of progressive contemporary art world, the artists in 'Culture in Action' were profoundly aware they were working with existing communities, originating another community for a time around a project. There was a consciousness, too, that everyone belongs to multiple communities, and these projects collectively transgressed community lines, bringing different constituencies of the city into some kind of recognition of or exchange with each other.

Today there is an acceptance that art can place the audience at the forefront. But artists who crossed that threshold two decades ago were agitatedly, even aggressively challenged. Some thought artists had no skill and no right to work in this way, and therefore were exploiting others for their own gain. Or they thought that the work they made *with* the public was not art. Successive generations stand on firmer ground and the explosion of practices is great. Still the fear of instrumentalising art remains. We found art could have meaning for others and could matter when they and the artist shared values, caring about the same things and about the promise of a democratic society.

We look back now at these ways of working as 'site specific', 'community based' or 'socially engaged art practice', but for me it wasn't about naming a movement. It was a necessary opening up of who could be the audience for contemporary art, a rethinking of the relationship of art to place and people.
—

Project, Programme or Exhibition
I came to use the term 'project' to refer to the artists' works, and 'programme' for the group of projects. Because the programme went on over years, it is hard to apply to it the term 'exhibition'. I guess I would say now that 'exhibition' was more a rhetorical device, a discourse I was having with myself and others in the field about what curators can do and how they can work outside museums. To me, all the components within and across projects – every forum, symposium, event and action that constituted each project and made up the overall programme – were part of the curatorial work.

At the same time, we were also trying to enact change on a national scale in regard to public art, though not by promoting a policy. It was about asking questions of the public art practice and sharing the thinking-and-doing process with others in the field. So we had a number of discussion sessions at different junctures that included those Chicagoans working with 'Culture in Action' artists on projects along with outside practitioners, critics and leaders in the art field. These think tanks helped the artists and myself think about what we were doing and what could be the cultural power of art and power of people in communities.

So was all this an exhibition? I find it unfortunate that when an exhibition includes a totality of thinking, making and experiencing, parts get labelled 'paracuratorial'. If I had to slice all of what happened in 'Culture in Action' between the curatorial and the paracuratorial, I would be cutting up a process that was organic and continuous. I think everything was fundamentally curatorial. I do not subscribe to a hierarchy by which the exhibition is at the apex; rather, the show might be a step in a process on the way to something else, even if that thing wasn't imagined at the outset. To me, the creative, generative, discursive, 'exhibit-able' and experiential are all part of what an exhibition affords. With 'Culture in Action', I worked from the belief that the exhibition was a format that could be expanded, adapted, even transformed, to follow what artists do, and to enable them further. The projects of 'Culture in Action' were not the first of their kind, to be sure, but practices of their kind were given a boost by having a frame placed around them. That frame was the exhibition.

The four months in the summer of 1993 when the show was 'on view' was just one period of the exhibition – one frame to present things to an audience made up of populations that had not been part of the process over the previous two years. Bus tours took place during this period. They offered a moment in the life of the projects and we tried to convey that what you were seeing that day at that location would, to some degree, be different tomorrow. They also were a way to see life in Chicago – not as a tourist attraction, or voyeuristic view into people's private lives but as continuous with the artists' work. At each location the audience got out and talked with people who made themselves available to share the projects and why they were important to them, what mattered to them and what needed to change in their situation to make things better. Then at the last stop, the Haha garden *Flood*, everyone had lunch together with those at the site, to talk about the overall experience. You had to want to go on a journey, it wasn't a quick look. It took five-and-a-half hours, but for some it had its rewards. fig.27–36

Still, the projects were not over at that point, after those four months. The book was published two years later, in 1995. And some projects lived on longer, some are still going. Street-Level Youth Media, the organisation that emerged from Iñigo Manglano-Ovalle's *Tele-Vecindario* project, had its twentieth anniversary recently and continues as a strong community organisation today. fig.45–56

—

A Learning Process
When you work with other people, the end result cannot be predetermined. You can't have a set plan and just implement it. You don't know what will emerge that can be an opportunity and direct the next move. You never know how things will turn out, not fully, and you never know what something might come to mean or do over time. You have to be open.

I had to keep the process open. The discussion with the board of Sculpture Chicago was a long conversation, but a real one. After the first encounter in January 1990, we met over and over for a year and a half – but we got there. This was before I invited a single artist. And all this time, I was also curating 'Places with a Past' in Charleston, South Carolina, which became a great learning process. We also got to know each other by working together on a temporary project, taking on an unexpected opportunity for which I brought in Ronald Jones – an artist I was working with in Charleston – to work with the City Park District. The result was an amazing park that became our home base for 'Culture in Action' in many ways. But as a process of planning, negotiation and implementation, it was also a great chance for the board and I to learn how to work together. p.*173*

But there was something else, something we all cared about that kept us together: the value of audiences' experiences. 'Why art matters to the everyday life of Chicago' became our meeting place. There was always the possibility, I said to them, that there might be no *artwork* to look at, but there would be artists working in the city's communities and that would matter just the same, maybe more. The board's decision to move ahead into the unknown, to let something happen not knowing what it was going to be, was a brave one, but the only possible one if we were really going to try something new. This was not just to be different, and certainly not because we were appealing to what others wanted to fund; it was because we were struggling together with questions around what art could do in public space.

For funders, the lack of demonstrable outcomes was problematic – so I made up plausible outcomes when I needed to in order to get the grant written and get the money to move ahead. Funders do not value organic, responsive, evolutionary processes. They fund according to articulated plans for implementation, an organisational strategy with clearly defined goals. So sometimes we didn't get a grant; at others a programme officer would find a way to take a risk, even feel inspired. In the case of the Rockefeller Foundation, I remember the revelation of its representative who came to actually experience the projects. Sitting next to me on the bus on the way back from the Haha garden, that programme officer said: 'I get it. It's bottom up, not top down.' Later that decade the Rockefeller Foundation launched the PACT grants: Partnerships Affirming Community Transformation.

Organic process is the process of life. I continually felt informed by the life of the city as it moved in and out of the foreground of the projects and the programme. There were steps in the process, but they are not so linear: sometimes you go backwards to go forward. No doubt, it was a messy, demanding process. I can't say we were always clear or made the best or smoothest moves at each point in the process. The long process that constituted 'Culture in Action' was a lived experience led by ideas and intuitions, and guided by listening.

There was a lot of listening *to* the process of being in dialogue with others with whom we share this city. In reflection and through my subsequent work, particularly in the early 2000s on the art experience and Buddhism,[6] I came to understand how process unfolds and how curating can be a mindful practice of caring for process.[7] This means keeping the aim of the programme in mind and clarifying that aim as you go along.

What the artists in 'Culture in Action' did changed over time as we met logistical obstacles and as ideas evolved. Lots of changes occurred, and at their best they were steered by a common aim: to see if public art could be more inclusive. We challenged each other on that score. In the end, the goal or outcome was dependent on that process, and also on multiple protagonists: as a curator I didn't hold all the cards. I am certain it was important to leave the process open. For instance, if we had started Iñigo Manglano-Ovalle's
fig.45–56 *Tele-Vecindario* with the goal of creating a permanent youth organisation, Street-Level Youth Media might well have never come about. In my experience you can work more fluidly by undertaking a project than launching an organisation. Without the creative space afforded by this project, what people cared about would not have emerged so palpably.

—

[6] At the core of this programme was an extended think tank among fifty museum professionals called 'Awake: Art, Buddhism and the Dimensions of Consciousness' (2001–03) which led to related projects at the participants' institutions and to a publication edited with my co-organiser Jacquelynn Baas. See J. Baas and M.J. Jacob (ed.), *Buddha Mind in Contemporary Art*, Berkeley: University of California Press, 2004.

[7] See M.J. Jacob, 'In the Space of Art', in *ibid.*, pp.164–69.

It had to be a co-learning process. In this case, after high school students, a social worker and Community TV Network (CTVN) employees had worked together, they did not want to go back to the way it was before, but to go on together. It was because of their determination that Street-Level Youth Media was founded – a reason and meaning arose for this new organisation.

Organic processes are the way we grow and learn. In the learning process that was 'Culture in Action' we were learning how to think and act more deeply through art about the values we cared about. We were not learning how to make a certain kind of art, how to develop what would later be called 'best practices' or how to teach how to do this work. Being in this process, I learned a lot. Most of all I learned to believe in art again, having lost hope working in museums. As life in Chicago fed the process of the programme, culture in action seemed to be everywhere, permeate everything. I felt we were touching something so essential, beyond art. Or maybe art was everywhere, everything. Maybe this is really the point: if you see the city consciously, as we do in seeing art, you can be the agent in your life, an agent for change. You don't have to be an artist – but it can help.

Mark Dion in correspondence with Stephanie Smith, May–July 2013

fig.1–13 *Stephanie Smith*: What were your initial hopes for the Chicago Urban Ecology Action Group [CUEAG]? What did you want to accomplish with the project – for yourself, for the student collaborators, for the Chicago audience – as a contribution to larger conversations about art, ecology and education?

Mark Dion: Although I was still a young artist when I conceptualised my participation in 'Culture in Action', I had already been working around issues in ecology for five or six years. At that time, when one surveyed the landscape of ecological and environmental news, there were remarkably few positive stories. Tales of biodiversity loss, habitat degradation and environmental racism were numerous. The many examples of human interaction with the environment that were based on destruction and corruption were utterly demoralising. Much of my early work was based on a drive to highlight these issues; it was very information based.

In this project, however, I wanted to get my hands dirty, to actually help sculpt a model for a positive relationship between individuals and the natural world. Working with the fellows in the project was great because they embodied this positive spirit. They were optimistic, intelligent, diligent, open and hopeful – all the qualities necessary to manifest a model contrary to dominant relations to nature. So that was my goal: to demonstrate that all human relations to the environment need not be based on spoliation, greed and waste: education, restoration and stewardship are also possible. I know it sounds rather grand, but I was young and aiming high.

SS: How did those goals play out in the actual experience of the project?

MD: For myself, the student participants, the organisations we worked with and Sculpture Chicago, I think the goals were indeed achieved. For instance, the environmental literacy of the group was significantly elevated. It certainly was for me. We also provided real help to organisations, as a small volunteer army working on projects like beach clean-up, prairie restoration
fig.6–13 and community-garden initiatives. Through activities at the CUEAG Headquarters in Lincoln Park, where we established a field station, we also built strong connections with many of those members of the public who chose to participate. However, in terms of providing a larger model for environmental action for either the art world or the ecology community, I cannot say we had tremendous impact.

That said, I do feel that many challenges raised by the exhibition in general have echoed significantly in the way art is practiced today. The fact that not a month goes by in which an art historian or critic does not write to me to obtain images or information related to 'Culture in Action' speaks to its lasting relevance.

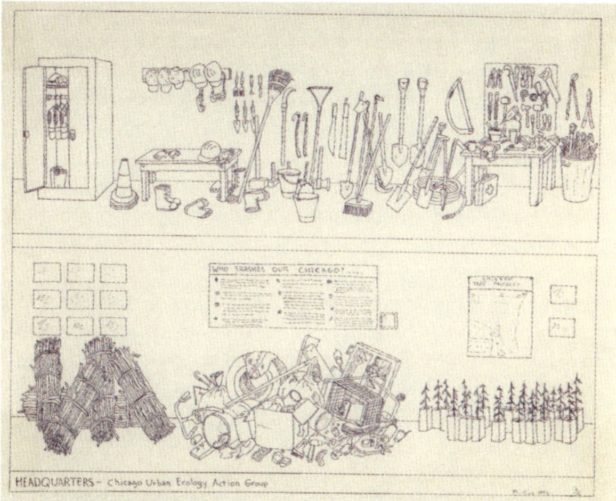

Mark Dion, *Headquarters – Chicago Urban Ecology Action Group*, 1993
Blueprint, 44.5 x 59.7cm (unframed), edition of 15
Photography: Jean Vong
Courtesy the artist and Tanya Bonakdar Gallery, New York

SS: Let's return later to that issue of the 'echo' in current practice. How did you see your project fitting within the larger frame of 'Culture in Action'? What interested you about Mary Jane Jacob's conceptual framing, her process, her approach to working with artists and within the city?

MD: Mary Jane wanted nothing less than to redefine what 'public art' meant. This was a full-frontal assault on corporate plop sculpture and other forms of public art that considered context and audience to be irrelevant. If that is your war, I say sign me up. This was perhaps the only moment in my life when I felt the excitement of an avant-gardist. It felt like something very important, like a paradigm-shifting project. Perhaps it was, but more likely it was a paradigm-splintering event. The exhibition was perhaps the first in the US to articulate a model of socially engaged public art, and thus provide for artists another arena to work in, beyond the gallery, alternative space, museum and classroom. This was not dissimilar to European models like documenta in Kassel, Sonsbeek in Arnhem and Sculptur Projekte Münster, but we really had nothing quite like that here, beyond what Mary Jane had done in Charleston.[1] It resonated as a template with other curators p.*15* and artists. I recall speaking with Anne Pasternak, Tom Finkelpearl and Lisa Corrin in great detail about the exhibition and its methodology.

SS: I want to push back a bit at the idea that 'Culture in Action' served as a primary lever to open socially engaged public practice as a viable alternative arena for artists. Maybe I'm misunderstanding what you're saying here? While Mary Jane certainly led the curatorial field in terms of making such a rich, huge exhibition focused on socially engaged

—

[1] 'Places with a Past: New Site-Specific Art at Charleston's Spoleto Festival', Charleston, South Carolina, 24 May to 4 August 1991, curated by Mary Jane Jacob.

public art, she was following the lead of artists. She took inspiration from artists like you who were developing new forms of process- and community-based art. She also drew on a long history of artist-led socially engaged public art – people like Suzanne Lacy who made complex projects without waiting for support or permission from institutions or even from independent curators. But all that said, Mary Jane certainly opened up possibilities for new ways of thinking about how curators and traditional organisations could support public and community-based projects.

MD: Mary Jane did not pull these ideas out of a hat. When you look at the artists she selected, they obviously had already worked in this method for quite some time. However, she did give this approach to artistic endeavour a platform as an exhibition. This allowed the projects to be highlighted very differently; it allowed the strategies and methods to be understood with more intention and consistency. Thus, rather than merely feeling like individual eccentric expressions, the notion of artists working in a social context could be presented as a real option, a legitimate form, despite the radical divergence of approaches and aesthetic resolution. She obviously had learned from large-scale international European exhibitions, from her own experiences in Charleston and very much from the artists themselves, but she, Eva Olson and the team from Sculpture Chicago took on a remarkably bold context – the megalopolis of Chicago itself. This was not a small city like Charleston, Kassel or Münster, or an urban park like Sonsbeek. This was Chicago.

SS: Did you have any anxieties going into the process?

MD: Yes, I undoubtedly had some anxiety about the project since it was such a significant endeavour and I identified with its goals. The exhibition had a very public face; the artists were asked to speak and present often. This was a great deal of pressure, since we were all really experimenting. There was no guide or model for how to do this kind of project.

SS: The issue of the 'public face' of the project is a thorny one. It's always challenging to figure out how best to welcome the public into the nuance of complex, site-and process-based projects – and it was surely more so in the early 1990s. For instance, you've noted elsewhere that there was relatively low visitation to the CUEAG field station/clubhouse, and also that visitors didn't know how to engage with a participatory project.[2] Could you say more about your observations of how people did (and didn't) respond to the public phase of the project?

MD: The art audience can be pretty lazy, and we were undoubtedly off the beaten track. With the notable exceptions of Mitchell Kane, Mike Paha, Dan Peterman and Joe Scanlan, I really cannot recall many artists coming to

—

[2] See Claire Bishop, *Artificial Hells: Participatory Art and the Politics of Spectatorship*, London: Verso, 2012, pp.203–04.

the clubhouse over the course of the summer. Most of the art public came on the tours, which took place on Saturdays, which was also the day the team and I were in the field working on community-garden projects, prairie restoration or trash-clean-up projects. Lots of the general public would drop in without prior knowledge of the work, and they could engage with us or not, depending on what we happened to be doing. If we were making things like houses for birds or bats, that was fine. If we had a lecture or guest speaker, it could be awkward. In the end, there were people who came back often to check in, but we did not see many art students, art writers or artists walk in the door. Since the project took the structure of an inclusive clubhouse (a model I still use a great deal today), rather than an exhibition space or classroom, it manifested a kind of hybridity which made it tricky for people to just plug in if they happened to come by. It worked best when we invited people. fig.11–13

SS: Suzanne Lacy made a helpful diagram in her book *Mapping the Terrain: New Genre Public Art* [1995], which came out around the same time as the book *Culture in Action*.[3] It's basically a series of concentric circles in which Suzanne lays out different modes of involvement – from initiator to collaborator to immediate audience to 'audience of myth and memory'. Part of her point is that projects like yours have to be critically assessed in relation to those modes. If we use her framing, it seems that the project was successful for you and the core collaborators, and has had a strong ripple effect in the space of 'myth and memory', but that it didn't work as well for the immediate public audience. Is that fair?

MD: Well, I have not seen that diagram but that is pretty much how I understand audience. No doubt I picked up this model from Suzanne and did not realise it until just now. I am not sure I would say that it didn't work for the broader audience, since I think it did resonate for many of them who actually showed up. My complaint, which I blame no one but myself for, was that the audience was not larger. I just did not know how to increase the numbers visiting the clubhouse. This was my fault, since I did not put much energy into it. It was not my priority, but it affected the reception of the work. However, the result of low participation from both the art audience and the general public was an amazingly intimate and powerful experience for the students I worked with, my guest speakers and seminar leaders and the friends who hung out on site. That was the core audience and we got the most out of that experience. Did it change lives? I can say without a second of doubt that it did. I later employed a similar model for the project 'The Tate Thames Dig' [26 October 1999 – 26 February 2000]: we had a core

—

[3] There were many lines of connection between *Mapping the Terrain* and *Culture in Action*, and both books were published within a year of each other by Seattle's Bay Press, an important if short-lived channel for disseminating thinking about this kind of art in the US during the 1990s. For more on the former, including a reproduction of Lacy's diagram, see Stephanie Smith, 'Mapping the Terrain, Again', *Afterall*, issue 27, Summer 2007, pp.66–73.

group of participating fellows, who of course got the most out of the project; we had a camp-like club, which hosted experts and seminar leaders; we conducted fieldwork; and we welcomed the public to observe and participate.

SS: How and why do you think the level of audience comfort with this kind of process-based participatory project has changed in the twenty years since 'Culture in Action'? Where do you think we're heading, for better or worse?

MD: Well, now there is quite a template for how one can attract a broader audience, but there is also a huge community of social-practice artists who share concerns, success stories, strategies and methods. In terms of changes over time, I find this significant. I am impressed with conferences like Open Engagement in Portland and the Creative Time Summit in New York City, which bring together such a remarkably different group of artists who share aspects of a commitment to art as a sociopolitical practice. This is a big deal: perhaps the most significant, sustained and inclusive meetings of international practicing artists that have ever happened. For me events like these and the discussions they generate are the antidote to the spirit-crushing proliferation of art fairs.

SS: Yes, I agree about their importance, although I wonder also about over-institutionalisation and over-production – especially when increasing interest from funders, museums and higher education is fuelling not only great new work but also a proliferation of poorly developed, 'lite' socially engaged art.

MD: I think social-practice work often enters art institutions today through the back door of education departments. These departments are often more receptive to new forms, and more experimental, and since they avoid the scrutiny of conservative donors, they tend to be more critical. Unfortunately they are also resource starved, and this can hamper projects. Art that is socially engaged should not be judged by less rigorous criteria than other art forms. There is excellent, challenging and well-conceived work, and poorly crafted and uninspired work as well. Good intentions should not be confused with good scholarship or execution.

SS: Agreed. It's a good time to reflect on all of these issues. One thing that seems especially important right now is the level of thoughtful exchange across different cultures and geographies, which ups the ante for all of us. International networks weren't very developed in 1993, though, so let's shift the frame back to that era. You were also involved in another major experimental exhibition of that time: 'PROJECT UNITE' in Firminy's Unité d'habitation.[4] Could you describe how you interacted (or didn't) with the immediate audience there?

—

[4] 'PROJECT UNITE', Firminy, France, 1 June to 30 September 1993, curated by Yves Aupetitallot.

MD: The methodology for 'PROJECT UNITE' could not have been more different from 'Culture in Action'. The first time I visited the site, I was just dropped off on Friday in this empty apartment – not able to speak a word of French, not having had anything to eat and being told someone would come get me on Monday. I had virtually no introduction to the site and its community beyond my initial tour of the building. I can only guess the organisers were attempting to demonstrate the concept of alienation.

I never understood 'PROJECT UNITE' as a community-based social-art project. It was merely an art exhibition in a context that had very strong political and historical parameters. For a number of artists in the exhibition who had a particularly harsh appraisal of modernist architectural fantasies based on life experience (here I would include Fareed Armaly, Christian Philipp Müller, Stephan Dillemuth, Art Orienté Objet and myself), it offered a situation in which to articulate our profound distrust of the modernist legacy. Like any exhibition of commissioned projects, I judge it by the success of the work produced, and there were some extraordinarily intelligent, beautiful and insightful projects in the exhibition. If the organisers had been perceptive enough to make a book as articulate and precise as *Culture in Action*, I am certain this exhibition would be better regarded and understood today.

> *SS*: Claire Bishop has described the US context for these exhibitions as more theorised and politicised than the European one. What's your take on that?

MD: It is hard to understand today, when there has been such a proliferation of biennials and site-specific projects around the world, how little there was in 1993. So events like Sonsbeek, the Venice Biennale, Skulptur Projekte Münster and documenta were much more important. There was nothing really like these in the US. Certainly those exhibitions were more broadly curated than 'Culture in Action', but they often had very political components to them that were based more on individual artists than on wider tendencies.

I think 'Culture in Action' had a very specific agenda, which was a direct challenge to the notion of what 'public art' is. This was an attempt to create another model. Mary Jane chose artists who were politically engaged, were not afraid to be didactic in a Brechtian sense and believed that great art could be accessible to a broad public. Essential to this vision of public art was the notion that art-making is a political act that can make things better, that can actively participate in or motivate change. I would agree with Claire that this particular exhibition was much more focused in its agenda, more overtly political, more theorised and polemical. I really cannot think of another exhibition in the country that was quite like it in the clarity of its agenda; perhaps only the 'Times Square Show',[5] which was particularly local in its focus.

That the art world did not embrace the entire endeavour was no surprise. We provided a remarkably challenging project that pushed the discourse of how art can function in relation to place. And I don't think any of the artists cared remotely about the art world's indifference or hostility. We expected it. What boils my blood is that many of the staunchest critics did not actually see the exhibition; they simply did not like the idea of it. In the end, for me this was still an art exhibition, and my participation was an artwork; therefore it was significantly important that it be seen in order to be judged effectively.

> *SS*: Could you say a little more about the indifference you perceived in the art world? 'Culture in Action' got national and international reviews and soon appeared in critical writing like Grant Kester's 'Aesthetic Evangelists' piece for *Afterimage*.[6] But it also had a strong impact on some of us who were just starting to work as curators (again, 'the audience of myth and memory', I suppose). I was just starting out in Houston then, and the book *Culture in Action* was a real source of inspiration, along with then-new local initiatives like Project Row Houses. 'Culture in Action' – or at least what we could understand of it from the book – provided a powerful counterpoint to traditional ways of thinking about art, about exhibitions, about the multifaceted roles that art plays in society. I think that was true for many other young artists and curators. We weren't indifferent.

MD: Well, in terms of your first point, I hardly think an article in *Afterimage* two years after the fact counts as bringing the exhibition and its concerns to the forefront of the art world. The art world's reception was minor during the exhibition – even with *The New York Times* review it received, which was thoughtful but also highly sceptical.[7]

The book was the key. From the start, Mary Jane perceived this as an endeavour that would live and resonate through the publication. I am sure she understood this much better than most of the artists. The book disseminated the concerns and methodologies of the exhibition. It is why we are talking today. This is part of Mary Jane's genius, honed through her experience in Charleston and the extraordinary publication she made there. But the response to 'Culture in Action' in my home context of New York City, prior to the book, was insignificant. The art community in New York is deeply provincial, and the meaning of the exhibition took time to gestate. It was crushing for me at the time to feel that we'd had so little impact.

—

[5] 'Times Square Show', New York, June 1980, curated by artists' group Colab (Collaborative Projects).

[6] Grant H. Kester, 'Aesthetic Evangelists: Conversion and Empowerment in Contemporary Community Art', *Afterimage*, January 1995, pp.5–11.

[7] Michael Kimmelman, 'Of Candy Bars and Public Art', *The New York Times*, 26 September 1993, section 2 (Arts & Leisure), pp.1 and 43–44. Online at http://www.nytimes.com/1993/09/26/arts/art-view-of-candy-bars-and-public-art.html?pagewanted=all&src=pm (last accessed on 14 April 2014).

SS: In response to the initial invitation to be interviewed, you wrote: 'I believe that there was truly excellent work produced in these projects, although the period also represented the beginning of the end for certain relationships.' What did you mean by this?

MD: It was around that time that a group of artists who had been very close began to fall apart. There had been a certain nexus of artists and critics related to the New York, Cologne and Chicago communities, some of whom were in 'Culture in Action', Sonsbeek and 'PROJECT UNITE', and our friendships and relations began to irrevocably disintegrate around this time. I felt like I was part of a team early in 1993, and felt I was on my own by the year's end.

SS: So your team for 'Culture in Action' was very much your student participants. I'd like to discuss the clubhouse you established with CUEAG in Lincoln Park. Mary Jane was proposing a challenge to traditional ideas of public sculpture, so your whole process-based project was being framed in part as a sculptural gesture. Maybe we could think of the clubhouse as a physical sculpture that housed a social sculpture. You retrofitted an existing park building – the former base for a fishing group – into a space that served many practical and pedagogical aims. I'm sure the students were very involved in the decisions about how it should be set up. But as far as I can tell from the documentation, the space also feels very 'Dion': a product of your ongoing interests in the history of display and in the ways that natural history and science are performed and made visible. This aspect of the work has generally been overshadowed by the process-based aspects of the project, but I'm sure a great deal of care went into the way the space looked and performed.[8] Could you talk about the visual and material aesthetic of the clubhouse and how that fits into your work more broadly? fig.6–10

MD: In thinking about this project I learned a great deal from the model of Tim Rollins and K.O.S.,[9] since it was the most prominent example I had for an artist working with young collaborators. Of course, not a single one of my high school team members was interested in being an artist, which was a salient distinction. I had always been less interested in the individual expressions from K.O.S.; I was more interested in what was happening in the workshop. So in Chicago I wanted to foreground the process rather than

—

[8] See, for instance, Joe Scanlan's article in *frieze*, where he thoughtfully addresses the clubhouse's materiality along with the beauty of the project's 'indefiniteness, its constant activity and non-productiveness a parallel for his fascination with and scepticism of scientific method. The same might be said of Dion's approach to art as social betterment.' J. Scanlan, 'Culture in Action', *frieze*, issue 13, November – December 1993, p.24; and reproduced in this volume, p.164.

[9] Since the early 1980s, when he initiated the Art and Knowledge Workshop, Tim Rollins has collaborated with a group of students in the Bronx who called themselves Kids of Survival (K.O.S.).

the product. That meant getting a public into the space, and also getting the space to speak. What we were talking about was the culture of nature; that topic was the fulcrum of all our activity and discourse. Therefore the space had to address that idea as well. Since it had been established for a fly-fishing club, we had a head start, but we also embellished it with our tools, apparatus and decorations, referencing spaces where people gather to participate in and generate the culture of nature – lodges, museums, field stations, visitors' centres. The space had to construct the experience. It was not a site where one came to look at sculpture or painting, but rather to become immersed in our circle. We wanted no spectators, only participants; to see the piece, one had to become part of it.

> *SS*: You also made a print that suggests some ways of organising the clubhouse's interior. It's one of only a few traditional 'art objects' to remain from the project. We've talked about your complex relationship to drawing in the past: you came of age at a time when concept was valued over craft, so you were trained to ask critical questions rather than to draw. Yet you quickly made drawing a key part of your work. It's a creative act that helps you to hone ideas; it's a tool to visualise and communicate what the static part of a project might look like; and it generates objects – like this one – that serve both as subjective forms of project documentation and as commodities. Could you talk about this particular image – how it fit into your working process for 'Culture in Action', and how the prints circulated after the fact? Are there other drawings connected to the project?

MD: I made drawings, some of which I turned into blue prints. Drawing for me is a critical tool to help me understand a space and what needs to be done to it. The blue print-drawings embody my discomfort with producing lasting works that leave my hands and become commodities. This was something I struggled with as a young artist, so while the print exists as an artwork it is extremely photo fugitive. The more it is exposed to light, the more quickly it changes and disappears. I exhibited one example quite recently and it was amazing how dramatically it changed over a few months.

> *SS*: Looking back now, twenty years on, which aspects of CUEAG and of your experiences with 'Culture in Action' have remained most relevant for your work?

MD: I took away a deeper understanding of the complexities of collaboration; of the importance of challenging models of pedagogy; and of the critical role a tangible art object can have as an ambassador for a complex, time-based project. For me and, I imagine, some of the other artists involved, this was an incredibly experimental project. I was not focused on other models of how to do this; I was attempting new things all the time. I really mean every day! Taking seventeen-year-olds – fourteen girls and one boy – to the central American jungle for two weeks... what was I thinking? This was the crucible for me as an artist, an environmentalist, a teacher and an orchestrator of complex collaborative projects. After the exhibition I was quite gun-shy about engaging with projects that had such a strong component of working closely with student collaborators. I really loved those kids I worked with and it broke my heart when I left Chicago, although I stayed in touch with some, and still have a wonderful relationship with at least one of them. But the depth of that engagement was something I have learned to manage. I ration my relation to such all-consuming projects. Their intensity is what makes them unforgettable, but also impossible to repeat. This project held seeds that germinated in my teaching methodology, my relationships with collaborators and finally with Mildred's Lane.[10]

—

[10] Mildred's Lane is a collaborative artist residency and think-tank project co-directed by Mark Dion and J. Morgan Puett, described online as 'a home and an experiment in living'. See http://mildredslane.com (last accessed on 14 April 2014).

Simon Grennan, of Grennan & Sperandio, in conversation with Lucy Steeds, September 2013

Lucy Steeds: Christopher Sperandio and yourself were the youngest artists invited to participate in 'Culture in Action', not long after your MA-degree show in Chicago.[1] Your current website characterises your ongoing joint practice with Sperandio in a way that chimes well with your contribution to 'Culture in Action'.[2] What did you learn from taking part in the exhibition?

Simon Grennan: One of the key things that we learned, given our lack of experience, even naïvety, at the time was the enormous difficulty that organisations like Sculpture Chicago or individual curators have in corporate and public environments. We considered 'Culture in Action' to be a big project, important and wealthy, but in fact it was hardly on the radar of anybody who was really affecting change. Mary Jane [Jacob]'s was a great achievement. Just managing to get to the position where she could curate an exhibition like that for Sculpture Chicago, and then, in doing it, changing its ethos and direction, putting down a marker in the field – she was at the top of the heap. And we were lower down, being artists. But then we saw that above her there was another set of horizons that were utterly unreachable – social and financial horizons – and from that perspective curating the exhibition was like running a local church fete.

LS: That sounds like a pretty grim realisation.

SG: No, not at all! We gained a fortuitous sense of perspective. It meant that we were able to locate our relationship to power. So the world got bigger for us – the horizon expanded. We were kids recently out of art school, and there were many places we'd never been, things we'd never seen, people we'd never met. We had to move from thinking that Mary Jane was God to understanding that of course she wasn't. And that happened very quickly. Mary Jane obviously understood, fundamentally and profoundly, how things worked, because otherwise she wouldn't have been able to do the show at all. So it was a great, expansive kind of experience – simply by doing the work with her, and with Sculpture Chicago.

—

[1] Simon Grennan and Christopher Sperandio graduated from the art department of the University of Illinois at Chicago in 1990. Grennan had moved to the US from the UK in order to take up his place at UIC in 1998.

[2] 'Two things remain constant in their practice: they always work together and their work invariably involves the authorial or editorial participation of other people – other members of the public. Their work often utilises media that are culturally compromised: chocolate, comic books and television, appearing at social sites of consumption in the home and store and on the street.' See http://www.kartoonkings.com (last accessed on 14 April 2014).

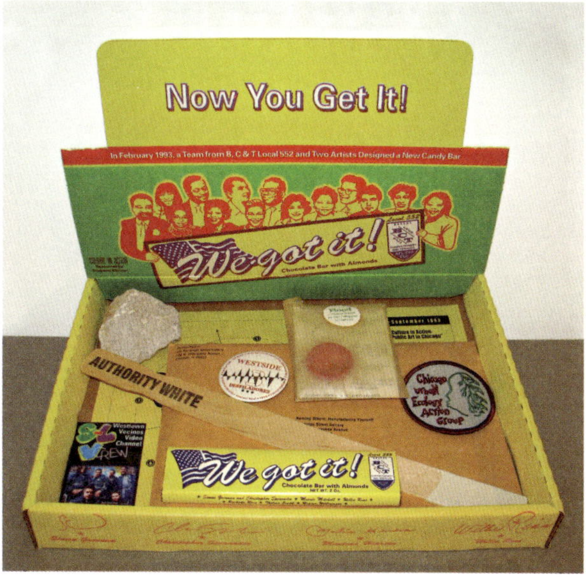

'Culture in Action' souvenir box of multiples and inserts. *We Got It!* box containing *We Got It!* candy bar, CUEAG badge, small rock from Wapanucka Oolitic Limestone Quarry, West Side Three-Point Marchers badge, *Eminent Domain* 'Authority White' paint stick, *Flood* condom with instructions and horticultural information, Street-Level Video press card and Robert Peters's survey booklet with 'multicultural crayons'. The box was assembled by Sculpture Chicago staff in an edition of 100–200 with objects identified and supplied by each artist, placed in the Grennan & Sperandio display box and distributed as a gift to artists, key collaborators, donors and board members. Commemorative watches were also produced and given to a wider circle of collaborators, volunteers and press.

LS: Before we come to your work for 'Culture in Action', can you tell me a bit about the Randolph Street Gallery? I know Robert Peters did an event there as part of his contribution to the show,[3] but the place seems to have a broader significance and I gather you showed work there while still a student.

SG: So, Maureen Sherlock [a visiting lecturer at the University of Illinois at Chicago] sometimes used to write and curate for Peter Taub, who co-directed Randolph Street Gallery, and she put me in a show there. There was a proliferation of not-for-profit galleries in Chicago at that time. Randolph Street was a kind of interventionist not-for-profit space, and was getting involved in all sorts of agitprop and community work. They also had a profound connection with the Chicago Imagist tradition. Do you know about that? Blue-collar, working-class visionary painting, which is fundamentally connected with vernacular painting from Puerto Rico and Mexico. You don't need a 'Culture in Action' in that kind of context, where people are already making and exhibiting their artwork! At Randolph Street Gallery there was a very keen awareness of that.

LS: It's interesting that 'Culture in Action' emerged in this context. It sounds a supportive and exciting situation for the project.

—

[3] See the description of Peters's contribution to the exhibition in this volume, pp.148–57, for further details.

SG: It certainly was, but in a sense I think Peter was critical of 'Culture in Action' – because he, Randolph Street Gallery and all the other folks were doing it already.

fig.17–26

LS: The participants listed for your 'Culture in Action' project in the exhibition literature are the twelve production-line workers who got a week's 'art leave' from a Nestlé factory in Chicago in order to work together with you to design a new chocolate bar and plan its advertising. Actually, I think they're all also named on the bars themselves. Jethro Head, the local union president, was a key figure too, as I understand it, and also Charles E. Brashears, the factory manager, but these individuals are not listed in the same way.

SG: Jethro purposefully didn't join the crew and Brashears wasn't invited. And, well, where does the list of participants end? There are lots of folks who were involved in the whole thing at various levels of participation, who impacted crucially, vitally.

LS: Maybe it fetishises the factory worker to only list them as your participants – is that a problem?

SG: You could choose to see it as a problem. But they were the ones that came up with the sort of bar that got made and with the wrapper and billboard design.

fig.19–21

LS: I wanted to ask you about the visual design. The bold lettering, blocks of bright colours and bold diagonal – did you relate to Constructivist graphics in any way?

SG: No! There has been some subsequent discussion of the aesthetics, but at the time we had a person-in-the-street approach to design.

LS: Joshua Decter has suggested the design anticipates your later work with Sperandio, on the visual languages of cartoons. I know your doctoral thesis, which is relatively recent, focused on the making of meaning in comic strips. But thinking as and for the person-in-the-street could also describe the work of the Constructivists, with their ambition to mass appeal.

SG: You're talking about audience, while I'm thinking about production. Our design work was do-it-yourself. We didn't know what we were doing and it was pretty freewheeling, reckless and unskilled. There was a kind of punk aesthetic. Chris and I had instructions from the crew on how to design the wrapper – what they wanted – and so we folded that in, without drawing on any design training or particular expertise.

LS: What were the design priorities that emerged from the crew?

SG: Well, there was unanimous agreement, which is interesting as they were quite a heterogeneous group. But their aesthetic concerns – the things they liked visually – were quite homogenous. For instance, there was a moment when a woman on the team, or rather what she was wearing, suddenly became the focus: Barbara's blouse-and-skirt combo of dark purple and yellow was much admired, and the fundamental colour combination of the chocolate wrapper was decided on the basis of everyone liking that. It was pretty unreflective.

LS: They were your focus group – or their own…

SG: Yes, the idea was that because they liked it, the people who they wanted the bars to reach would like it too.

LS: Tell me about the design of the chocolate bar itself, inside the wrapper.

SG: Well, the group wanted a cream-filled bar in an unusual shape, but that proved technically unfeasible. Instead they just set the levels of sugar and cocoa and added almonds.

LS: As well as being sold in shops in Chicago, the bars were handed out to all the factory workers – and there are pictures of Jethro Head doing this himself. fig.26

SG: Yes. He created a real buzz about 'the worker bar', 'the line-worker chocolate'. He had a much deeper understanding of what we were doing than we did. When you talk about the local union president and the local factory manager – local here doesn't mean small. Outside the art milieu, Brashears was a much more powerful figure than Mary Jane, and he had access to and was involved in negotiations with people who were affecting a global social situation. Our whole project was strategy for him, and it was strategy that almost got out of hand, because there was push and pull with Jethro, who was also strategising. One was a very experienced plant manager, and the other was a very experienced union boss – and both were extraordinarily helpful, while furthering their causes. The chocolate bar was kind of neutral ground for them to manoeuvre in. Jethro was working on some key issues in the factory, and our project allowed him to press those.[4]

LS: I was going to ask you if you had doubts about having instrumentalised the factory workers for the sake of your project, your practice, but now I want to ask if we could say Head instrumentalised you and your project.

—

[4] For instance, it allowed Jethro Head to test a recent initiative by the employers, Nestlé: their 'Total Quality Management' programme was claiming to increase worker participation in decision-making but was perceived as a move to limit union activity.

SG: Well, it depends on what social model you follow. The idea of instrumentalisation assumes there's an exploitative relationship, one way or another, and that's not necessarily accurate. I tried to explore this in reference to a broader practice, beyond our own, in a recent essay, following the writing of Erving Goffman.[5] I think it's more productive to look at the situation in terms of people having expertise in leading their own lives, or in being themselves, becoming themselves as subjects, by performing their expertise. Goffman talks about the self as having public and private aspects, and he does this kind of loose and reckless thing, which I think is fabulous, where he applies a theatre rationale, discussing onstage and offstage development of subjectivity. The members of the team that we worked with in Chicago had their own expertise, and then their experiences on the project along with all their other experiences developed that. There was a kind of selfishness in what Chris and I were doing as well: we were just interested in seeing what would happen if we inserted ourselves into a new environment, into other people's lives. You know, I'd never been in a chocolate-bar factory in my life – entering into this project, for us, was about developing our performed expertise.

LS: Is there a question then about responsibility – or irresponsibility – aside from instrumentalisation?

SG: I don't know if we acted irresponsibly because there wasn't much at stake – I mean that's what we quickly learnt, as I've said. If a church fete goes wrong, there's a bit of embarrassment, but nobody's lost their actual job. Nobody was really in control anyway. And it was all framed in such a way that at any point those involved could walk away. There's a way in which our work, and it's continued like this, is a kind of entertainment. Often for us, and definitely for others, it falls into a kind of leisure activity.

LS: Isn't that instinct partly what allowed the Labour government in the UK in the 1990s to impose on funded art an agenda of social inclusion?

SG: Well, whether the government wants it to or not, it doesn't work like that. Cultural participation as social palliative is fiction. Nothing gets achieved that way. Every report I've read about public art work is fictional: this impacted those people in that way to make them feel better about themselves; because they worked with so and so, they've had an opportunity that they wouldn't otherwise have had. Actually, no, not really. The plan for employing culture to produce social change in a way that could be termed instrumentalisation – it doesn't work.

LS: I'm interested that you've turned to Goffmann, a sociologist. You've said before that Maureen Sherlock's teaching was important for

—

[5] See Simon Grennan, 'Competence in Your Own Enactment: Subjectivity and the Theorization of Participatory Art', in Julia Round and Bronwen Thomas (ed.), *Real Lives, Celebrity Stories: Narratives of Ordinary and Extraordinary People Across Media,* London: Bloomsbury, 2014, pp.79–93.

you, and that this took a sociological approach to discussion of art and especially film. Wasn't it she who asked testing questions such as 'Why are there no black people in your class?'

SG: Yes, that was Maureen. I came to Goffmann through social anthropology. We were introduced very early to Pierre Bourdieu – and one of the problems with Bourdieu, when you are a twenty-year-old, is learning that things that appear natural, inevitable to you at that age, are actually the product of some kind of ideology. Loïc Wacquant, Bourdieu's star pupil, was also in Chicago at that time. He was working on this project, on the South Side of Chicago, to undertake a social anthropology of boxing, and he'd joined a boxing gym. It's like, I could have passed him in the street! So this is an occasional but connected chain of stuff in our thinking, which has always had a kind of neo-Marxist sociology slant.

LS: And the work you produce is a working-through of some of that in an untheorised way?

SG: Yes, absolutely. It's just a part of the environment in which we start to think things up. But it's only a part, so the theory is not an engine for us at all.

LS: And when other people theorise your work?

SG: I suppose there is a proprietorial sense that we have in our work, which is partly professional and partly personal. We have a sense of ownership of it, with everything that might imply – good and bad. And so when somebody says something about it that we think is wrong, it irritates us.

LS: And that didn't come with Nicolas Bourriaud and relational aesthetics at the time? I'm thinking of the exhibition he curated, 'Traffic',[6] which you and Sperandio were in, and about its catalogue, where he writes about relationality.

SG: Bourriaud was cack-handed, but he wasn't wrong. It's different with Claire Bishop['s recent critique].[7] What she's saying is reactionary – she wants to revert to a safe critical and art-historical distance that's just not tenable. She argues that the experience of a participant-viewer is theoretically beyond the discourse of the artwork, other than as a distinct situation in which, alone, a view can be taken. Her argument is very self-consciously presented as something that nobody else will say for professional reasons – but she's not contributing to the debate, she's hauling herself up the ladder. Actually, I've never made so much of an effort to work through our position before, explicitly – or to verbalise it. It's interesting, because what motivated me to work through it in more detail was that book getting my goat. Er, thank you, Claire!

—

[6] 'Traffic', 26 January to 24 March 1996, CAPC musée d'art contemporain Bordeaux.
[7] See Claire Bishop, *Artificial Hells: Participatory Art and the Politics of Spectatorship*, London: Verso, 2012.

LS: Claire Bishop has clashed with Liam Gillick in print on the subject of relational aesthetics,[8] and I just went back to his comments on 'Traffic', because he was also in that show. I was interested in the way he clearly felt keenly at the time that it was being misunderstood. He seems to have worried that Bourriaud was being made into an artist-curator and that, while he wasn't necessarily claiming that, he was colluding with it.

SG: Absolutely. I think all of that makes some kind of sense. There's also the idea that Nicolas didn't actually know what we were doing at all. That he was on the edge of understanding his own sense of where this was going. And therefore there was an enormous amount of speculation in the show. It wasn't a consolidation of something, but then it gets crystallised and suddenly it becomes a kind of mantra, and then a brand, and then you're done and on to the next thing.

LS: I've led us away from 'Culture in Action', a speculative show in a different sense, and one that didn't attempt to nail a label to the practices it grouped.

SG: There were different problems. Of course 'Culture in Action' had to be a show, but how do you take something that really shouldn't be, or couldn't be, or won't be a show and turn it into a show? It's an impossible thing to resolve. Without exception, everyone I met who visited had their expectations confounded; they got frustrated – they'd come to see an opera, and there was no one up on stage! And Mary Jane and her team were working furiously to try and get something into view for people. In any normal sense, 'Culture in Action' was a terrible exhibition!

LS: For me she was rethinking what an exhibition might be – but it seems that wasn't conveyed. Perhaps it could have been positioned more explicitly as an attempt in that direction, asking for more critical generosity?

SG: Yes! And no. I mean, she didn't know how to do it, because it'd never been done. And the problems that we threw up had to be dealt with – practically, quickly. Even though there seemed to be an enormous amount of money, she couldn't have been pre-prepared. Nobody could.

LS: I'm interested about your relationships with other artists in the show. If you'd all been installing in a gallery, with individuals or groups all there together, side-by-side, I guess there'd have been a chance to share tools, tips, drinks or whatever – but that doesn't necessarily happen in the situation for 'Culture In Action'.

SG: Absolutely. Essentially, Sculpture Chicago was running the projects separately. So you'd overlap with folks, and people would be brought

—

[8] See Liam Gillick, 'Contingent Factors: A Response to Claire Bishop's "Antagonism and Relational Aesthetics"', *October*, no.115, Winter 2006, pp.95–107.

together at certain points, but actually, because of the logistical complexity of the whole thing, there were folks you wouldn't see for three, four, six months – even while we were all working at the same time.

LS: You were brought together for public presentations, I think?

SG: There were various meetings we had, where people were drawn together. But because a lot of the artists weren't in town, that was difficult. Practically difficult. But we knew Haha, because they were 'local artists', like us.

LS: And Iñigo Manglano-Ovalle, too. In fact, together with Richard House, from Haha, you were the international artists. Otherwise this was quite narrowly a show of US artists.

SG: Of course I wasn't really local at all – I'd actually left Chicago by the time we were invited to take part in the show. But I did know about Haha. We knew who they were and what they were doing. We'd scrutinised them closely when we were students – it was quite a competitive environment!

LS: You shared a common core of influences, I think, and a context of institutional critique?

SG: Absolutely. But I think they thought we were just rubbish! Or, to put it another way, we thought that they were stuck-up. We were at the state university and they were at the Art Institute [of Chicago]. And we were quite critical of their work, because we thought it sometimes did one of the things that Bishop says this kind of work can do, which is use people as raw material. And also, you know, they were trendy, they were – now I'm going to quote Shakespeare, and I don't usually do this – the 'curled darlings of our nation'. They were middle-class folks, properly into their idea of community, and we were knock-about, sharky, low and rough. So we didn't like them. And they didn't like us [laughs].

LS: What about other artists in the show?

SG: We had a kind of respect for Daniel Martinez, because his attitude was 'I don't care where I am, I am the community, now give me the money'. He was very straightforward that way, so we thought, 'Bloody hell, that's cool.' And we had fruitful exchanges with Kate Ericson and Mel Ziegler, who were much gentler in their approach, much more ruminative about what they were doing. Haha were trendy; Kate and Mel were gentle, homespun; and Daniel Martinez was, kind of, Keith Richards... Oh, and Suzanne Lacy. She's an amazing artist, I think...

LS: A role model?

SG: Well, she struggles for the work, and that's what we admired her for. And she was also very aloof from the whole administrative thing.

LS: She'd been making work in a certain way for a while and others were only catching up?

SG: I think that's true… I mean: she *had* been there before the rest of us! There was a kind of infectious sense of a working set of relationships that produced the show.

LS: And there were working conversations?

SG: Well, exchanges may have taken place where we understood the whole – and about what we were doing. And we were looking at what others were doing.

LS: Sperandio was quoted in the local press at the time as saying, 'This is a chance to take the artistic resources we normally have at our disposal and hand them over to people who wouldn't normally have those resources';[9] also, 'We delivered them a platform to express their creativity, and they utilised it.'[10] Does this capture an underlying ambition of your work for the show?

SG: Not really! We never thought that was true, and when Chris was saying it, I don't think he thought it was true either [laughs]. No, we were all trying to produce a show for Mary Jane, and that was the 'Art makes us better' show, the 'Art makes us nicer' show, the 'Art brings the people together' show…

LS: And that's the kind of the rhetoric that became widespread in the UK, under the New Labour government of Tony Blair.

SG: It was PR. But one way to think about those particular statements is that they weren't a method, they were a problem. 'What happens if you…?', 'Is it possible to…?' It wasn't to say 'This is what we tried to do', because that's not true; we didn't do that at all. What we got, though, was the handover of a week of paid leave for the factory crew [laughs]… That's good actually – an achievement.

LS: Can you tell me how the chocolate bar you produced in Chicago made it into Andrea Rosen's gallery in New York?

SG: That was a little later. The bar was in *The New York Times*, on the front of the culture section, before Andrea ever asked for some. Sperandio was living in Manhattan, and she was one of the people he bumped into. And of course, being a proper hipster, she thought, 'Wouldn't it be cool if people could take one of the chocolate bars in the gallery?' – it just makes the gallery cooler. We didn't have a show with her, a box of the bars just sat on the counter there for a bit. Who knows what she was thinking, but there was

—

[9] See Lewis Lazare, 'Candy Workers: We Got It! Nestlé: You Keep It', *Chicago Reader*, 30 April 1993.

[10] See L. Lazare, 'Sweet Sculpture: Workers Step Up to the Drawing Board', *Chicago Reader*, 14 January 1993.

a moment when we seemed to have arrived on an international scene. But that was all. And it went away very quickly.

LS: The attention was prompted by 'Culture in Action'?

SG: And Chris was out and about peddling our work in Manhattan. Actually, you know that he and I appeared on the Mark Radcliffe Show?

LS: Really, on BBC Radio 1, in amongst music and DJ chat?

SG: Yes, it was just after Sculpture Chicago, and it was about Sculpture Chicago. I was in the studio with Mark Radcliffe in Manchester, and we had Jethro on the line from Chicago [laughs]. *Wh-why!?* Mark Radcliffe was like, 'Who's put this on my sheets?'

LS: Some relatively big names in the art world covered the show too: Dan Cameron, Lynne Cooke, Lisa Corrin, Michael Kimmelmann... Maybe not all the coverage was read in the US, but there was significant UK coverage, although *frieze* was not as established then as it is now, of course.

SG: There weren't acres of press, but there were some very well-focused, very perspicacious reviews. I think Mary Jane did that. She had a press reach beyond that of a lot of the artists involved. And the UK angle might have been part of an explicit strategy that she had, maybe thinking she might have trouble getting it into the press in the US.

LS: Do I gather you eventually sold your contribution to 'Culture in Action', or some version of it? Moving on from the bars just being given away in a gallery...

SG: Colin de Land sold the project archive to a couple of collectors in New York in the late nineties. They got a billboard and boxes of chocolates as part of it. Chris lived around the corner from American Fine Arts and he probably just walked in there one day and got talking to Colin. Colin was always looking for the happy accident.

LS: So he represented you?

SG: We worked with him for five or six years. We had two shows with him. Colin was so interesting. And it was he who turned our Chicago project into an artwork and sold it. The last time I saw the work it was in the collectors' house, in custom-made cabinets.

LS: Well, I gather that Robin Klassnik keeps one of the chocolate bars in the freezer at Matt's Gallery in London – mythically next to his peas.

SG: I reckon they'll last forever, chilled or whatever: they've got so much sugar in them, just as the crew wanted.

'Culture in Action' Revisited: Daniel J. Martinez in conversation with Michael Brenson[1]

Michael Brenson: We have a strong sense of the way 'Culture in Action' has been written into art history, and I think I can speak for both of us when I say that what we actually lived through, what we experienced and what we thought is unrecognisable from the way it's been written about. So our purpose is to speak from our own experience and try to talk about this from an experiential level at that particular moment, contextualise it in that moment, and in the process hopefully open up different ways of thinking about it.

Daniel J. Martinez: What we're trying to do here is look at 'Culture in Action' in a much more complicated way, through a personal lens. And it's important for you to know that our involvement suggests a certain trajectory. We were there. We are deeply committed to what 'Culture in Action' represents and what it was. It's a point of view and a perspective, I think, that is unique and has not been able to be brought to life at this point, or at least in the criticism that has been levelled against 'Culture in Action'.

Michael and I are not talking about social practice – that came later and that is another discussion. We are talking about 'Culture in Action' and we're talking about 1993.

In order to actually understand 'Culture in Action', one would have to revisit or think about each of the artists' projects individually. It's very dangerous to think about 'Culture in Action' as a collective. While there is a curatorial view of 'Culture in Action', I think the priority was that of the individual artists for the projects they created, which means that they have to be examined in a close reading of what the intent and objectives of those artists were, because it was like a number of one-person shows.

The proposition that Mary Jane [Jacob, curator] made to me didn't seem unusual or peculiar to me at all, and that's probably because there was a very clear division that existed in the art world in the 1980s. There were two parallel, equally valid systems or methods of the production of art. One was a commercial view and the other was a non-profit view. Artists that existed within a non-profit world in the United States were able to sustain the validity of their ideas without affirmation by sales of their work. It freed a group of artists to exist autonomously from these other economic or social structures that I think now have come to play a much more dominant role.

In the 1980s there was also a war going on, and for anyone who doesn't remember, that war was very distinct, like the Cold War. You saw very clearly

—

[1] This is an edited transcript from the symposium 'Culture in Action: Public Art in Chicago Twenty Years Later', organised by Threewalls and held at the University of Chicago, 5 October 2013.

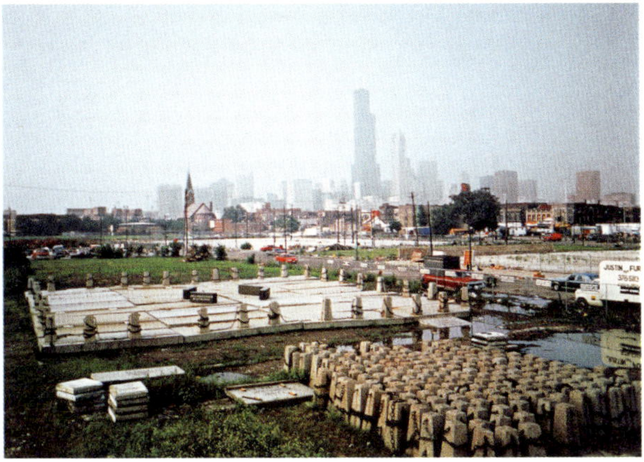

Daniel J. Martinez, *100 Victories / 10,000 Tears*, 1993, with Chicago skyline in the background. This photograph was used for the cover of the 'Culture in Action' exhibition catalogue in 1995.

who the enemy was and you made a decision as to what side you were on. Everyone knew where you stood in relation to culture production, who you associated with and the ways you wanted to organise, produce your ideas and interact within a larger social landscape. So the creation of art was something where the possibility of the unknown existed: the possibility of propositions into unknown aesthetic spaces that had not been previously visited.

I unknowingly came to 'Culture in Action' with the idea that the proposition of working at the level of cities was normal. It didn't seem to me new, and this is the reason why. Simultaneous with 'Culture in Action' I was in the 1993 Whitney Biennial.[2] Both were no longer about producing an autonomous art object, but intervening into the national landscape. Another concurrent project was 'Revelations', at Cornell University, which caused a riot and the takeover of Day Hall, similar to the 1968 takeover of this administration building by black students in order to ask for changes in faculty and curriculum.[3] Because of 'Revelations', this happened again in 1993. In 1991, I had been part of what was considered to be one of the first of these interventionist projects, 'In Public' in Seattle, but which actually had nothing to do with the history of this kind of social interaction or community-based projects.[4] p.38

I believe I was invited to participate in 'Culture in Action' in order to both develop and extend the ideas I was working on in relation to civic and social

—

[2] '1993 Biennial Exhibition', Whitney Museum of American Art, New York, curated by Thelma Golden, John G. Hanhardt, Lisa Phillips and Elisabeth Sussman, 5 March to 13 June 1993.

[3] 'Revelations/Revelaciones: Hispanic Art of Evanescence', Cornell University, Ithaca, New York, curated by Chon Noriega and José Piedra, 6 November to 19 December 1993. Among its eight site-specific pieces was Martinez's *The Castle is Burning*.

[4] 'In Public: Seattle 1991' was a public art programme organised by Diane Shamash and the Seattle Arts Commission. See note on p.38 in this volume.

space and its immanent potential for public/political exchanges. This then became the basis of the collaboration with Mary Jane to create 'Culture in Action'.

My perception of the world I existed in came from a minority discourse. And the minority discourse has to do with – and I would say particularly in Chicago, even though I come from one of the most racist cities in this country, LA – race and class. There was an urgent necessity to bring forward ideas of race and class; this needed to be a priority. It's a conversation we had a great difficulty with then and continue to even now.

MB: This was a time of potential for provocation. I was at *The New York Times* from 1982 to 1991. With Skulptur Projekte Münster in 1987, 'Magiciens de la Terre' in Paris in 1989 and the 'Decade Show' in New York in 1990, and then Mary Jane's 'Places with a Past' in Charleston in 1991,[5] all of which I saw, the concept and frame of 'the exhibition' were broken open. Exhibitions like these radically questioned what museums were showing, their make-ups, what art was and who audiences were. Many people believed that if we wanted to understand what art could do, we had to go outside them.

p.15

I continue to think about the rise and fall of the East Village art scene of the early 80s. Works came out of those streets – pretty rough streets. There was a lot of crime down there, a lot of poverty, a lot of gritty communal energy and a lot of vitality in the art. Much of the work was being shown in storefront galleries. There was a good deal of potential in work that came out of such neighborhoods and was connected to the streets of the city, and it was thwarted, truncated when it was almost immediately taken into the system. There was a loss for me in that, a feeling that something dynamic and necessary wanted to happen but couldn't.

I remember being in a SoHo gallery soon after it had moved from the East Village and hearing its owner, referring to work on the wall, use the phrase – this was the first time I'd heard it – 'it's like printing money'. I knew the artist. I saw the gap between the profit being made on certain kinds of artists and the actual lives of artists. I was becoming attuned to artists like Adrian Piper, who spoke about galleries as a refuge, not a place where people went to learn about the world or be in touch with themselves in the world, but to escape from it.

—

[5] Skulptur Projekte Münster, Münster, 14 June to 4 October 1987 (see note on p.20 in this volume); 'Magiciens de la Terre', Centre Pompidou and the Grand Halle at the Parc de la Villette, Paris, 18 May to 14 August 1989; 'The Decade Show: Frameworks of Identity in the 1980s', New Museum, Museum of Contemporary Hispanic Art and The Studio Museum in Harlem, New York, 12 May to 19 August 1990; 'Places with a Past: New Site-Specific Art at Charleston's Spoleto Festival', Charleston, South Carolina, 24 May to 4 August 1991.

I think it's also essential to mention the crisis of the National Endowment for the Arts. Daniel was talking about the possibility for a climate of experimentation. The NEA gave artists money and said do with the money what you want. Artists didn't have to be accountable. It was theirs and they could experiment. Spaces for experimentation had existed in the past, and now this central one was under siege. The necessity of experimental work had to be asserted that much more strongly.

So you put these things together and then we get to the end of 1991, and I'm out of the *Times*. I'm on my own, ready for pretty much anything, when Mary Jane asked me to be involved with 'Culture in Action'. I had no idea what I would be doing, but I had followed the trajectory of Mary Jane's career. 'Places with a Past' changed my life, and I was ready for the adventure she was opening up – this movement into an unknown. Like Daniel was saying, there was no language for this work but the time was ripe.

DJM: Even though only a relatively small number of artists received NEA grants, the idea of NEA grants and support of major non-profit institutions in every city in the United States cultivated artists to think differently about the possibility of what and how they could engage themselves and the kind of art that they wanted to produce. This was a kind of freedom that was unique because it laid the foundational groundwork for things to occur in ways and for artists to think about things in ways that were not otherwise possible.

The opportunities the NEA provided allowed something else to occur: it supported a minority discourse that was formidable. So the opportunity to be able to act within that is something important to be noted about the time.

Quite honestly, the art world had been and continues to be extremely hegemonic and divisive. As we moved towards the end of the 1980s, the NEA started to collapse. As the culture wars intensified via Jesse Helms and through a conservative political component in the government and the rise of the Christian Right, the NEA became a scapegoat, and the eventual net result was the defunding of the NEA's individual artists fellowship programme, to many the heart and soul of the agency.[6]

I think 'Culture in Action' took risks in areas that nobody had been willing to risk previously because there wasn't a language. Mary Jane came to artists and she actually trusted us. She asked us what we wanted to do. She had created a new type of relationship with the host organisation Sculpture Chicago. There was no staff and the two full-time people hired, the director Eva Olson and assistant Karen Paluzzi, came on board to work just on this programme. The programme and organisation were one. And with this new

—

[6] For a journalistic account of right-wing senator Jesse Helms and his role in the arts funding debates of that period, see Richard Bolton, *Culture Wars*, New York: New Press, 1992.

singular focus on 'Culture in Action', Sculpture Chicago openly accepted a new way of working with artists, acting as a support system, making connections, organising events and sometimes offering suggestions without interfering in the trajectory of the development of the idea or projects. Mary Jane's curatorial vision depended upon experimentation. There was no institutional framework, no preconceived idea of how we were supposed to operate. They trusted artists. What an idea that is: trust artists in your culture! I don't think that happens anymore.

> *MB*: I want to mention Richard Serra's *Tilted Arc* at Federal Plaza in New York – installed in 1981, the public hearing about it in 1985 and its removal in 1989. The hearing exposed and deepened a schism between the art world and the non-art world; it was bitter. Towards the end of the 1980s I began to feel that people like me, who were part of the art world and supported Serra as a great sculptor, had to think differently about the issue of multiple audiences and about people who were not connected with the professional art world, who felt hostile to it, often for good reasons. I remain uneasy with mass culture, but the old modernist dichotomy had become intolerable.
>
> 'Culture in Action' was a chance to actually move out and deal with people who were not connected to the professional art world, and step into this schism. This, I think, is a factor behind 'Culture in Action', part of the particular necessity of working with communities throughout the city, of bringing artists in touch with all sorts of people and having them work together and see what would happen.
>
> *Tilted Arc* may be the end of a certain idea of art-making: the idea that individual artists can make a work that lays claim to a site and obliges people to live with it, and where the work has domination over site and its everyday reality. Something in me will always want to believe in that possibility. There's always a need for art that refuses to accommodate itself to the system it enters, particularly now, given the tyranny of likeability. I think *Tilted Arc* was an unforgettable work, but it was always going to assert itself in an untransformative way in front of that bureaucratic building, on that plaza, surrounded by other official buildings. Maya Lin's Vietnam memorial was a year later,[7] with a similar experiential sculptural language, but with an entirely different attitude towards its public. That's a historical hinge point if you see those works together.

DJM: I think there was fertility in these parallel worlds we're speaking of, where *Tilted Arc* was the signal towards the end of a way of the individual artist and the aggressiveness of work in relation to the people who use that site. So if it signals an end to a certain kind of art-making, the possibility of another way of thinking about art was the opportunity for multiple ways of

—

[7] *Vietnam Veterans Memorial*, designed by architect Maya Lin in response to a public design competition, was installed in Constitution Gardens, Washington DC in 1982.

thinking not in the dominant discourse. Something else was occurring that was not identified; it was not labelled, not organised, actually. It was at a very grass-roots level among artists who were trying to initiate ways that were being glossed over by the dominant view in this country and, therefore, pushed into this minority view. But, ultimately, 'Culture in Action' was ridiculed and criticised in the same way as *Tilted Arc* – and this is the point I want to bring to you. What was it that was ripped open by 'Culture in Action'? Why did it solicit such venomous detractors? Why were the established modes of critical thinking so afraid of what the exhibition represented? I think 'Culture in Action' was putting an end to one discourse and attempting to initiate another that was outside of the aesthetic dogmas of the time.

> *MB*: Talking about why 'Culture in Action' had such a big effect on our lives may be the place to go from here. I felt like I was in over my head all the time with 'Culture in Action', even though I wasn't working with it the way you were, day in and day out to try to make something work among people you did not previously know, many of whom had never spoken to one another. You developed two major projects: a parade that went through three different sites, including the Maxwell Street Market; and the second part, sited there, a kind of agora put together with banished granite blocks from the University of Illinois at Chicago.

fig.57–63

fig.65–67

DJM: Your sense of being overwhelmed, I would say for me, was not dissimilar. Attempting to organise groups of people and individuals to utilise the apparatus of collective street intervention, which has a tremendous history around the world either in protest or in celebration – it was nothing but a challenge to recognise and follow in that particular history. You think you're not actually going to be able to do this, but that doesn't mean that you're not going to try, because you believe the results – the aggregate reading of that intervention – extends itself beyond that place and time. Today Maxwell Street Market is gone. There's a mall and a baseball field there. It's impossible to recognise or trace the previous histories, the political and individual actions and events that made Maxwell Street Market and the surrounding area, and that were so important.

fig.64

There was also a real capacity for failure. I'm also thinking about the project of Iñigo Manglano-Ovalle, who made work where he lived, with residents who are involved with issues of daily survival. This is where the people you work with could be disappointed – so if you failed, it was a type of failure with real, everyday consequences, different than the failure of a gallery show. This element of risk and disappointment, the possibility of letting down or having people you work with feel used, was significant. So this form of art-making contained a proposition that demanded new ideas, approaches and methods of working that required a new form of commitment on our part as artists.

fig.45–56

I think of all the different communities and people who were involved in all the 'Culture in Action' projects now recognising how willing they were to give themselves over to an idea that had the possibility of that kind of failure. Why would you do that? Why would you put yourself at risk in such a way? I didn't know anybody here. I'd never been to Chicago before. Why trust someone unknown from LA? But they did without question – that was what was so fantastic and unique. Perhaps this is where the raw power of hope and desire is laid bare. It is the potential to be open to new experiences that can be made possible by these types of exchanges.

MB: This leads me back to the art question. Interviewing people who worked with you and the other 'Culture in Action' artists, I would ask myself about them. Why would you give yourself to an artist? Why would you give yourself to this kind of collaboration? It was important for me to think about this belief in the artist and this belief in the power of art. Museums did not lead me to these questions. It is interesting to ask the question, where does this belief come from? I think artists still have a place in legend and in this society that leads or encourages many people to cooperate with them, to want to be in their presence, in the hope that something out of the ordinary and potentially transformative will come out of it.

DJM: I don't think it is overstating it to say that the ability of a civil society to succeed and prosper depends upon the communities of which it is constructed. Community is wide-ranging; it is the full spectrum of groups of individuals with a whole variety of intersecting interests. If that's the case, I think one of the propositions of 'Culture in Action' was to look back at the construction of a civil society in which the general public, educated or not to the ideas of art, recognises that the place of the artist is integral to the health of that ecosystem. Even if they don't understand what the artist is doing, they know artists need to be there. And with artists something can actually change the way you think about the way you live in the world. I am not talking about solving the social ills of a society with art – that's impossible. I am talking about something more subtle. I am talking about being affected by experiences with art, poetry and philosophy which are created by artists working in and interacting with the world in which we live.

MB: I don't know if I would agree that everyone knows that artists are integral to society. I think that pretty much everyone assumes that artists have power. I think one of the consequences of the attacks on the NEA, on [Robert] Mapplethorpe, [Andres] Serrano and the NEA Four (Karen Finley, Tim Miller, Holly Hughes and John Fleck), was to affirm that art had power.

Twenty years later I remember your work. I remember almost every project to various degrees. To talk about memory and the way these projects work in memory is to talk about effect. Your projects are among my strongest memories: one is a collective memory, a communal one; the other solitary. Perhaps they're both at once. The suddenness of the parade moving through the street, with its high school marching
fig.63 bands, was like a vision. Hundreds of people getting off buses; then on

the street, encountered by other people, all surprised; then they board the buses and move elsewhere. The parade around Maxwell Street was like a spell, almost a charm, cast around the market; then this one, too, was gone. The enchantment of that performative suddenness in the city, in urban space, seemed to bring with it a new kind of eruptive possibility within the fabric of the city. It was communal in shape and scope and personally experienced. fig.59–61, 63

For me, standing in the agora that you had built out of these massive granite blocks, standing alone amid the signs of Chicago labour history, looking over the distant skyscrapers, including the Sears Tower, I felt I was in a dream space. The agora was a platform, a speakers' corner. I was standing on stone, with signs of dramatic historical events, looking at a city that seemed both reality and vision. Both projects connected self to city. Both felt historically and physically grounded, and poetic. fig.65–67

DJM: When we were marching down the street in the Garfield Park neighbourhood, we came up to the intersection. Coming the opposite way was a funeral hearse. There was one moment in which a decision had to be made: whether this parade full of life was going to go or the celebration of this death was going to pass by first. As you know, everything stops for hearses and the convoy of cars that follows. There was just one glance between me and this very beautifully dressed man who got out of the hearse. He looked down the street and saw the parade. He looks at me. He gives a nod. He gets into his car. They wait and we go by. You don't plan that. That's what I would suggest is your reference about poetry. It's these brief moments that are exquisite and beautiful.

MB: I think that these projects are constructed in such a way – using your language to bring in the notion of wonder – as to give them the possibility of being transformative, the possibility of lasting. The 'Culture in Action' projects required improvisation. This built into them the capacity for play. Basically you had to figure it out day-to-day as you went along, with all the persistence and negotiation, and periodically joy and discovery, that happened.

DJM: The consequences of the gesture of 'Culture in Action' are not to be quantified through the vernacular of the critical art apparatus. Therefore, I think it's beneficial for us to attempt to conjure languages and terminology that are not about pinpointing, but actually continuing to unpack and free these projects from the constraints of the tools of criticism. And that's a question for you: how do we move from the position of criticism as it functioned, say, when you were at the *Times*, and criticism of something that is an ephemeral gesture, a gesture that is not only ephemeral but also sustainable? That's the thing – 'Culture in Action' isn't any one thing. That's why I said, if you want to talk about 'Culture in Action', you have to talk about every single project and then talk about it collectively and then go back again. You're never going to sum it up because it's everywhere; it's around you; it's in you. It's human.

MB: The rhetoric of social service and piety can't do justice to 'Culture in Action', although an intense desire to make the world better may be part of the motivational drive that brought the projects into existence. The languages of the social sciences can't do justice to the experiences of discovery and surprise. No single scheme can account for all the projects, which, as you said, were very different. This was the first art programme that I was aware of that was shaped by the scale of the city. I mean, the ambition of it was –

DJM: Fantastic.

MB: Extraordinary. Within the conventions of criticism, how do you think about all this? What critical apparatus can do justice to all this? It was imperative to be *with* the work, and then, to the best of your ability, give it time. You had to let the projects reveal themselves for what they were, because if you imposed on them an existing frame, writing about them was, at least for me, impossible. My catalogue essay was just a beginning. The possibilities that 'Culture in Action' opened up for writing have barely begun to be explored.

'Culture in Action' was raw. That's what I think people forget, because this work is so institutionalised now and spoken about within institutional languages. But that's not the way it was lived. It felt completely raw.

DJM: It was raw. It was alive. It was form and formlessness. Like a palpitating heart in open-heart surgery, it was just beating in front of you. I know that sounds like some kind of exaggeration, but if you had been there during that time you would understand. I think it was genuine. I think it was honest. And I know that is maybe a peculiar word to use in relation to art, but I find that there's a lot of plain dishonesty currently.

MB: For Miwon Kwon and Claire Bishop, the critic, the art historian, winds up being in a position of authority over the curator, as well as the artist, and all this is done in their books without full engagement with the projects.[8] These critic-scholars don't trust artistic and curatorial intention. They don't seem present with the projects, or to have been open to them at all. There's a belief that you could take them on through comparative projects and histories of site specificity, through the rhetoric around and the writing on this work, and through structures of critical theory. I'm not saying writers can't make intelligent and necessary observations from this distance – Bishop and Kwon do – but there's hardly an ounce of curiosity in their critiques. Their critiques are disembodied.

DJM: So you have an ideological war. For instance, Kwon persists in critically attacking 'Culture in Action' in Los Angeles, where she continues to teach about the failure of 'Culture in Action'. Ultimately it's a form of ideological assassination. I take issue with their condescending absoluteness and their perceived intellectual superiority. There is something powerful about 'Culture in Action' that disrupts their world view, so their only recourse is to attack it. I object to their narrow-minded view of art, and I will not be bullied into a corner by someone who thinks they're morally and intellectually superior to me.

'Culture in Action' posited a position of the social and the political as a priority while testing, but not discarding, the aesthetic. So it's a war, and the war in my opinion is over art history. If people do not understand that art history is a blood sport, it is. And artists are fighting for the position to sustain themselves within that art history.

> *MB*: I'm interested in what kind of language people writing about this kind of work think is appropriate. The languages that are adopted for these projects in those books – and they're both significant books – are intended to diminish and control the projects. This raises the question of what kind of language and which kinds of publications could meet the challenges of this kind of work.
>
> 'Culture in Action' was treated as an institution from the moment it began, perhaps because of the funding it received, perhaps because the cultural industry had quite rapidly embraced some of its key ideas. But in a profound sense 'Culture in Action' was not institutional, if not non-institutional. I think to actually go back and recreate that moment would give the writing more suppleness and honesty. I wonder why writers don't look at Mary Jane's curatorial practice? She didn't do 'Culture in Action' again. To talk about her trajectory from Gordon Matta-Clark, Magdalena Abakanowicz, Jannis Kounellis and Christian Boltanski to 'Places with a Past', 'Culture in Action' and 'Conversations at the Castle'[9] – she didn't make an idea into a territory. She did not institutionalise herself. She moved from unknown to unknown.

DJM: So the question is, how are new generations of artists thinking through the possibilities of art-making, because it will be up to this new generation to rethink what's possible after 'Culture in Action'? I'm open to the broadest range of critical apparatuses. I just wish that there were more views present, so that those who were not there had the opportunity to think through these projects in different ways. I'm against the current

—

[8] See Miwon Kwon, *One Place After Another: Site-Specific Art and Locational Identity*, Cambridge, MA: The MIT Press, 2004; and Claire Bishop, *Artificial Hells: Participatory Art and the Politics of Spectatorship*, London: Verso, 2012.

[9] At the Museum of Contemporary Art (MCA), Chicago, Jacob curated 'Magdalena Abakanowicz' (1982), 'Gordon Matta-Clark: A Retrospective' (1985), 'Jannis Kounellis Retrospective' (1986) and 'Christian Boltanski: Lessons of Darkness' (1988), all of which toured to other locations. In 1991, she organised 'Places with a Past', Charleston, South Carolina; and, in 1996, 'Conversations at the Castle', for the Arts Festival of Atlanta, Georgia. See, for example, Michael Brenson and M.J. Jacob (ed.), *Conversations at The Castle: Changing Audiences and Contemporary Art*, Cambridge, MA: The MIT Press, 1998.

mode of classification and categorisation of art and artists in general. I'm against it because as soon as we move into trendy terminologies, you see them collapse upon themselves. This was clear with relational aesthetics. So what I'm seeking is operational or experiential modes that allow for complex engagements with this work. At the core, what we're talking about is the unknown possibilities for art-making. Can we suspend the definitions of art so that they're always in flux, always changing, always redefining themselves? Can we have a culture in which art-making is not so narrowly defined as I perceive it currently is? What will it take for art and artists to maintain genuine freedom and autonomy in the twenty-first century? What are we willing to risk?

Authors' biographies

Michael Brenson is a critic, scholar and teacher. He received an MA in Creative Writing and a Ph.D in art history from Johns Hopkins University, and was an art writer for *The New York Times* from 1982 to 1991. His publications include *Visionaries and Outcasts: The NEA, Congress, and the Place of the Visual Artist in America* (2001); *Acts of Engagement: Writings on Art, Criticism, and Institutions, 1993–2002* (2004); edited (with Mary Jane Jacob) *Conversations at the Castle: Changing Audiences and Contemporary Art* (1998); edited (with Rhea Anastas) *Witness to Her Art: Art and Writings by Adrian Piper, Mona Hatoum, Cady Noland, Jenny Holzer, Kara Walker, Daniela Rossell and Eau de Cologne* (2006). He is a Getty scholar and Guggenheim Fellow, a Visiting Senior Critic in the University of Pennsylvania's School of Design's Department of Fine Arts and a member of the sculpture faculty in Bard College's Milton Avery Graduate School of the Arts. He is writing a biography of David Smith.

Joshua Decter is a New York-based writer, curator, art historian and theorist. Decter's book *Art is a Problem: Selected Criticism, Essays, Interviews and Curatorial Projects (1986–2012)* was recently published by JRP|Ringier, and encompasses seven chapters: 'Institutional Critique® and its Discontents', 'Aporia (art as politics, the politics of art)', 'Everything is Social', 'Convoluted Cities', 'The (Un)De-definition of Art','What Do We Want from Exhibitions?', and 'On the Curatorial Road'. He has curated exhibitions such as 'a/drift' at the Center for Curatorial Studies at Bard College, 'Transmute' at the Museum of Contemporary Art in Chicago, 'Tele[visions]' at The Kunsthalle Vienna, and 'Dark Places' at The Santa Monica Museum of Art. Decter was a curatorial interlocutor for inSite_05, 'Interventions' (Tijuana/San Diego), and has organised symposia such as 'The Situational Drive: Complexities of Public Sphere Engagement' at Cooper Union, New York, in 2007. Decter founded the MA Art and Curatorial Practices in the Public Sphere programme at USC in 2011, and has also taught at CCS Bard, the School of Visual Arts in New York, the School of the Art Institute of Chicago, New York University, UCLA and Art Center College of Design in Pasadena.

Mark Dion was born in New Bedford, Massachusetts in 1961. Dion's work examines the ways in which dominant ideologies and public institutions shape our understanding of history, knowledge and the natural world. The job of the artist, he says, is to go against the grain of dominant culture, to challenge perception and convention. Appropriating archaeological and other scientific methods of collecting, ordering and exhibiting objects, Dion creates works that question the distinctions between 'objective' ('rational') scientific methods and 'subjective' ('irrational') influences. He is the co-director of Mildred's Lane, an innovative visual art education and residency programme in Beach Lake, Pennsylvania. For over two decades Dion has worked in the public realm on a wide range of scales, from architecture projects to print projects in newspapers. Recent projects include large-scale permanent commissions for dOCUMENTA(13) in Kassel, Germany, for the Montevideo

Biennal in Uruguay and for the Port of Los Angeles. Dion lives with his wife and frequent collaborator Dana Sherwood in New York City and works worldwide.

Helmut Draxler is an art historian and a cultural theorist based in Berlin. He publishes extensively in the field of art, politics and theory and occasionally also works as a curator. From 1992 to 1995 he was director of the Kunstverein in Munich and from 1999 to 2012 he was Professor for Aesthetic Theory at the Merz Academy, University for Art, Design and Media in Stuttgart. He is currently Professor for Art Theory at the Academy of Fine Arts in Nuremberg. He is author of *Gefährliche Substanzen. Zum Verhältnis von Kritik und Kunst* (Berlin: b-books, 2007) and editor of publications such as *Theorien der Passivität* (Munich: Fink, 2013) in collaboration with Kathrin Busch and *Film, Avantgarde und Biopolitik* (Vienna: Schlebrügge Editor, 2009) in collaboration with Sabeth Buchmann and Stephan Geene. He has curated exhibitions which have included 'Shandyism. Authorship as Genre', Secession, Vienna, 2007 and 'The Content of Form', Generali Foundation, Vienna, 2013.

Simon Grennan and Christopher Sperandio have run an art practice together exclusively since 1990. Known as pioneers of interventionism, new genre and post-relational art, Grennan & Sperandio work in publishing, broadcast media and events, arranging situations in which participants and audiences are creatively dis-habituated. They have worked with Museum of Modern Art New York, Channel 4 Television, Fantagraphics Books and English Heritage, among many others. Simon was Director of Viewpoint Photography Gallery Salford and Public Art Forum (now IXIA). Chris is Associate Professor of Fine Art at Rice University, Houston. Grennan & Sperandio's website is www.kartoonkings.com.

Mary Jane Jacob is a curator who, through hundreds of exhibitions, site-specific and community-based projects and public programmes, has actively worked with artists to expand the practice and public discourse of art as a shared process. Her study into the nature of the art experience has lead to anthologies *Buddha Mind in Contemporary Art* (2004), *Learning Mind: Experience into Art* (2009), *The Studio Reader: On the Space of Artists* (2010) and *Chicago Makes Modern: How Creative Minds Changed Society* (2012). As Professor and Executive Director of Exhibitions and Exhibition Studies at the School of the Art Institute of Chicago, she spearheaded a major research project on Chicago social practice since the 1880s which culminated in exhibitions and a publication series in 2014.

Daniel Joseph Martinez has engaged in an investigation of social, political and cultural mores through artworks that have been characterised as 'nonlinear multidimensional propositions'. His works range from the digital to the analogue, ephemeral to the solid. Using forms of strategic engagement Martinez employs mutation and schizophrenia as a form of confusion directed toward the precondition of the coexistence of politics as radical beauty. Ongoing themes in the work are contamination, history, nomadic power, cultural resistance, dissentience and systems of symbolic exchange. He represented the United States in the American Pavilion in the 2006 Cairo Biennale. Martinez is Professor of Theory, Practice, and Mediation of Contemporary Art at the University of California, Irvine; he teaches in the Graduate Studies Program and the New Genres Department. He lives and works in the Crenshaw District of South Los Angeles.

David Morris is a writer, researcher and teacher. He is co-editor, with Sylvère Lotringer, of *Schizo-Culture: The Event, The Book* (Semiotext(e) / The MIT Press, 2014). He has been working with the Semiotext(e) archive since 2011. He is co-organiser, with Katherine Waugh and Paul Pieroni, of the exhibition project 'Cracks in the Street', SPACE, London, 2014. His writing has been published in a range of publications including *Cabinet, Art Monthly, frieze, A Circular* and the *Los Angeles Review of Books*, as well as exhibition texts and catalogue essays. He is an associate editor at Afterall and an associate lecturer at University of the Arts London.

Paul O'Neill is a curator, artist, writer and educator based in New York and Bristol. He is Director of the Graduate Program at the Center for Curatorial Studies, Bard College in New York. Paul has co-curated more than fifty exhibition projects across the world. He has been international tutor on the de Appel Curatorial Program in Amsterdam since 2005 and he has held numerous research and lecturing positions at Goldsmiths, University of London; Middlesex University; the Graduate School of Creative Arts and Media, Dublin; and the University of the West of England, Bristol. Paul's writing has been published in many books, catalogues, journals and magazines and he is a regular contributor to *Art Monthly*. He is reviews editor for *Art & the Public Sphere* journal and is an editor of Afterall's *Exhibition Histories* series. He is on the editorial board of *The Exhibitionist* and *The Journal of Curatorial Studies*. He is editor of the curatorial anthology, *Curating Subjects* (2007), and co-editor of *Curating and the Educational Turn* with Mick Wilson (2010), both published by de Appel and Open Editions (Amsterdam and London), and author of *Locating the Producers: Durational Approaches to Public Art* (Amsterdam, Valiz, 2011), edited with Claire Doherty. He is author of the critically acclaimed book *The Culture of Curating and the Curating of Culture(s)*, (Cambridge, MA: The MIT Press, 2012). His forthcoming book *Curating Research* (de Appel and Open Editions) co-edited with Mick Wilson will be published in 2014.

Joe Scanlan is an artist living in New York, where writing is an integral part of his studio practice. In addition to solo museum exhibitions at K21 in Düsseldorf, the Van Abbemuseum in Eindhoven, and Ikon Gallery in Birmingham, he has published more than fifty articles and reviews in *frieze*, *Artforum* and *Parkett*, and has published seventeen artist's books under the imprint of his website, thingsthatfall.com. He is currently the director of the Program in Visual Art at Princeton University.

Stephanie Smith works at the intersection of contemporary art, experimental museum practice and the public sphere. As Deputy Director and Chief Curator at the University of Chicago's Smart Museum of Art, her projects include 'Feast: Radical Hospitality in Contemporary Art' (2012), 'Heartland'(2008–09, in collaboration with Van Abbemuseum, Eindhoven) and 'Beyond Green: Toward a Sustainable Art' (2005). Smith is also an editor at *Afterall* journal, and co-directs New Projects – an urbanism studio, research centre and exhibition space. She has lectured at venues from Arizona State University to the Sharjah Biennial (UAE), and, in addition to extensive publications through the Smart, her writing has appeared in journals and books including *Afterall, Parkett, Service Media* (2012) and *Land, Art: A Cultural Ecology Handbook* (2006).

Lucy Steeds specialises in the history and theory of recent exhibitions of contemporary art. She is a writer, teacher and editor, and manages Afterall's *Exhibition Histories* book series while sharing the post of Pathway Leader for MRes Art: Exhibition Studies at Central Saint Martins, University of the Arts London, with Pablo Lafuente. She has a doctoral degree in cultural history from Goldsmiths College, University of London, and is working on a book, *Exhibition*, for the 'Documents of Contemporary Art' series (Whitechapel Gallery and The MIT Press, 2014).

Hafþór Yngvason is the Director of the Reykjavik Art Museum, Iceland, where he is responsible for the operations and artistic direction for the museum's three exhibition venues: Hafnarhús, Kjarvalsstaðir and the sculpture museum and park Ásmundarsafn. He was the Director of Public Art at the Cambridge Arts Council in Cambridge, Massachusetts from 1995 to 2005. He has curated several exhibitions, including a retrospective of Santiago Sierra's films and videos (2012), and large-scale public projects, including Yoko Ono's *Imagine Peace Tower* in Viðey, Iceland (2007) and Santiago Sierra's *The Black Cone, Monument to Civil Disobedience* in front of the Icelandic Parliament (2012). Among books that he has edited is *Foundation, Katrín Sigurðardóttir, The Pavilion of Iceland at the Venice Biennale 2013* (Milan: Marsilio Editori, 2013).

Selected bibliography

'Art and the Social: Exhibitions of Contemporary Art in the 1990s', Afterall and Former West symposium, Tate Britain, 30 April 2010, recordings available at http://www.formerwest.org/ResearchSeminars/ArtAndTheSocial (last accessed on 14 April 2014). Claire Bishop's contribution was revised for publication in C. Bishop, *Artificial Hells: Participatory Art and the Politics of Spectatorship*, London: Verso, 2012

Yves Aupetitallot (ed.), *PROJECT UNITE, Vol.1–3* (exh. cat.), Firminy, 1993

Homi Bhabha, 'Conversational Art', in Mary Jane Jacob and Michael Brenson (ed.), *Conversations at the Castle: Changing Audiences and Contemporary Art*, Cambridge, MA: The MIT Press, 1998, pp.38–47

Claire Bishop, 'Antagonism and Relational Aesthetics', *October*, no.110, Fall 2004, pp.51–79; Liam Gillick, 'Contingent Factors: A Response to Claire Bishop's "Antagonism and Relational Aesthetics"', *October*, no.115, Winter 2006, pp.95–107

Claire Bishop, 'The Social Turn: Collaboration and Its Discontents', *Artforum*, vol.44, no.6, February 2006, pp.178–83; Grant H. Kester, 'Another Turn' and C. Bishop, 'Claire Bishop Responds', *Artforum*, vol.44, no.9, May 2006, pp.22–24

Will Bradley and Charles Esche (ed.), *Art and Social Change: A Critical Reader*, London: Afterall and Tate Publishing, 2007

Jan Brand, Cadelijn de Muynck and Valerie Smith (ed.), *Sonsbeek 93* (exh. cat.), Ghent: Snoeck-Ducaju & Zoon, 1993

Arthur C. Danto, 'Museums and the Thirsting Millions', *After the End of Art: Contemporary Art and the Pale of History*, Princeton, NJ: Princeton University Press, 1997

Claire Doherty (ed.), *Contemporary Art: From Studio to Situation*, London: Black Dog, 2004

Nina Felshin (ed.), *But is it Art?: The Spirit of Art as Activism*, Seattle: Bay Press, 1995

Tom Finkelpearl, *What We Made: Conversations on Art and Social Cooperation*, Durham, NC: Duke University Press, 2013

Brigitte Franzen, Kasper König and Carina Plath (ed.), *Sculpture Projects Muenster 07* (exh. cat.), Cologne: Verlag der Buchhandlung Walther König

Suzi Gablik, 'Removing the Frame: An Interview with "Culture in Action" Curator Mary Jane Jacob', *New Art Examiner*, vol.21, no.5, January 1994, pp.14–18

Mary Jane Jacob (ed.), *Culture in Action: A Public Art Program of Sculpture Chicago* (exh. cat.), Seattle: Bay Press, 1995

Grant H. Kester, 'Aesthetic Evangelists: Conversion and Empowerment in Contemporary Community Art', *Afterimage*, January 1995, pp.5–11

Grant H. Kester, *The One and the Many: Contemporary Collaborative Art in a Global Context*, Durham, NC: Duke University Press, 2011

Miwon Kwon, *One Place After Another: Site-Specific Art and Locational Identity*, Cambridge, MA: The MIT Press, 2004

Suzanne Lacy, *Mapping the Terrain: New Genre Public Art*, Seattle: Bay Press, 1995

Bruno Latour and Peter Weibel (ed.), *Making Things Public: Atmospheres of Democracy* (exh. cat.), Cambridge, MA: The MIT Press, 2005

Lucy R. Lippard, *The Lure of the Local: Senses of Place in a Multicentered Society*, New York: The New Press, 1997

Paul O'Neill and Claire Doherty (ed.), *Locating the Producers: Durational Approaches to Public Art*, Amsterdam: Valiz, 2011

Gerald Raunig and Gene Ray (ed.), *Art and Contemporary Critical Practice: Reinventing Institutional Critique*, London: Mayfly, 2009

Olga Stefan and Catalin Gheorghe (ed.), 'Social Curating and Its Public: Curators from Eastern Europe Report on Their Practices', *ONCURATING.org*, issue 18, 2013, available at http://www.on-curating.org/index.php/issue-18.html#.UwTrMl6mU7B (last accessed on 14 April 2014)

Nato Thompson (ed.), *Living as Form: Socially Engaged Art from 1991–2011* (exh. cat.), New York and Cambridge, MA: Creative Time Books and The MIT Press, 2012

Brian Wallis (ed.), *Democracy: A Project by Group Material*, Seattle: Bay Press, 1990

Michael Warner, *Publics and Counterpublics*, New York: Zone Books, 2002

What, How and for Whom (WHW) (ed.), *Kollektive Kreativität / Collective Creativity* (exh. cat.), Frankfurt a.M.: Revolver Archiv für Aktuelle Kunst, 2005

Picture credits for the project descriptions

Unless noted below, all photography by John McWilliams for Sculpture Chicago and courtesy Mary Jane Jacob

Photography: Marc PoKempner (fig.1–5)

Photography: Mark Dion (fig.11)

Photography: Melissa Ann Pinney (fig.41 and 42)

Photography: Iñigo Manglano-Ovalle (fig.47, 48, 50 and 51)

Photography: Antonio Perez (fig.52, 56, 58 and 61)

Photography: Loren Santow (fig.71)

Courtesy Mark Dion and Tanya Bonakdar Gallery (fig.2 and 11)

Courtesy Simon Grennan (fig.23)

Courtesy Suzanne Lacy (fig.37–44)

Courtesy Wendy Jacob / Haha (fig.28, 31–34 and 36)

Courtesy Robert Peters (fig.68–70 and 72–74)

Courtesy *Chicago Reader* (fig.71)

Acknowledgements

The editors would like to thank the authors, artists, curators and photographers for their contributions to this book.

For support in the research process that led to this publication we are additionally grateful to: Fareed Armaly; Doug Ashford; Julie Ault; Yves Aupetitallot; Judith Barry; Jack Becker, Forecast Public Art; Claire Bishop; Doro Boehme, John M. Flaxman Library Special Collections, SAIC; Michael Brenson; AA Bronson; Christine Clinkx, Museum van Hedendaagse Kunst Antwerpen; Joshua Decter; Mark Dion; Eugenio Dittborn; Goran Djordjevic; Helmut Draxler; Richard Embray, Four Corners Books; Andrea Fraser; Rosalind Furness, *frieze*; Renée Green; Simon Grennan; David Hammons; Paul Higgins, *Chicago Reader*; Richard House; Lauren Hudgins, Tilton Gallery; Jim Isermann; Mary Jane Jacob; Wendy Jacob; Ronald Jones; Yoko Kanayama, Asher Trust; Rebecca Keller; Michael Kimmelman; Suzanne Lacy; Louise Lawler; Michael Leitgeb, Universalmuseum Joanneum; Iñigo Manglano-Ovalle; Daniel J. Martinez; Allan McCollum; Sarah Mendelsohn; Louise O'Hare; Laurie Palmer; Antonio Perez, Chicago Tribune; Robert Peters; John Ploof; Marc PoKempner; Jessica Rath; Lauran Rothstein, Jeff Koons LLC; Emily Ruotolo, Tanya Bonakdar Gallery; Loren Santow; Joe Scanlan; Julia Scher; Stephanie Smith; Christopher Sperandio; Haim Steinbach; Penelope Truitt, Free Agent Media; Morgan Rae Walsh; Hafþór Yngvason.

Joshua Decter would like to thank Lilian and Olivia, as well as his late parents, Paula and Moshe.

For her support of the project from the outset the editors would like to thank Marie-Claude Beaud.

The *Exhibition Histories* series has been generously supported by: the Academy of Fine Arts Vienna; Central Saint Martins, University of the Arts London; the Center for Curatorial Studies, Bard College; MUDAM Luxembourg, Musee d'Art Moderne Grand-Duc Jean; the National Lottery through Arts Council England; and Van Abbemuseum, Eindhoven.

Index

Notes